SAMS

The *Sams Teach Yourself in 24 Hours* Series

Sams Teach Yourself in 24 Hours books provide quick and easy answers in a proven step-by-step approach that works for you. In just 24 sessions of one hour or less, you will tackle every task you need to get the results you want. Let our experienced authors present the most accurate information to get you reliable answers—fast!

HomeSite Keyboard Shortcuts

The following are the standard keyboard shortcuts. Shortcuts can be customized through the Customize dialog.

File Management Shortcuts

KEY	ACTION
Ctrl+N	New file
Ctrl+O	Open file
Ctrl+P	Print file
Ctrl+S	Save file
Shift+Ctrl+S	Save as
Ctrl+W	Close file
Shift+Ctrl+W	Close all files

Editor Shortcuts

KEY	ACTION
Ctrl+A	Select all
Shift+Ctrl+A	Insert <A> tag
Ctrl+B	Insert <B> tag
Shift+Ctrl+B	Insert tag
Ctrl+C	Copy
Shift+Ctrl+C	Center text
Ctrl+E	Open tag chooser
Shift+Ctrl+E	Open Expression Builder*
Ctrl+F	Find
Shift+Ctrl+F	Extended find
Ctrl+G	Go to line
Ctrl+H	Toggle Quick Bar
Ctrl+I	Insert <I> tag
Shift+Ctrl+I	Insert <IMG> tag
Ctrl+J	Insert code template
Ctrl+K	Toggle bookmark
Shift+Ctrl+K	Go to next bookmark
Shift+Ctrl+L	Toggle results window
Ctrl+M	Find matching tag
Shift+Ctrl+M	Insert comment
Shift+Ctrl+P	Insert <P> tag
Ctrl+Q	Repeat last tag
Shift+Ctrl+Q	Execute document as script
Ctrl+R	Replace
Shift+Ctrl+R	Extended replace
Ctrl+U	Insert <U> tag
Ctrl+V	Paste
Ctrl+X	Cut
Shift+Ctrl+X	Special characters
Ctrl+Y	Delete line
Ctrl+Z	Undo
Shift+Ctrl+Z	Redo
F1	Help for selected tag

continues

Teach Yourself HomeSite 4 in 24 Hours

Key	Action
F3	Find next
Ctrl+F4	Edit current tag
F9	Toggle resource tab
Shift+F9	Toggle resource tab focus
F12	Toggle browse mode
Shift+F12	Toggle design mode
Ctrl+F12	Toggle full screen
Shift+Ctrl+.	Indent
Shift+Ctrl+,	Unindent
Ctrl+[	Go to previous start tag
Ctrl+]	Go to next start tag
Ctrl+,	Start brackets
Ctrl+.	End brackets
Ctrl+Backspace	Delete previous word
Ctrl+Delete	Delete to end of word
Ctrl+Enter	Insert and a new line
Shift+Ctrl+Space	Non-breaking space
Ctrl+Tab	Next document
Shift+Ctrl+Tab	Previous document
Ctrl+double-click	Select current tag
Shift+Ctrl+double-click	Select entire tag

Tools Shortcuts

Key	Action
Ctrl+D	Open document in Macromedia Dreamweaver
Ctrl+Alt+F	CodeSweeper
F2	Display Tag Tips
Shift+F2	Toggle Tag Insight
F4	Open Tag Inspector
F6	Validate current tag
Shift+F6	Validate document
F7	Spell check
Shift+F7	Spell check all files
Ctrl+F7	Mark spelling errors
F8	Settings
Shift+F8	Customize
F11	Open document in external browser

Debugger Shortcuts*

Key	Action
Alt+B	Breakpoints
Alt+K	Tag stack pane
Alt+M	Mappings
Alt+P	Output pane
Alt+Q	Variables pane
Alt+R	Recordsets pane
Alt+W	Watches
Alt+X	Toggle breakpoint
Alt+Y	Debug settings
Ctrl+F5	Start or continue debugging
Alt+F5	End debugging
Alt+F6	Clear all breakpoints
Ctrl+F8	Step into
Ctrl+F9	Step over
Ctrl+F10	Step out
Ctrl+F11	Run to cursor

*Only available in ColdFusion Studio.

SAMS

HomeSite 4
in 24 Hours

Hour	Title	Content
1	Understanding HomeSite	Understand what makes the Web tick, Web Server and Web Browser overview, introduction to HomeSite
2	Getting Started	Install HomeSite, take a guided tour of the editor
3	Getting Help	Learn how to get help when you need it
4	Customizing HomeSite	Make HomeSite work the way you do
5	Creating a Web Page	Create your first Web page, use the wizards
6	Designing a Web Page	Design and lay out a Web page
7	Working with Fonts and Colors	Use fonts and colors to format your text
8	Using Images	Add images to your pages
9	Linking Pages	Link pages together; after all, links are what make the Web the Web
10	Working with Tables	Create tables for greater layout control
11	Working with Frames	Use frames to create multi-window interfaces
12	Creating Forms	Learn how to use forms to collect information from visitors
13	Using the Design Mode	Use the Design mode to simplify HTML element manipulation
14	Editing Your Pages	Perform searches and replaces, clean up your code, and use the CodeSweeper
15	Using Style Sheets	Learn all about style sheets and how to use them
16	Validating and Testing Your Pages	Check your code and test your pages
17	Using Snippets and Templates	Reuse code blocks to save precious time
18	Managing Your Web Site	See the bigger picture, monitor download times, and make sure links remain linked
19	Working Remotely	Set yourself up for remote development and hosting
20	Managing Your Projects	Organize your development efforts with projects
21	Introducing ColdFusion Studio	Learn all about HomeSite's big brother, ColdFusion Studio
22	Developing Against Remote ColdFusion Servers	Learn how to use ColdFusion's Remote Development Services
23	Using the SQL Query Builder	Build SQL queries using the SQL Query Builder
24	Working with the Integrated Debugger	Debug your applications from anywhere

Ben Forta

SAMS Teach Yourself

HomeSite 4

in 24 Hours

SECOND EDITION

A Division of Macmillan Computer Publishing
201 West 103rd St., Indianapolis, Indiana, 46290 USA

Sams Teach Yourself HomeSite 4 in 24 Hours

Copyright © 1999 by Sams

International Standard Book Number: 0-672-31560-2

Library of Congress Catalog Card Number: 99-60195

Printed in the United States of America

First Printing: May 1999

00   99   98   4   3   2   1

Trademarks

Warning and Disclaimer

EXECUTIVE EDITOR
Bryan Gambrel

ACQUISITIONS EDITOR
Angela Kozlowski

DEVELOPMENT EDITOR
Susan Shaw Dunn

MANAGING EDITOR
Lisa Wilson

PROJECT EDITOR
Rebecca Mounts

COPY EDITORS
Kim Cofer
Pat Kinyon

INDEXER
Aamir Burki

PROOFREADER
Mary Ellen Stephenson

TECHNICAL EDITOR
Jason Wright

SOFTWARE DEVELOPMENT SPECIALIST
Todd Pfeffer

INTERIOR DESIGN
Gary Adair

COVER DESIGN
Aren Howell

LAYOUT TECHNICIANS
Ayanna Lacey
Heather Miller
Amy Parker

Contents at a Glance

Contents

About the Author

Ben Forta is Allaire Corporation's Product Evangelist for the ColdFusion product line. He has more than 15 years' experience in the computer industry in product development, support, training, and product marketing. Ben is the author of *The ColdFusion 4.0 Web Application Construction Kit* (now in its third edition) and the more recent *Advanced ColdFusion 4.0 Application Development*, both published by Que Corporation. He co-authored the official Allaire ColdFusion training courses, writes regular columns on ColdFusion and Internet development, and now spends a considerable amount of time lecturing and speaking on ColdFusion and Internet application development worldwide. Born in London, England, and educated in London, New York, and Los Angeles, Ben now lives in Oak Park, Michigan, with his wife and their five children. Ben welcomes your email at ben@forta.com and invites you to visit his Web site at http://www.forta.com.

Dedication

Dedicated to the memory of Josh Dowdell - a popular and active member of the Allaire and ColdFusion communities, and my very first technical editor.

Acknowledgements

First of all I must thank Nick Bradbury for HomeSite. I'm not sure if even Nick realized the incredible demand for the tool he created, and the entire Internet development community owes him a debt of gratitude.

Thanks to everyone at Macmillan who helped out on this book. Special thanks to my Developer, Susan Dunn, and my Project Editor, Rebecca Mounts, for their incredible dedication and attention to detail. A very special thank you to my Acquisitions Editor, Angela Kozlowski, for help and support well beyond the call of duty. Once again, Angela, I could not have done it without you.

Thanks to my Technical Editors, Jason Wright, Jo Torgessen, and Kim Stevens, for catching all those errors I deliberately put in the text just to check that they were doing their job properly. :-)

And finally, thank you to my wonderful wife Marcy for enabling me to walk down this path yet again. Although it is my name that goes on the cover, it is she who works the hardest to make my work a reality.

Tell Us What You Think!

As the reader of this book, *you* are our most important critic and commentator. We value your opinion and want to know what we're doing right, what we could do better, what areas you'd like to see us publish in, and any other words of wisdom you're willing to pass our way.

As an Associate Publisher for Sams, I welcome your comments. You can fax, email, or write me directly to let me know what you did or didn't like about this book—as well as what we can do to make our books stronger.

Please note that I cannot help you with technical problems related to the topic of this book, and that due to the high volume of mail I receive, I might not be able to reply to every message.

When you write, please be sure to include this book's title and author as well as your name and phone or fax number. I will carefully review your comments and share them with the author and editors who worked on the book.

Fax: 317-581-4770

Email: adv_prog@mop.oom

Mail: Brad Jones
          Associate Publisher
          Sams Publishing
          201 West 103rd Street
          Indianapolis, IN 46290 USA

Introduction

The World Wide Web is an exciting place and everyone wants to be a part of it. Everyone wants a Web presence, and that trend shows no sign of abating anytime soon. Whether you are about to launch your corporate presence on the Web or are creating a personal family site, you are becoming part of an ever-growing family of developers, all dedicated to the growth of the phenomenon called the Internet.

Fortunately, creating Web sites is easy; unfortunately, creating quality Web sites is not. Most development tools restrict us developers, opting to insulate us from more complex fine-tuning features rather than provide us with tools that could be misused. And so many developers resort to using simple text editors that do not restrict them, but also don't really help them.

But all that has changed.

What Is HomeSite?

HomeSite is an editor, and a very good one at that. Unlike most other text editors, HomeSite was designed with Web development in mind. Its claim to fame is how it gracefully handles seemingly opposing goals:

- Providing tools that simplify Web page development
- Providing developers with complete control over their code

From humble shareware beginnings, HomeSite has grown to be the most popular HTML editor on the market with hundreds of thousands of loyal users the world over. The press also loves HomeSite as much as Web developers do, showering it with awards including the following, but involving many, many more:

- CNET Award for Internet Excellence
- CNET BUILDER.COM Editors' Choice
- NewMedia Hyper Award
- *PC Magazine* Editors' Choice
- *Win98 Magazine* Editor's Choice
- *Windows Magazine* WinList award

If you have not yet experienced HomeSite, you owe it to yourself to do so immediately.

Who Should Use This Book?

This book is for anyone who is now using HomeSite (or ColdFusion Studio), as well as for anyone who is planning to. If you are new to Web development, you've picked the right tool to start with. If you are an existing Web developer who's new to HomeSite, this book will teach you all you need to know to get up and running in just a few hours. If you already are a HomeSite user, you'll find the tips, tricks, and advice spread throughout the book to be invaluable. And if you are a ColdFusion user—using the ColdFusion Studio development environment—this book will be an invaluable tutorial and guide.

To run HomeSite, you need a computer running Windows 95, Windows 98, or Windows NT. You should also have a connection to the Internet.

What's on the CD-ROM?

 The CD-ROM contains a non-expiring evaluation version of HomeSite. I'll walk you through the installation process in Hour 2, "Getting Started."

How to Use This Book

This book is designed to teach you topics in a series of lessons, each of which should take an hour (or less) to learn. All the books in the *Sams Teach Yourself* series enable you to start working and become productive with the product as quickly as possible. This book will do that for you too!

Each lesson starts with an overview of the topic to be taught. The overview helps you determine the nature of the lesson and whether the lesson is relevant to your needs.

Each lesson concludes with a set of questions and answers, and a quiz just to make sure you were paying attention. (The answers to the quiz questions can be found in Appendix A, "Answers to Quiz Questions," so you can check your responses.)

Interspersed in each lesson are special elements that provide additional information:

Notes present interesting side information related to the discussion.

Tips offer advice or show you an easier way of doing something.

Cautions alert you to possible problems and give you advice on how to avoid or fix them.

This book covers both HomeSite and ColdFusion Studio. The latter is HomeSite's big brother, an editor designed specifically for ColdFusion developers. Although most of the book covers both HomeSite and ColdFusion Studio, the last four lessons cover ColdFusion Studio exclusively.

This special icon indicates a new term that's defined and explained in a paragraph. The term being defined is formatted in *italic*.

The Input icon identifies code that you type yourself; the icon usually appears next to a code listing. (Anything that you need to type will appear in a special **`boldfaced monospace`** typeface.) The Output icon highlights the output produced by running the code. On occasion, you'll also see a combined Input/Output icon.

Part I
Getting Started

Hour

HOUR 1

Understanding HomeSite

In a relatively short amount of time, the World Wide Web (the *Web* for short) has become a household word. Business cards and letterheads contain Web site addresses, television commercials end with the trailer "See us on the Web at…" and even household items such as shampoo and light bulbs proudly display their home page addresses on their packaging.

What has facilitated this phenomenal growth? Actually, it's a combination of things, the most significant of which is HTML—the Hypertext Markup Language—used to publish information on the Web. We'll look at HTML later in this hour, but for now it's enough to say that HTML is a powerful and capable language, yet is extremely easy to learn. HTML makes publishing information on the Web easy and fun and, as such, wherever you turn, individuals and organizations are rolling out Web sites.

In this hour you'll learn the following:

- What the Internet is, and what intranets and extranets really are
- How Web servers and Web browsers work their magic
- What HomeSite is and what it *isn't*

Understanding the Internet

Much ambiguity and confusion surrounds the Internet, so we'll start with a definition. Simply put, the Internet is the world's largest network.

The networks found in most offices today are local area networks, (LANs), comprised of a group of computers in relatively close proximity to each other and linked by special hardware and cabling (see Figure 1.1). Some computers are clients (more commonly known as *workstations*), others are servers (also known as *file servers*). All these computers can communicate with each other to share information.

FIGURE 1.1

A LAN is a group of computers in close proximity linked by special cabling.

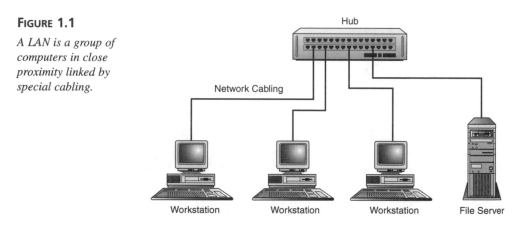

Now imagine a bigger network, one that spans multiple geographical locations. Larger companies, with offices in multiple locations, typically use this kind of network. Each location has its own LAN that links the local computers together. All these LANs are, in turn, linked to each other via some communications medium. The linking can be anything from a 28.8bps modem to high-speed T1 connections and fiber-optic links. The complete group of interconnected LANs (see Figure 1.2) is called a WAN, or wide area network. WANs are used to link multiple locations within a single organization.

Suppose that you need to create a massive network that links every computer everywhere. How would you do this? You'd start by running high-speed backbones, connections capable of moving large amounts of data at once between strategic locations—perhaps large cities or different countries. These backbones would be similar to high-speed, multilane, interstate highways connecting various locations. You'd build in fault tolerance to make these backbones fully redundant so that if any connection broke, at least one other way to reach a specific destination would be available.

FIGURE 1.2

A WAN is made up of multiple interconnected LANs.

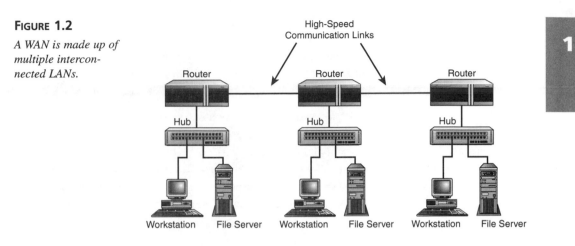

Next, you'd create thousands of local links that would connect every city to the backbones over slower connections—similar to state highways or city streets. You'd allow corporate WANs, LANs, and even individual users with dial-up modems to connect to these local access points. Some would stay connected at all times, whereas others would connect as needed.

You'd create a common communications language so every computer connected to this network could communicate with every other computer.

Finally, you'd devise a scheme to uniquely identify every computer connected to the network. This would ensure that information sent to a given computer would actually reach the correct destination.

Congratulations, you've just created the Internet!

Okay, so I'll admit that this is something of an oversimplification, but the truth is that this is exactly how the Internet works.

The high-speed backbones do exist. Most are owned and operated by the large telecommunications companies.

The local access points, more commonly known as POPs (Points of Presence), are run by phone companies, cable television providers, online services, and local Internet service providers (also known as ISPs).

NEW TERM The common language is IP, the Internet Protocol, except that the term *language* is a misnomer. A *protocol* is a set of rules governing behavior in certain situations. Foreign diplomats learn local protocol to ensure that they behave correctly in another country. Protocols ensure that there are no communication breakdowns or serious misunderstandings. Computers need protocols, too, to ensure that they can communicate with each other correctly and to be sure that data is exchanged correctly. IP is the protocol used to communicate across the Internet, so every computer connected to the Internet must be running a copy of IP. (All modern operating systems—including Windows, Windows NT, MacOS, and UNIX—come with a built-in copy of the IP software.)

The unique identifiers are IP addresses. Every computer, or host, connected to the Internet has a unique IP address. These addresses are made up of four sets of numbers separated by periods—for example, 208.193.16.250. Some hosts have fixed (or *static*) IP addresses; others have dynamically assigned addresses. Regardless of how an IP address is obtained, no two hosts connected to the Internet can use the same IP address at any given time. That would be like two homes having the same phone number or street address. Information would end up in the wrong place all the time.

Every time you request a Web page (or perform any other Internet-based transaction), data is being sent back and forth between your host (your computer) and the remote host (the computer you're requesting the data from). The data being sent back and forth passes through computers, hubs, routers, and other equipment.

To see just how you're connected to the remote host, use the TRACERT program that comes with Windows and Windows NT. To use TRACERT (short for Trace Route), go to a command prompt and type **TRACERT** *HOST*, replacing the word *HOST* with the host name or IP address of the host you want to trace to (for example, TRACERT www.forta.com). You'll be amazed at where your data actually travels to get to you.

Internet Applications

The Internet itself is simply a massive communications network that offers very little to most users, which is why it took 20 years for it to become the phenomenon it is today.

The Internet has been dubbed the Information Superhighway, and that analogy is quite accurate. Highways themselves aren't nearly as exciting as the places you can get to by traveling them—and the same is true of the Internet. What makes the Internet so exciting are the applications that run over it and what you can accomplish with them.

The most popular application now is the World Wide Web, which single-handedly transformed the Internet into a household word. In fact, many people mistakenly think that the World Wide Web *is* the Internet. This is definitely not the case, and Table 1.1 lists some of the more popular Internet-based applications.

TABLE 1.1 POPULAR INTERNET-BASED APPLICATIONS

Application	Description
Email	SMTP (Simple Mail Transfer Protocol) is the most popular email delivery mechanism; POP (Post Office Protocol) is one of the most popular protocols used to retrieve email.
FTP	File Transfer Protocol transfers files between hosts.
Gopher	This menu-driven document-retrieval system was popular before the creation of the World Wide Web.
IRC	Internet Relay Chat enables real-time, text-based conferencing over the Internet.
NFS	Network File System is used to share files among different hosts.
Newsgroups	These threaded discussion lists (of which there are thousands) are built on the NNTP protocol.
Telnet	Telnet logs in to a host from a remote location.
WWW	The World Wide Web has almost become synonymous with the Internet itself.

NEW TERM   All these different applications, and many others, use IP to communicate across the Internet. The information transmitted by these applications is broken into *packets*, or small blocks of data, and sent to a destination IP address. The application at the receiving end processes the received information.

> Depending on what programs you're running, your computer could be connected to multiple hosts at any given time. You can display a list of all active IP connections by using the NETSTAT program. Go to a DOS command prompt and type **NETSTAT -A** to display a list of all connections, the protocol being used, the ports that the connection is on, and the status of the connection.

Intranets and Extranets

Intranets and extranets are now two of the industry's favorite buzzwords. Not too long ago, most people thought "intranet" was a typo; in a very short period of time, however, intranets and extranets have become recognized as legitimate and powerful new business tools.

NEW TERM　An *intranet* is nothing more than a private Internet. In other words, it's a private network, usually a LAN or WAN, that enables the use of Internet-based applications in a secure and private environment. As on the public Internet, intranets can host Web servers, FTP servers, and any other IP-based services.

Companies have been using private networks for years to share information. Traditionally, office networks haven't been information-friendly. Old private networks didn't have consistent interfaces, standard ways to publish information, or client applications that could access diverse data stores. The popularity in the public Internet has spawned a whole new generation of inexpensive and easy-to-use client applications. These applications are now making their way back into the private networks. Intranets are gathering so much attention now because they are a new and cost-effective solution to an old problem.

NEW TERM　Extranets take this new communication mechanism one step further. *Extranets* are intranet-style networks that link multiple sites or organizations by using intranet-related technologies. Many extranets actually use the public Internet as their backbone and employ encryption techniques to ensure the security of the data being moved over the network.

The two things that distinguish intranets and extranets from the Internet are who can access them and from where they can be accessed. Don't be confused by hype surrounding applications that claim to be "intranet-ready." If an application can be used over the public Internet, it will work on private intranets and extranets too.

DNS, the Domain Name Service

IP addresses are the only way to uniquely specify a host. When you want to communicate with a host—for example, a Web server—you need to specify the IP address of the Web server you're trying to contact.

As you know from browsing the Web, you rarely specify IP addresses directly. You do, however, specify a host name, such as `www.forta.com`. If hosts are identified by IP addresses, how does your browser know which Web server to contact if you specify a host name?

The answer is the Domain Name Service (DNS), a mechanism that maps host names to IP addresses. When you specify the destination address of `www.forta.com`, your browser sends an address resolution request to a DNS server asking for the IP address of that host. The DNS server returns an actual IP address—in this case, 208.193.16.250. Your browser can then use this address to communicate with the host directly.

1

If you've ever mistyped a host name, you've seen error messages telling you that the host couldn't be found, or no DNS entry was found for the specified host. These error messages mean that the DNS server couldn't resolve the specified host name.

DNS is never needed. Users can always specify the name of a destination host by its IP address to connect to the host. There are, however, some very good reasons not to use the IP address:

- IP addresses are hard to remember and easy to mistype. Users are more likely to find www.forta.com than they are 208.193.16.250.

- IP addresses are subject to change. For example, if you switch service providers, you might be forced to use a new set of IP addresses for your hosts. If users identified your site only by its IP address, they never could reach your host if the IP address changed. Your DNS name stays the same, even if your IP address switches. You need to change only the mapping so that the host name maps to the new correct IP address.

- Multiple hosts, each with unique IP addresses, can all have the same DNS name. This allows load balancing between servers, as well as the establishment of redundant servers.

- A single host, with a single IP address, can have multiple DNS names. This enables you to create aliases if needed. For example, ftp.forta.com and www.forta.com might point to the same IP address, and thus the same server.

DNS servers are special software programs. Often your ISP will host your DNS entries so that you don't need to install and maintain your own DNS server software.

You can host your own DNS server and gain more control over the domain mappings, but you inherit the responsibility of maintaining the server. If your DNS server is down, there's no way of resolving the host name to an IP address, and no one will be able to find your site.

Understanding Web Publishing

As mentioned earlier, the most commonly used Internet-based application is now the World Wide Web. The recent growth of interest in the Internet is the result of the growth of interest in the World Wide Web.

The World Wide Web is built on the Hypertext Transfer Protocol (HTTP). HTTP is designed to be a small, fast protocol that is well suited for distributed multimedia information systems and hypertext jumps between sites.

Information on the World Wide Web is stored in pages. A page can contain any of the following:

Text	Tables
Headers	Forms
Lists	Graphics
Menus	Multimedia

NEW TERM   A *Web site* is simply a collection of Web pages along with any supporting files (such as GIF or JPG graphics). Creating a Web site thus involves creating one or more Web pages and linking them. The Web site is then saved on a Web server.

Web Servers

The Web consists of pages of information on hosts running Web-server software. The host is often referred to as the *Web server*, which is technically inaccurate. The Web server is actually software and not the computer itself. Versions of Web server software can run on almost all computers, and although most Web server applications have minimum hardware requirements, no special computer is needed to host a Web server.

Originally, all Web development was performed under different flavors of UNIX. Most Web servers still run on UNIX boxes, but this is changing. There are now Web-server versions for almost every major operating system. Web servers hosted on high-performance operating systems, such as Windows NT, are becoming more and more popular because UNIX is still more expensive to run than Windows NT and is also more difficult to use for the average user. Windows NT has proven itself to be an efficient, reliable, and cost-effective platform for hosting Web servers. As a result, Windows NT's slice of the Web server operating system pie is growing dramatically.

So, what exactly is a Web server? It's a program that serves up Web pages upon request. Web servers typically don't know or care what they're serving up. When a user at a specific IP address requests a specific file, the Web server tries to retrieve that file and send it back to the user. The requested file might be the HTML source code for a Web page, a GIF image, VRML worlds, .avi files, and so on. The Web browser determines what should be requested, not the Web server. All the server does is process that request, as shown in Figure 1.3.

Pages on a Web server are stored in different directories. When requesting a Web page, a user may provide a full path (directory and filename) to specify a particular document.

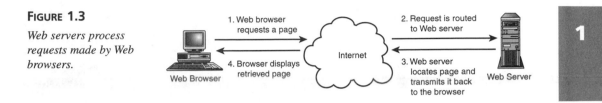

FIGURE 1.3

Web servers process requests made by Web browsers.

Web servers enable you to specify a default Web page, a page that is sent back to the user when only a directory is specified, with a Web server. These default pages are often called index.html or default.htm. If no default Web page exists in a particular directory, it either returns an error message or a list of all available files, depending on how the server is set up.

Web Browsers

Web browsers are the programs used to view Web pages. The Web browser has the job of processing received Web pages, parsing the HTML code, and displaying the page to users. The browser attempts to display graphics, tables, forms, formatted text, or whatever the page contains. The most popular Web browsers now in use are Netscape Navigator (see Figure 1.4) and Microsoft Internet Explorer (see Figure 1.5).

FIGURE 1.4

Netscape Navigator runs on more platforms (operating systems) than any other browser.

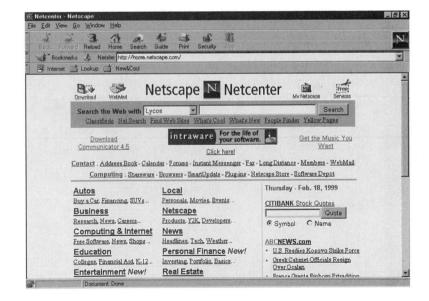

FIGURE 1.5

Microsoft Internet Explorer is the most popular browser among users of Windows and Windows NT.

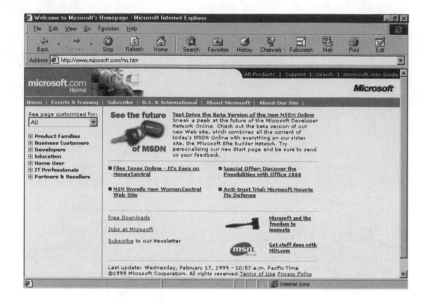

Web-page designers must pay close attention to the differences between browsers because different Web browsers behave differently. Unfortunately, no single browser supports every feature of the HTML language. Furthermore, the same Web page often looks different on two different browsers because every browser renders and displays Web page objects differently.

For this reason, most Web page designers use multiple Web browsers and test their pages in every one to ensure that the final output appears as intended. Without this testing, some Web site visitors can't correctly see the pages you publish.

Most Web browsers also provide users with tools to manage a list of favorite sites (usually called *bookmarks* or *favorites*), as well as the capability to print pages and save shortcuts to specific Web pages.

To request a Web page, browser users must specify the address of the page. The address is known as an URL.

URLs

Every Web page on the World Wide Web has an address. This is what you type into your browser to instruct it to load a particular Web page.

These addresses are called Uniform Resource Locators (URLs). URLs aren't only used to identify World Wide Web pages or objects. Files on an FTP server, for example, also have URL identifiers.

As seen in Figure 1.6, World Wide Web URLs consist of up to five parts:

- The protocol to use to retrieve the object. This is always `http` for objects on the World Wide Web.
- The Web server from which to retrieve the object. This is specified as a DNS name or an IP address.
- The host machine port on which the Web server is running. If omitted, the specified protocol's default port is used; for Web servers, this is port 80.
- The file to retrieve or the script to execute. The filename often includes a complete file path.
- Optional script parameters, also known as the *query string*.

FIGURE 1.6

URLs are made up of multiple parts, the minimum of which is the host name.

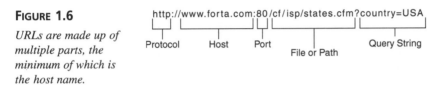

To understand how URLs work, look at a few examples:

- `http://www.forta.com` points to a Web page on the host `www.forta.com`. Because no document or path was specified, the default document in the root directory is served.
- `http://www.forta.com/cf/books/` also points to a Web page on the host `www.forta.com`, but this time the directory `/cf/books/` is specified. Because no page name was provided, the default page in the `/cf/books/` directory is served.
- `http://208.193.16.250/cf/books/` points to the same file as the preceding example, but this time the IP address is used instead of the DNS name.
- `http://www.forta.com/cf/books/news.cfm` again points to a Web page on the `www.forta.com` host. Both a directory and a filename are specified this time. This retrieves the file `news.cfm` from the `/cf/books/` directory, instead of the default file.
- `http://www.forta.com/cf/isp/states.cfm?country=USA` points to a script, rather than a Web page. `states.cfm` is a ColdFusion page that is executed when requested. Anything after the `?` are parameters that are passed to the script. In this example, a single parameter called `country` is being passed with a value of `USA`.

Links in Web pages are references to other URLs. When a user clicks a link, the browser processes whatever URL it references.

Understanding HTML

Web pages are plain text files constructed with HTML, the Hypertext Markup Language. HTML is implemented as a series of easy-to-learn *tags*, or instructions. Web page authors use these tags to mark up a page of text. Browsers then use these tags to render and display the information for viewing.

As stated earlier, HTML is very easy to learn. As long as you understand tags and attributes, you're all set.

HTML tags are always placed in between < and >. For example, to force a paragraph break, you would specify <P>.

Many tags are part of tag pairs that surround content. For example, to display the word *hello* in boldfaced text, you would specify the following code:

```
<B>hello</B>
```

Here the <B> tag turns bold on, and </B> turns it off again. End tags are always named with the same name as the start tag, preceded by a / character.

Some tags take one or more parameters in the form of attributes. Attributes are used to specify optional or additional information to a tag. For example, the <BODY> tag defines the body content of a Web page. <BODY> takes an optional attribute called BGCOLOR that specifies the page background color. So to create a page with a blue background, you could use the following code:

```
<BODY BGCOLOR="blue">
```

Some tags have no attributes, some have many. Attributes are almost always optional and can be specified in any order you want. Attributes must be separated from each other by a space, and attribute values should ideally be enclosed within double quotation marks.

HTML is constantly being enhanced with new features and added tags. To ensure backward compatibility, browsers must ignore tags they don't understand. For example, if you were to use the <MARQUEE> tag to create a scrolling text marquee, browsers that don't support this tag will still display the marquee text, but it won't scroll.

Web pages also can contain hypertext jumps, which are links to other pages or Web sites. Users can click links to jump within a page, or to jump to other pages on the same Web site or any page on any site.

The word *Web* in World Wide Web refers to the way that pages are all linked and cross-linked (kind of like a spider's web). This facilitates your ability to jump to any Web page on any Web server, and back again.

Introducing HomeSite

So now you know that Web sites are simply collections of Web pages, and that Web pages are plain text files. As such, you can create and edit your Web pages in any text editor or word processor.

But that is definitely the masochistic way to create pages. There now are dozens of products designed to simplify Web page development. These tools are often referred to as *page editors* or *authoring tools*, and the two aren't alike at all.

Editing Versus Authoring

Web page authoring tools are built around the premise that you, the page developer, don't want to learn or know HTML. As such, authoring tools provide fancy, graphical-based interfaces that enable you to interactively create your Web site. Under the hood, these tools are actually generating HTML code for you, but the authoring tool attempts to hide this fact. To provide this level of abstraction and isolation, authoring tools have to cut corners and support a subset of HTML's capabilities. Not all of HTML can be graphically represented within a GUI environment.

Authoring tools have their place in the market (some, like Microsoft FrontPage, sell very well). However, professional Web developers generally shy away from these tools for a simple reason—you can't do some things in HTML within an authoring environment. If you want total control over your Web pages, you can't and shouldn't ignore the underlying HTML. Manual fine-tuning of the tags and the attributes is often the only way to achieve specific results. Professional developers, therefore, use editors rather than authoring tools. Editors are programs used to manually create and manipulate HTML; they don't hide the HTML, they present it to you directly for you to edit.

So why use an editor if you have to edit the HTML manually anyway? Well, good Web page editors empower you with an array of tools that greatly simplify the Web site development process without compromising flexibility. In other words, you get the best of both worlds. You can edit the code manually so that you have all the power and flexibility you need, and you can also use tools and features that do lots of the grunt work for you.

So, what is HomeSite? HomeSite *isn't* an authoring tool. HomeSite *is* a Web page editor.

HomeSite is designed specifically for users who understand that you can't be scared of HTML if you want to develop professional Web pages. But HomeSite is also the most powerful and flexible Web page editor on the market. And by using HomeSite, you can create Web sites that are powerful, sophisticated, and professional, and you can do it all very easily.

Welcome to HomeSite.

Summary

During this first hour, you were introduced to some important Internet fundamentals. Understanding how the Internet does what it does is an important part of developing Web sites, and so the basics of Web servers, Web browsers, URLs, DNS, and HTML were explained. You also learned exactly what HomeSite is and what it isn't.

Before you can start experimenting with HomeSite, however, the product needs to be installed. Hour 2, "Getting Started," walks you through the installation process and introduces HomeSite.

Q&A

Q Why do some domains end with `.com`, while others end with `.net` or `.org`?

A The text after the final period in a host name is called the top level domain. `.com` is used for commercial domains (most domains fall into this category), `.org` is reserved for non-profit organizations, `.net` is used by Internet service providers (ISPs), `.edu` is used by universities or colleges that grant four-year degrees, `.gov` is used by the U.S. government, and `.mil` is used by the U.S. military. Other countries have domains that end with a two-letter country designator.

Q I see you have a domain named `forta.com`. How can I get my own domain?

A The basic rule is that if a domain name isn't currently taken, you can have it. The InterNIC is the organization responsible for assigning domains that end with `.com`, `.org`, `.net`, and `.edu`. The InterNIC charges a $35 annual fee for assigning your domain name. To obtain a domain name, simply fill in forms at the InterNIC's Web site at `http://www.internic.net`. However, obtaining a domain name isn't enough. To actually use your domain name, it needs to be hosted on a DNS server. You can set up your own DNS servers (you must have at least two of them) if you have your own permanent Internet connection; otherwise, you'll need to have your ISP host it for you.

Q Most of the Web sites I visit have host names that begin with www. Is this required?

A Actually, you can name a host anything you'd like. Before the Web ever existed, the Internet was already being used to share information. Protocols such as FTP and Gopher were used to access data on other hosts. Because single organizations would often offer multiple forms of data access, they named the machines by the service they offered (such as `ftp.forta.com`). This practice carried over into the Web, and is still prevalent.

Workshop

The Workshop contains quiz questions and activities to help reinforce what you've learned in this hour. If you get stuck, the answers to the quiz questions can be found in Appendix A, "Answers to Quiz Questions."

Quiz

1. What's the difference between the Internet, intranets, and extranets?
2. True or false: Every page on the Internet has a unique address.
3. True or false: Every host connected to the Internet has a unique DNS name.

Exercise

Want to find out more about a domain you visit regularly? The WHOIS utility returns information about registered domains. You can try this out at `http://whois.internic.net/cgi-bin/itts/whois/`.

Hour 2

Getting Started

By now I hope you are impatiently waiting to try HomeSite. But before you can do so, HomeSite must be installed on your computer.

In this hour you'll learn the following:

- What hardware and software you need to run HomeSite
- How to install HomeSite
- How to navigate HomeSite

 Even though I refer extensively to only HomeSite, the instructions in this hour (and indeed, the entire first three sections of this book) apply to both HomeSite and ColdFusion Studio equally. ColdFusion Studio users can follow all the HomeSite instructions, and then continue to the final section of this book for specific coverage of ColdFusion Studio.

Installing HomeSite

HomeSite is installed by using a standard Windows installation program. The installation process creates all the needed directories, installs files, and establishes default options and settings so that you can get up and running immediately.

HomeSite has an integrated browse mode that enables you to preview your pages while you are working on them. To use this feature, you must have Microsoft Internet Explorer 3.01 (or later) installed on your computer. If you don't have Microsoft Internet Explorer installed, you might want to install that first. You can download a copy directly from Microsoft at `http://www.microsoft.com/ie`. HomeSite's design mode also requires that Microsoft Internet Explorer 4.01 or later be installed. If you are running an older version of Internet Explorer, you might want to upgrade.

Note that the pages created with HomeSite may be viewed in any browser, but the integrated browse mode requires Microsoft Internet Explorer.

Hardware and Software Requirements

To run HomeSite, you must have the following hardware and software:

- A Pentium class computer (or better)
- Windows 95, Windows 98, or Windows NT 4 (on an Intel platform)
- At least 16MB RAM (although I personally recommend at least 32MB if you are running Windows 95/98, and at least 64MB if you are running NT)
- 10MB of free disk space
- A modem or network connection (if you intend to do any remote development or deployment to production and hosting servers)

Although HomeSite runs only on Windows platform computers, pages and sites created with HomeSite can be deployed and hosted on machines running any operating system.

Obtaining a Copy of HomeSite

HomeSite is a commercial product developed and sold by Allaire Corporation. HomeSite is available from many software distributors, as well as from Allaire directly at `http://www.allaire.com/products/homesite`.

 The accompanying CD contains a non-expiring evaluation version of HomeSite. You can use this copy of HomeSite to learn and experience the product, and to determine how well it fits your needs. If you decide that HomeSite works for you, you must register your copy with Allaire and purchase a license. However, the evaluation software isn't limited in any way and doesn't expire, even beyond the evaluation period.

The Installation Process

To start the installation process, locate the file HOMESITE40.EXE on the accompanying CD (or wherever you saved it if you downloaded it from the Allaire Web site), and double-click it. This launches the installation program as seen in Figure 2.1. Click Next to continue. You are then prompted to read and accept the license agreement; after you read it, click Yes to proceed.

2

FIGURE 2.1

The HomeSite installation program walks you through the process of installing HomeSite on your computer.

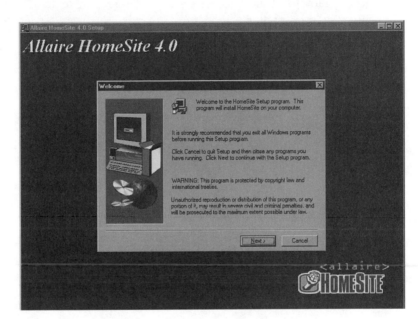

The installation program prompts you for your name, company name, and serial number, as seen in Figure 2.2. If you are installing an evaluation version of HomeSite, the word evaluation appears in the serial number field. After you fill in these fields, click Next.

FIGURE 2.2

Your HomeSite installation is personalized with the name, company name, and serial number provided during the installation process.

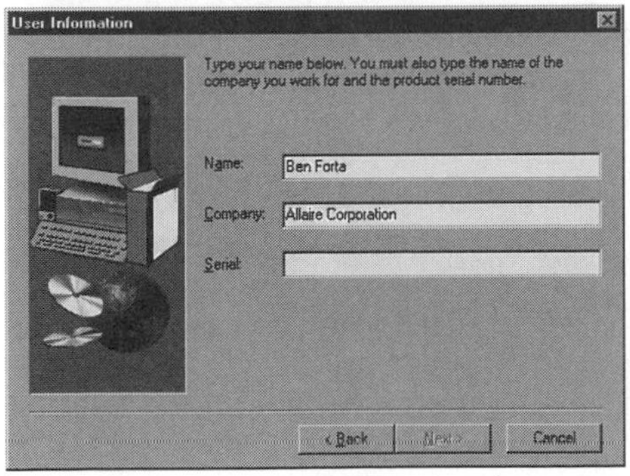

Upgrading an evaluation version of HomeSite to the full, licensed version requires that you reinstall the licensed software over the evaluation version.

Next, you're prompted for the location of the directory into which to install HomeSite (see Figure 2.3). Unless you have a compelling reason to do otherwise, I suggest that you just keep the default directory. If the directory specified does not already exist, it will be created for you automatically. Click Next to continue.

FIGURE 2.3

The default installation directory, as suggested by the installation program, should generally be used.

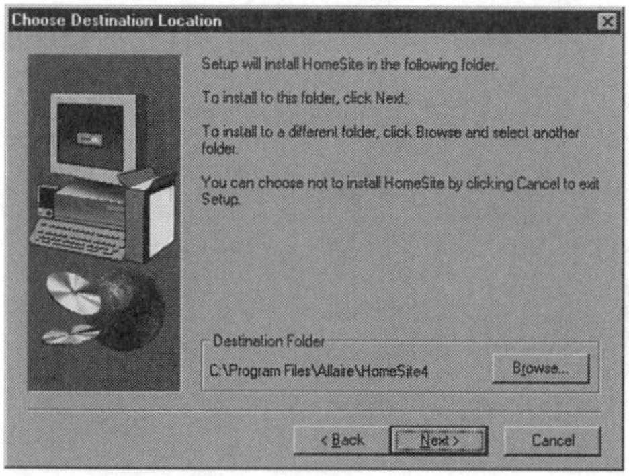

Now you must specify what you want installed. The dialog in Figure 2.4 shows the two options available to you. The first, HomeSite Program Files, is HomeSite itself (obviously, this must be installed to use the program). The second, Documentation, is the online documentation. Unless you are low on disk space, you should install the documentation because this will soon become one of your primary sources of development help. Make your selections, and click Next to continue.

FIGURE 2.4

Unless disk space is limited, both the HomeSite Program Files and the Documentation should be installed.

Next, you're prompted for the name of the Windows program group to be created. The default value will work just fine, so click Next, and you're prompted for a final confirmation before actual file installation begins. Verify the options, and click Next to begin the installation.

The installation program creates directories, copy files, program groups, and whatever else it needs, all the while displaying information banners describing HomeSite and some of its features. When the installation program is complete, you might be prompted to restart your computer, as seen in Figure 2.5. If you are prompted to do this, save any open work, close all programs, select Yes, I Want to Restart My Computer Now, and click Finish.

FIGURE 2.5

If you are prompted to restart your computer, do so before running HomeSite for the first time.

That's all there is to it. HomeSite is installed, ready, and waiting. And so now it's time to look at HomeSite itself.

> To ensure that you are always using the latest and greatest version of HomeSite, the product can itself check to see if newer versions are available. You can access this option by choosing Check for New Version from HomeSite's Help menu.

Getting to Know HomeSite

To start HomeSite, select the HomeSite 4.0 option from the HomeSite 4.0 Program menu off the Windows Start button. A splash screen is displayed for a few seconds while the program loads, and then you see the HomeSite program window (see Figure 2.6).

Browse tab

Toolbars   Edit tab   Design tab   Quick Bar

FIGURE 2.6

The HomeSite program window is divided into several different panes and windows.

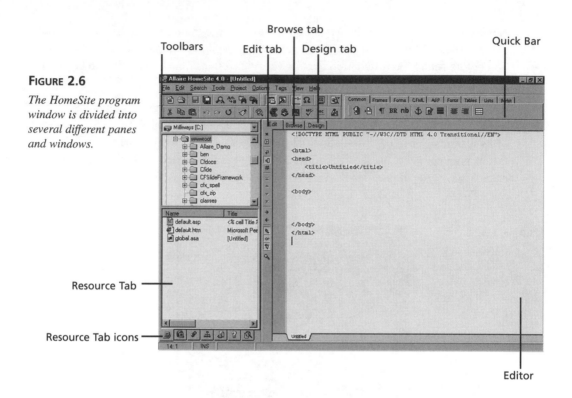

Resource Tab

Resource Tab icons

Editor

Now take a quick look at each major component of the HomeSite program window.

The Editor

As already explained, HomeSite is an editor. As such, the editor itself accounts for most of the HomeSite screen real estate. The editor window is where you write and browse your code.

HomeSite is an MDI (multiple document interface) editor, which means you can have multiple documents open within it at any given time. Each file is represented by a tab at the bottom of the editor window. To switch between open files, just click the appropriate tab.

The file tabs at the bottom of the editor window are used primarily for document selection, but they also serve another important use. The document name within the tab changes color, indicating whether a file has been saved. If a file has not been saved, the filename is displayed in blue with a blue × in front of it. After a file is saved, the filename is displayed in black.

Along the left side of the editor window is the Editor toolbar. Table 2.1 lists the buttons in this toolbar.

TABLE 2.1   EDITOR TOOLBAR BUTTONS

Button	Description
	Close the currently active document.
	Show list of currently open files.
	Toggle word wrap on and off.
	Hide or show gutter (the gray bar at the left of the editor window).
	Hide or show line numbers.
	Go to first open document.
	Go to previous open document.
	Go to next open document.
	Go to last open document.
	Indent selected text.
	Unindent selected text.
	Toggle Tag Insight (explained in Hour 3, "Getting Help").
	Toggle Tag Completion (explained in Hour 3).
	Toggle tag validation.
	Hide or display browser window beneath the editor (explained later). This button is available only in HomeSite, not in ColdFusion Studio.

2

HomeSite features all sorts of options that you can use to customize the behavior of the editor. Hour 4, "Customizing HomeSite," looks at some of these.

Menus, Buttons, and Toolbars

Almost every feature in HomeSite can be accessed in more than one way. Standard Windows menus provide access to most functions. Toolbars and buttons provide shortcuts to menu operations. If you're more comfortable typing (as opposed to using the mouse), you can use shortcut key combinations or menu selections.

> The tear-out card at the front of this book contains a list of hot keys and shortcuts.

Almost all HomeSite toolbars can be dragged, dropped, and anchored anywhere onscreen. If your screen does not look exactly like the ones in the figures, don't worry. It just means that they were moved, and in Hour 4 I show you how to do just that (along with other customizations).

Table 2.2 lists the standard set of four toolbars. Also, a very important toolbar is the Quick Bar, a tabbed set of toolbars that usually appears at the top right of the HomeSite screen. The Quick Bar contains multiple toolbars that you select by clicking their tabs, and each toolbar contains one or more buttons.

TABLE 2.2   TOOLBAR BUTTONS

Button	Description
Standard Toolbar Buttons	
	Create a new file by using the default template.
	Open a file, display the file selection dialog.
	Save the currently selected (active) file.
	Save all open files.
	Perform a search.
	Perform a search and replace operation.

Button	Description
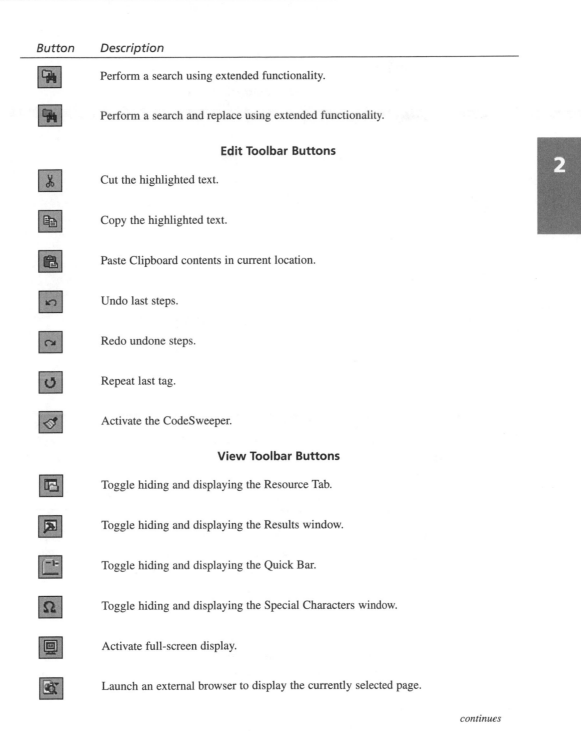	Perform a search using extended functionality.
	Perform a search and replace using extended functionality.

Edit Toolbar Buttons

	Cut the highlighted text.
	Copy the highlighted text.
	Paste Clipboard contents in current location.
	Undo last steps.
	Redo undone steps.
	Repeat last tag.
	Activate the CodeSweeper.

View Toolbar Buttons

	Toggle hiding and displaying the Resource Tab.
	Toggle hiding and displaying the Results window.
	Toggle hiding and displaying the Quick Bar.
	Toggle hiding and displaying the Special Characters window.
	Activate full-screen display.
	Launch an external browser to display the currently selected page.

continues

TABLE 2.2   CONTINUED

Button	Description

Tools Toolbar Buttons

Button	Description
	Display the Color Palette.
	Verify links in a page.
	Validate the active document.
	Display the image thumbnail viewer.
	Spell check the active page.
	Toggle the highlighting of misspelled words while you type.
	Launch the Stylesheet Editor.

The Integrated Browser

The only guaranteed way to preview what a Web page will look like in a browser is, well, to view it in a browser. Rather than require you to keep saving your changes and then view them in a separate browser, HomeSite integrates with Microsoft Internet Explorer (if you have it installed) to display the pages within a browser right within HomeSite.

Because the integrated browser is an actual Web browser (rather than a simulated preview), the page displayed within it is exactly what is displayed to visitors when your site is deployed. Furthermore, the browser is fully functional, and all HTML elements (images, tables, links, frames, and so forth) are displayed correctly with in it.

This integrated browser is accessible in two different ways:

- To display a full-size browser window (complete with browser navigation buttons), click the Browse tab in the editor mode selector. The browser, seen in Figure 2.7, is displayed in place of the editor. To toggle back to the editor, click the Edit tab.

- The browser can also be displayed directly beneath the editor window (see Figure 2.8). In this mode, page changes are reflected in the browser as the code is changed in the editor window. To enable this browser, click the Show Browser Below Editor button on the Editor toolbar (refer to Table 2.1). To close the browser window, click the button a second time.

FIGURE 2.7

HomeSite is fully integrated with Microsoft Internet Explorer, allowing pages to be previewed directly within the editor.

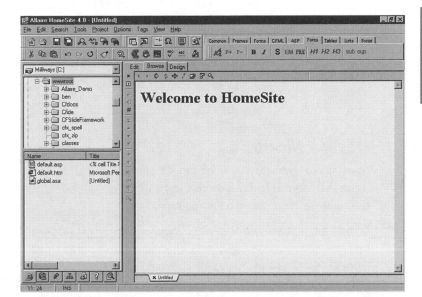

FIGURE 2.8

The integrated browser can be displayed beneath the editor window, so that code changes can be seen as they are made.

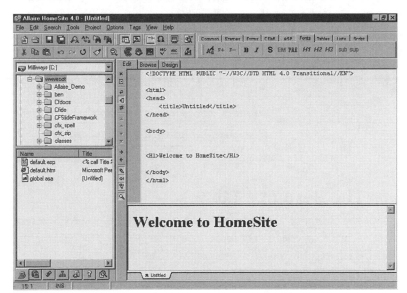

The Show Browser Below Editor option is available only in HomeSite, not in ColdFusion Studio.

In addition to integrated browser support, HomeSite supports the viewing of pages in multiple external browsers. This enables you to check how a page will appear in many different browsers. More on this in Hour 16, "Validating and Testing Your Pages."

 To toggle between Edit and Browse modes, press the F12 key.

Design Mode

Even though HomeSite is an editor, not an authoring tool, HomeSite's creators understood that some HTML elements can be tricky to code purely by hand. As such, HomeSite 4.0 introduced a Design mode.

Design mode is *not* a WYSIWYG layout tool, nor is it supposed to be one. Design mode can, however, provide a graphical representation of some HTML elements, allowing them to be created and manipulated graphically rather than coded by hand. The key difference is that Design mode is simply a way to generate blocks of HTML code that are inserted back into your page. When you go back to Edit mode, notice that HomeSite has generated cleanly formatted HTML and embedded it into your page for you.

To use Design mode, simply click the Design tab in the editor mode selector. You'll see a screen similar to the one shown in Figure 2.9.

In Hour 13, "Using the Design Mode," we'll look at Design mode in detail.

 To toggle between Edit and Design modes, press Shift+F12.

The Resource Tab

The Resource Tab is the block on the left of the HomeSite screen. The Resource Tab is actually a collection of tabbed resources, selected by clicking the tabs beneath it. The Resource Tab has seven tabs within it, as listed in Table 2.3.

FIGURE 2.9

Design mode provides a graphical interface to some common HTML layout tasks.

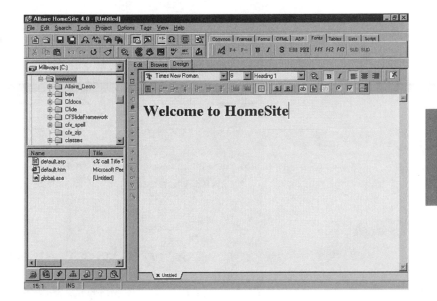

2

TABLE 2.3   RESOURCE TAB ICONS

Tab	Description
	The Local Files tab provides an Explorer-style tree control that you can use to browse and open files. Local files can also be files on a network drive, as long as you have rights to those files.
	The Remote Files tab provides access to files on a remote server (via an FTP connection).
	Use the Project tab to create and manage development projects.
	The Site View tab provides access to site management features.
	Use the Snippets tab to save and access *code snippets* (blocks of reusable code).
	The Help tab provides access to the integrated help system.
	The Tag Inspector tab provides a hierarchical tag based on the view of the page being edited.

    ColdFusion Studio users will notice one additional tab, the Database tab. This is discussed later in the book, in the hours dedicated to ColdFusion Studio.

We'll be using the Resource Tab extensively throughout this book.

 To temporarily hide the Resource Tab (to increase the size of the editor window), press the F9 key. Press F9 again to restore the Resource Tab.

Summary

This second hour walked you through installing HomeSite on your computer, and introduced you to HomeSite by giving you a quick tour of its screen and windows.

Q&A

Q HomeSite seems very code-centric. Am I going to have to write everything by hand?

A HomeSite is code-centric, that is true. But no, you aren't forced to do everything by hand. HomeSite comes with menus, toolbars, tag selection features, wizards, and more to do much of the work for you.

Q HomeSite looks incredibly feature rich. Will HomeSite do everything I need when creating Web sites, or will I need other tools and utilities too?

A HomeSite is an editor, the best in its class. HomeSite provides you with all the editing features you require, but you will need other tools as well. Probably the most important tool you'll need is a graphics manipulation program, something you can use to create and manage graphics.

Workshop

The Workshop contains quiz questions and activities to help reinforce what you've learned in this hour. If you get stuck, the answers to the quiz questions can be found in Appendix A, "Answers to Quiz Questions."

Quiz

1. Why does HomeSite feature an integrated Web browser and support for multiple external browsers as well?

2. True or false: HomeSite's Design mode is a full-featured WYSIWYG design tool.

Exercise

HomeSite is chock-full of toolbars and buttons. If you hold your mouse over any of them, a text description of the button will pop up. Take a few moments to get to know which buttons are on which toolbar, and what they do.

2

Hour **3**

Getting Help

As I've already explained, HTML editors don't hide the underlying code from you. Rather, they expose all HTML code to you so that you have complete and utter control over the end result. Although HTML is not a difficult language to learn, remembering all the tags and their attributes can be difficult. So that you always have the information you need when you need it, HomeSite comes with a sophisticated and extensive set of help features.

In this hour you'll learn the following:

- How to use Tag Editor dialogs to simplify tag usage
- How to get inline and pop-up help when you need it
- How to use the online help system

Help Is Never Far Away

You know the expression, "Good help is hard to find"? Well, whoever penned that one was definitely not a HomeSite user. Allaire has included extensive help within HomeSite and provided many different ways to access it:

- The Tag Chooser to help you find the tag you are looking for
- Tag Editors to simplify using tag attributes
- The Tag Inspector to simplify using tag attributes and events, as well as to provide a clear understanding of what tags are being used within a page
- Tag Tips for quick attribute lists
- Tag Insight for rapid keyboard-based attribute (and value) selection
- Tag Completion to help prevent mismatched (or unclosed) tags
- Traditional searchable online help
- Web-based help (live from the Allaire Web site)

To ensure that you have the help you need when you need it, let's look at how to get help within HomeSite.

Tag Chooser

HTML is a tag-based language. Most tags are intuitively named (for example, <BR> for a line break and <TABLE> for a table)—most, but not all. Furthermore, although some tags are used over and over, developers rarely use others. To help you find the tag you want (even if you can't remember its name), HomeSite features the Tag Chooser.

There are three ways to activate the Tag Chooser:

- Right-click in the editor window and select Insert Tag
- Press Ctrl+E
- Select Tag Chooser from the Tools menu

The Tag Chooser (see Figure 3.1) is a tree-style control that enables you to locate tags by functionality. The tree contains not just HTML tags, but also HDML (Handheld Device Markup Language), VTML (Visual Tool Markup Language), CFML (ColdFusion Markup Language), and more. To locate the tag you need, expand the language and then click a category to display the tags within it. Then simply select the desired tag and click the Select button.

Tag Editors

When you know the tag you want to use, the most commonly needed help is attribute related. As such, one of the most frequently used HomeSite help systems is the Tag Editors. These tag-specific pop-up dialogs interactively prompt you for tag attributes and values.

FIGURE 3.1

*The Tag Chooser sim-
plifies tag selection.*

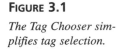

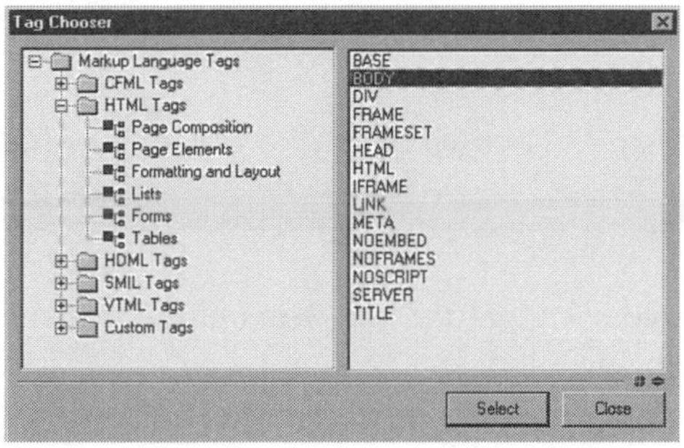

There are multiple ways to display a Tag Editor:

- Right-click a tag within the editor window and select Edit Tag
- Select any tag within the editor window and press Ctrl+F4
- Select any tag within the editor window, and then select Edit Current Tag from the Tags menu
- Select a tag from the Tag Chooser

Tag Editors, like the one in Figure 3.2, enable you to edit and specify tag attributes, without having to remember their individual names. Even better, the dialog fields are context aware, meaning that they intelligently prompt for the right kind of information. For example, the color attributes in the <BODY> tag enable you to select a color from a drop-down list or specify a custom color (as an RGB value).

FIGURE 3.2

*The <BODY> Tag Editor
prompts for colors,
margins, and even
browser-specific
options, as indicated
by the Internet
Explorer icon.*

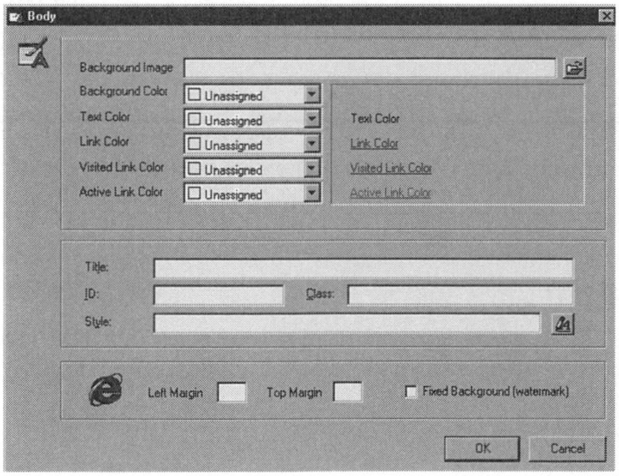

3

Many Tag Editors contain embedded help as well. For example, look at the <TABLE> Tag Editor:

1. Place the cursor in the editor window on any blank line (that's where the tag will be inserted).

2. Click the Tables tab on the Quick Bar.

3. Click the Table dialog button (the one with the Tbl text and a blue-and-white bar above it) to display the <TABLE> Tag Editor.

4. At the bottom right of the Tag Editor window (right above the Cancel button) are two little buttons (shown in Figure 3.3). Click the right one to toggle the embedded help (see Figure 3.4).

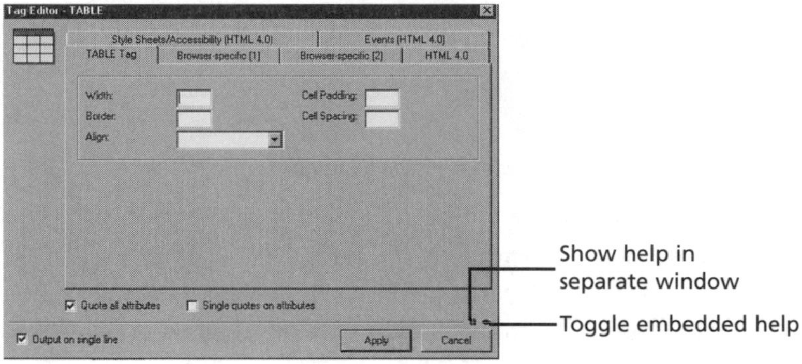

FIGURE 3.3

Many Tag Editors contain embedded help, which can be accessed by clicking either of the two help window buttons.

Show help in separate window

Toggle embedded help

5. To display help in a separate pop-up window, click the left button (again, indicated in Figure 3.3). The help window remains open until you close it by clicking the close button (the × on the window's title bar).

Some Tag Editors (such as the <TABLE> one we just looked at) are tabbed dialogs with options in multiple tabs. When this is the case, you'll find that the most frequently used options and attributes are on the first tab.

FIGURE 3.4

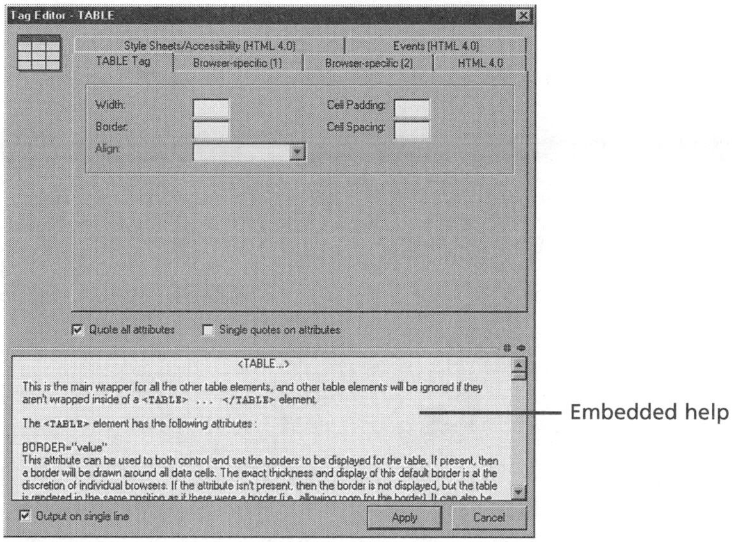

Tag Editor help can be displayed embedded with the Tag Editor window (as shown here) or in a separate pop-up window.

Embedded help

3

Tag Inspector

The Tag Inspector provides an alternative way to edit tag attributes and properties. The Tag Inspector is part of the Resource Tab (we looked at that briefly in Hour 2) and is selected in one of the following ways:

- Click the Tag Inspector tab at the bottom of the Resource Tab.
- Select Inspect Current Tag from the Tags menu.
- Press F4 (if the editor window cursor is on a tag, the Tag Inspector will open with a tag selected).

The Tag Inspector window (see Figure 3.5) consists of two panes. The upper pane contains a tree control that lists all the tags within a page. You can expand and close branches by clicking the + or – symbol next to them. You also can select any tag simply by clicking it. When a tag is selected, the tag within the editor window is highlighted, and the lower pane in the Tag Inspector displays a list of the tag's attributes and events.

To try out the Tag Inspector, do the following:

1. Click the <BODY> tag in the editor window.
2. Press F4 to activate the Tag Inspector for the currently selected tag (the <BODY> tag you just clicked).
3. Click any attribute and event to set their values. Click the BGCOLOR attribute to specify the page background color.

FIGURE 3.5

*The Tag Inspector pro-
vides a tree view of all
tags within a page and
enables you to edit
their attributes and
events directly.*

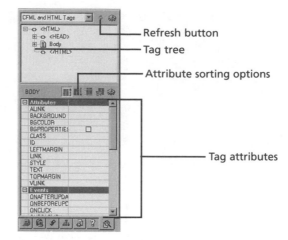

— Refresh button

— Tag tree

— Attribute sorting options

— Tag attributes

4. Because BGCOLOR is a color field, HomeSite displays a drop-down color selector
    box (see Figure 3.6). Select any color from the list to set the page background
    color.

5. Click any other field. Your color selection is updated in the <BODY> tag in the editor
    window.

FIGURE 3.6

*The Tag Inspector sim-
plifies the process of
specifying attribute
colors by embedding a
color selector drop-
down list box.*

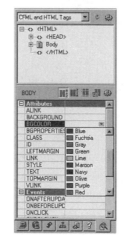

If you manually change the code in the editor window while the Tag
Inspector is active, you might have to instruct the Tag Inspector to refresh its
tag list. Do this by clicking the Refresh button at the top of the Tag
Inspector window (refer to Figure 3.5).

The attributes and elements listed in the Tag Inspector can be sorted in several ways by using the buttons identified in Figure 3.5.

Tag Tips

Another form of help is Tag Tips, little pop-up boxes right within the editor window (see Figure 3.7) that contain tag attributes. To display a Tag Tip, do the following:

1. Click the <BODY> tag in the editor window.

2. Press F2 to display the Tag Tip for the currently selected tag (the <BODY> tag you just clicked).

3. Press Esc (or click the mouse) to remove the box.

FIGURE 3.7

Tag Tips are little pop-up help boxes that display a list of tag attributes.

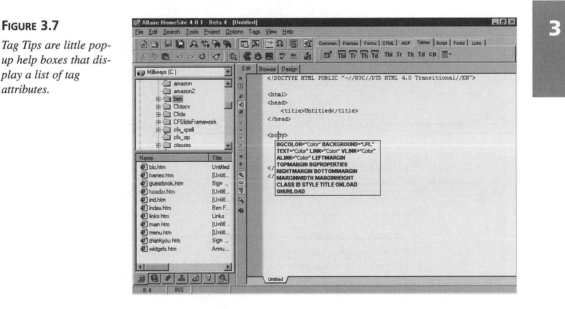

Tag Insight

Another form of pop-up help is Tag Insight. This intelligent feature detects when you need help, and pops up selections automatically in a list box. The best way to see this feature is to try it:

1. Position your cursor right in front of the <BODY> tag's > in the editor window.

2. Press the spacebar (as though you were entering a space before another attribute).

3. Wait a second or two until a pop-up box (like the one in Figure 3.8) appears.

4. Make a selection by clicking any attribute or by scrolling with the cursor keys and pressing Enter.

FIGURE 3.8

HomeSite intelligently provides pop-up help in the form of Tag Insight when it detects that you need it.

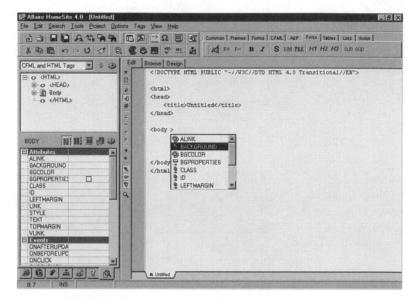

Attributes that have known value sets (such as colors) automatically display a second Tag Insight box when the attribute is selected.

By default, HomeSite waits one second before displaying Tag Insight. If this is too fast, you can change this interval in the HomeSite Settings dialog by selecting Settings from the Options menu.

Tag Insight appeals primarily to users who prefer working with the keyboard instead of the mouse.

Tag Insight can be turned on and off by using the button on the Editor toolbar (see Hour 2, "Getting Started").

If Tag Insight pops up when you don't want it, press Esc to close it.

Tag Completion

The final form of automatic help is Tag Completion. This feature is designed to prevent you from introducing mismatched tags. Try the following:

1. Position your cursor anywhere between the <BODY> and </BODY> tags.

2. Type **<TABLE>**. As soon as you type the > character, HomeSite automatically inserts a </TABLE> tag for you.

To turn Tag Completion on and off, use the button on the Editor toolbar (see Hour 2).

The Online Help System

In addition to all the help features mentioned up until now, traditional application help is also available within HomeSite. The online help system (see Figure 3.9) is accessed via the Resource Tab (discussed in Hour 2). All help documents are actually HTML documents, which are viewed by using the integrated Web browser.

3

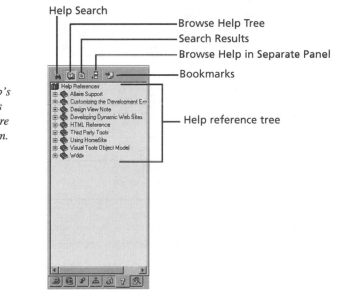

FIGURE 3.9

*The Resource Tab's
Help tab provides
access to the entire
online help system.*

Help Search
Browse Help Tree
Search Results
Browse Help in Separate Panel
Bookmarks
Help reference tree

The Bookmarks button allows you to save a list of help pages for future reference.

To access the online help system, click the Help tab in the Resource Tab (the one with the yellow question mark on it). The Help tab provides access to help in two ways:

- Help documents can be browsed by using a document tree.
- To find specific help documents, you can use the search dialog.

Suppose that you needed help creating HTML tables. The following steps walk you through browsing the help tree to find the document you need:

1. Click the Help Reference Tree button to display the help tree (see Figure 3.10).

FIGURE 3.10

The Help tab enables you to easily browse available online help documents.

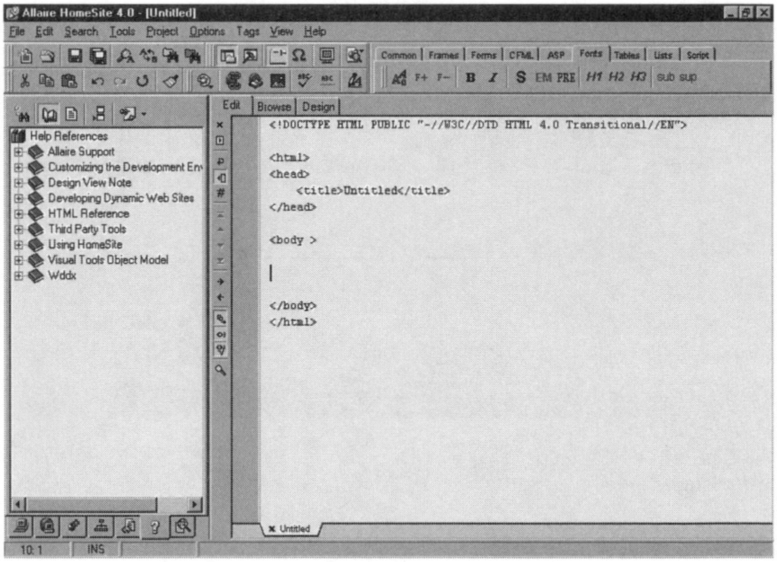

2. Expand the HTML References branch and scroll to find the Tables entry.
3. Expand Tables to display a list of documents, and then double-click the document titled Table Examples to view it in the integrated browser (see Figure 3.11).
4. Sometimes it is more convenient to browse help in a separate window so that you can work on your code at the same time. To display the help right within the Resource Tab (see Figure 3.12), click the Browse Help in Separate Panel button (refer to Figure 3.9 if you need help finding this button).

FIGURE 3.11

By default, help documents are displayed full screen in the integrated browser.

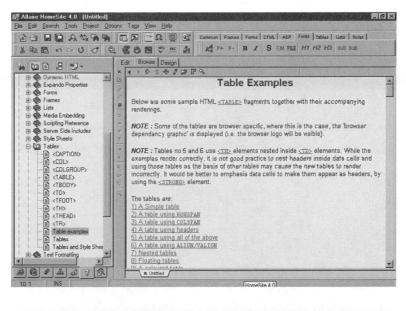

FIGURE 3.12

Help documents can be displayed in a panel within the Resource Tab, enabling you to work on your code while reading the help.

Help displayed
in separate
Resource Tab
pane

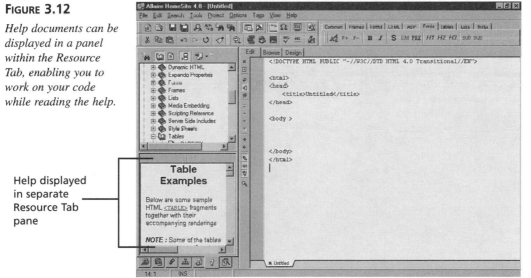

Now see what's involved in finding the same help by using the Search feature:

1. Click the Search button to display the Search Help References dialog (see Figure 3.13).

The Search Help References dialog lets you specify the text to search for, as well as the documents to be searched.

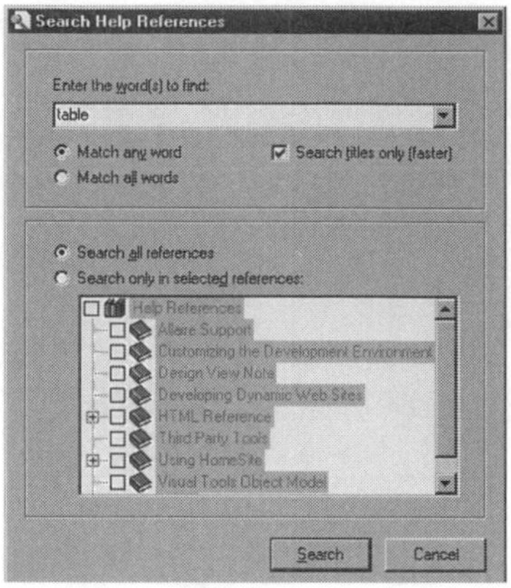

2. Type **TABLE** in the Enter the Word(s) to Find text box.

3. Click the Search button to perform the search. The results are displayed in a Search Results list in the Resource Tab's Help tab (see Figure 3.14).

4. Double-click the Table Examples document to open it.

FIGURE 3.14

Search results are displayed in the Resource Tab. Double-clicking any matching document opens it in the integrated browser.

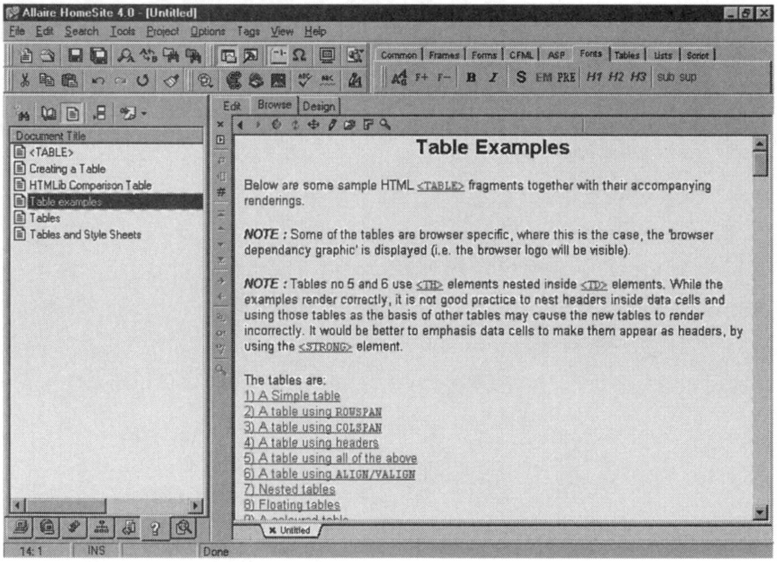

HomeSite on the Web

HomeSite comes with extensive help, enough to provide you with the answers to almost any problem or question. But if that isn't enough, there's more. The Allaire Web site contains all sorts of links, tips, and advice for HomeSite users, all accessible right from within HomeSite.

To access the Web-based help extensions, select HomeSite on the Web from HomeSite's Help menu. This selection will enable you to

- Purchase a live (non-evaluation) copy of HomeSite
- Download free add-ons
- Access the HomeSite Developer Center, which is chock-full of useful tips, tricks, and links

Summary

This hour introduced the HomeSite help features. By ensuring that the help you need is at your fingertips at all times, HomeSite can greatly simplify your development efforts, saving you lots of precious time.

Q&A

Q I'm using several third-party products in my Web pages, some of which use tags not natively supported by HomeSite. Is there a way to add Tag Editors for these tags?

A HomeSite Tag Editors are created by using a special XML-based language called VTML (Visual Tool Markup Language). While coverage of VTML is beyond the scope of this book, the online help system does explain this language, as well as provide examples and instructions for creating your own Tag Editors.

Q Is it possible to add my own help document to the online help system?

A The help documents in the online help system are HTML files, and you can add any HTML files of your own to the help system. To add help documents, just place them in folders beneath the HomeSite Help directory (usually C:\Program Files\Allaire\HomeSite4\Help).

Q New Web technologies are being released all the time, and I'd like to keep the HomeSite help system up-to-date. Where can I find documents describing these new technologies?

A The best place to start is the W3 Consortium Web site at `http://www.w3.org`. Another valuable resource is the HTML Writers Guild at `http://www.hwg.org`.

Workshop

The Workshop contains quiz questions and activities to help reinforce what you've learned in this hour. If you get stuck, the answers to the quiz questions can be found in Appendix A, "Answers to Quiz Questions."

Quiz

1. Which HomeSite feature would you use to ensure that you close all tags correctly?
2. What three HomeSite features can you use to interactively specify tag attributes?

Exercise

As you work with HomeSite, you'll develop a preference for some help features over others. By using the steps we walked through in this hour, experiment with the various help features to familiarize yourself with them and to determine which ones work best for you.

HOUR 4

Customizing HomeSite

HomeSite is a highly flexible and customizable product. Rather than force you to work a specific way, it's designed to adapt to the way you want to work.

In this hour you'll learn the following:

- How to use the HomeSite configuration options
- How to configure the editor
- How to manage and configure toolbars

Customizing and Configuring HomeSite

Most HomeSite customization and configuration is performed by using the Settings and Customize dialogs:

- The Settings dialog is used for everything except toolbar and shortcut configuration. It's activated by clicking F8 or by choosing Settings from the Options menu.

- The Customize dialog is used for toolbar and shortcut configuration. It's activated by clicking Shift+F8 or by choosing Customize from the Options menu.

General Settings

You use the General page of the Settings dialog (see Figure 4.1) to configure general HomeSite editor behavior. Some options are extremely important, so let's look at a few of them right now. I'm not actually going to walk through every one of them—there are far too many options for that—just the ones that I think are most important.

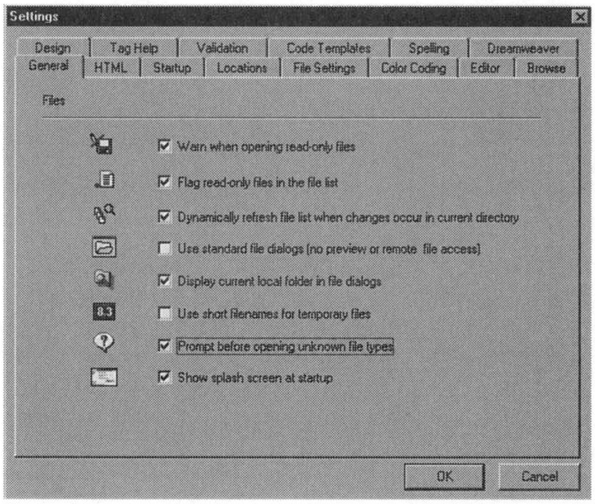

FIGURE 4.1

Use the General settings to control general HomeSite options.

Warn When Opening Read-Only Files

If you open a file that's flagged as read-only, HomeSite won't let you make any changes to it. To prevent you from trying to edit a file that can't be edited, you can tell HomeSite to pop up a warning message (like the one in Figure 4.2) each time you try to open a read-only file. I recommend that you always keep this option checked.

FIGURE 4.2

HomeSite can warn you if you attempt to open a read-only file for editing.

Flag Read-Only Files in the File List

The read-only warning in Figure 4.2 is extremely useful, but it also can be very annoying if you're working in a directory that contains many read-only files that you inadvertently click. To save you from repeatedly opening read-only files, turn the Flag Read-Only Files in the File List option on. Now read-only files will be flagged as such in the file list on the Resource page.

Show Details in File List

The file list in the Resource page can display simple filenames, or filenames accompanied by page title, file size, and other useful information. Obtaining this information (especially the HTML <TITLE>) is a time-consuming process, so depending on how large your file directories are and how fast your computer is, you might want to turn the Show Details in File List option off. However, unless it's a real inconvenience from a performance perspective, I suggest you keep this option turned on.

Dynamically Refresh File List When Changes Occur in Current Directory

The Resource page displays a list of files in a selected directory. By default, after HomeSite reads the file list (when the directory is selected), that list isn't automatically updated. If you're working in a network environment (where multiple users share the same directories) or are using other programs that could be modifying files as well, you might want to turn on the Dynamically Refresh File List When Changes Occur in Current Directory option. But be warned: Turning on dynamic refreshing slows down HomeSite, particularly if the files are accessed over slow connections.

> If you opt to not turn on this option, you can still force HomeSite to update the file list by clicking within the file list window and pressing F5.

HTML Settings

The HTML page of the Settings dialog (see Figure 4.3) enables you to control how HomeSite generates and embeds HTML code within your pages. Again, I'm not going to cover all the options on this page, just the ones that I think are most important at this time.

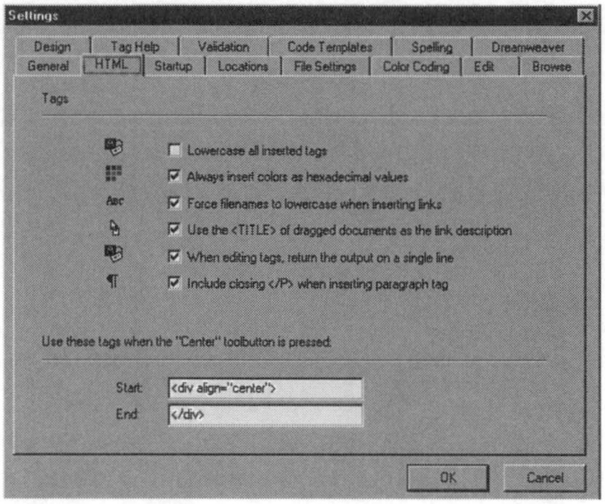

FIGURE 4.3

FIGURE 4.3

*Use the HTML page of
the Settings dialog to
control how HomeSite
generates HTML code.*

Lowercase All Inserted Tags

HTML developers need to pick a standard convention as to how tags and attributes
should appear within their pages. Some developers like all HTML tags to be inserted in
uppercase:

```
<TABLE BORDER="3" CELLPADDING="2" CELLSPACING="2">
```

Others prefer to use lowercase:

```
<table border="3" cellpadding="2" cellspacing="2">
```

There is no right or wrong case for tags within your pages, but you should be
consistent—pick a standard and stick with it.

To force HomeSite to embed all tags in lowercase, check the Lowercase All Inserted
Tags box. To force HomeSite to embed all tags in uppercase (the way I personally prefer
it), uncheck this box.

Always Insert Colors as Hexadecimal Values

You can refer to colors in HTML in two ways. There are standard color names that many
(but not all) browsers support, enabling you to specify colors as follows:

```
<BODY BGCOLOR="blue">
```

The other way to specify colors is by their RGB values, as follows:

```
<BODY BGCOLOR="#0000FF">
```

RGB values are explained thoroughly in Hour 7, "Working with Fonts and Colors," but for now it will suffice to say that every color has a unique six-character value that identifies it.

Color names are definitely more convenient (everyone knows what fuchsia is, but how many of you know that FF00FF is the RGB value for fuchsia?). Many older browsers don't understand color names, however, so they'll ignore the color altogether if a name is encountered.

HomeSite supports both methods of color specification. To use color names whenever possible, uncheck this box. To always use RGB values, check this box.

Not all colors have names, so even if you do use color names you will have to resort to RGB values occasionally.

When Editing Tags, Return the Output on a Single Line

HomeSite Tag Editors (discussed in Hour 3, "Getting Help") enable you to interactively specify tag attributes. When the Tag Editor is closed, HomeSite pastes the generated code into your page.

HomeSite can write generated HTML in two ways:

- With each attribute on a separate line:

```
<table width="100%"
       border="2"
       valign="TOP"
       nowrap>
</table>
```

This makes your HTML far more legible (and easier to edit), but it also increases the page size slightly, which in turn increases the time it takes to download your page.

- With the tag and its attributes on one long line:

```
<table width="100%" border="2" valign="TOP" nowrap></table>
```

This is less legible (and thus more difficult to edit, especially when a tag has many attributes), but it keeps the page size down a bit.

To have HomeSite generate tags on a single line, check the When Editing Tags, Return the Output on a Single Line box. To generate code on multiple lines, uncheck it.

4

Many developers actually use both styles. During page development, when you're continuously editing pages, multiline output is preferred. However, when the site is complete and is about to be deployed, you can reformat the file with tags formatted using single line output, which will improve download time.

Use These Tags When the "Center" Toolbutton Is Pressed

In HTML's early days, there was no easy way to center elements on a page. Although not the officially correct way to center elements, the popular browsers added support for a tag named <CENTER>. Anything between the <CENTER> and </CENTER> tags would be centered on the page.

Now there's finally an officially approved method to center elements—using the <DIV> tag. The only problem with <DIV> is that many older browsers don't support it.

By default, when you click the Center button (in the Common Quick Bar toolbar), HomeSite generates <DIV> code. If support for older browsers is a concern, you might want to tell HomeSite to use the <CENTER> tags instead. To do this, enter **<CENTER>** in the Start text box and **</CENTER>** in the End text box.

Startup Settings

The Startup options of the Settings dialog (see Figure 4.4) configure HomeSite's behavior on application startup. These options enable you to automatically restore previously used files for editing and to check for new versions of the HomeSite software.

Restore Last Opened Documents at Start-Up

Many developers find themselves working on a set of files over an extended time period, often the duration of a project or development effort. If you find yourself manually opening the same files repeatedly, you'll find the option Restore Last Opened Documents at Start-Up useful because it tells HomeSite to automatically reopen all files that were open the last time you quit HomeSite. Of course, if you work with different files all the time, enabling this option can be more of burden than a benefit. The choice is yours.

FIGURE 4.4

Use the Startup page of the Settings dialog to configure HomeSite's behavior on program startup.

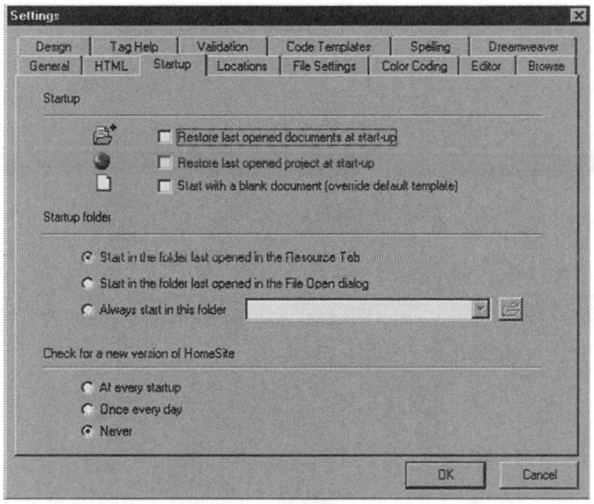

Restore Last Opened Project at Start-Up

NEW TERM *HomeSite projects* are groups of files that are opened and manipulated as a set. (Hour 20, "Managing Your Projects," looks at projects in detail.) HomeSite lets you restore open projects just as it does open files. To enable this option, check the Restore Last Opened Project at Start-Up box.

Check for a New Version of HomeSite

Allaire Corporation is constantly improving and enhancing HomeSite. To ensure that you're using HomeSite's latest and greatest version, you can have HomeSite automatically check to see if a new version is available. Depending on the option you select, HomeSite will perform this check once a day (at application startup) or every time you start HomeSite.

Checking for new versions of HomeSite requires that you be connected to the Internet. If you connect to the Internet on demand via an ISP and aren't connected at all times, you shouldn't use automatic update checking because this will cause HomeSite to force a connection to your ISP.

If you opt not to have HomeSite automatically check for new versions of the software, you can still perform this check on demand by choosing Check for New Version from HomeSite's Help menu.

The version-checking feature described here is available only in HomeSite, not in ColdFusion Studio.

Configuring the Editor

I'm sure I've said this before, but just in case—HomeSite is an editor. Because HomeSite users spend most of their time within the editor itself, the editor is designed to be highly configurable and customizable.

Color Coding

You've probably noticed that text in the editor window is displayed in different colors. HomeSite supports the use of automatic color coding so that different page elements (tags, attributes, comments, literal text, tables, and so forth) are displayed in different colors. Color coding is an extremely useful development tool for several reasons:

- It makes pinpointing specific lines of code easier.
- It breaks the monotony of long pages of code.
- It helps you locate errors. If a tag shows up in the wrong color, it indicates a typo, missing quotation mark, or some other error.

HomeSite uses color schemes to define colors. The default scheme is the one that you've seen already (with literal text in black and most HTML tags in dark blue). Color schemes are automatically associated with file extensions, so if you're editing files with an HTM or HTML extension, the HTML color scheme is used. If the extension is JS (a JavaScript file), the JavaScript scheme is used. Similarly, if the file has an ASP or ASA extension, the ASP scheme is used. Color scheme selection occurs automatically—when you open the file, HomeSite uses the appropriate color scheme.

If you don't like the default colors being used in a scheme, HomeSite lets you change them. Color schemes are configured by using the Color Coding page of the Settings dialog (see Figure 4.5).

To modify a color scheme, follow these steps:

1. On the Color Coding page of the Settings dialog, double-click the scheme to be edited to display the color selection window.
2. Click Edit Scheme to display the scheme editor (see Figure 4.6).

FIGURE 4.5

Use the Color Coding page to edit editor color schemes.

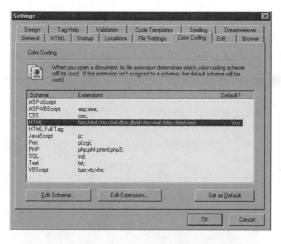

FIGURE 4.6

The color scheme editor prompts for colors for each scheme element and previews what the scheme would look like.

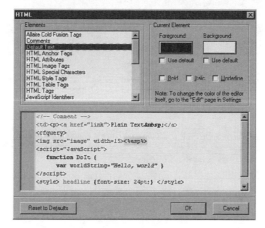

4

3. Click any element in the Elements list to select the element to update.

4. Specify the foreground, background, bold, italic, and underline settings for this element.

5. Repeat steps 3 and 4 for all elements you want to update.

6. When you're done, click OK to save your changes.

> Don't be scared to experiment with color schemes to pick one that works best for you. If you end up with a scheme that you don't want to use, you can always restore the default settings by clicking the Reset to Defaults button in the scheme editor.

Editor Fonts

HomeSite lets you select the font (and size) for text within the editor window. Font selection is made by using the Edit page of the Settings dialog (see Figure 4.7). After you make your selection, click OK to save it.

Settings dialog showing the Editor tab with Font set to Courier New, a font dropdown list showing David, David Transparent, Fixed Miriam Transparent, Fixedsys, Garamond, Georgia, Haettenschweiler. Options include Auto indent, Insert tabs as spaces, Allow text drag-and-drop, Treat HTML dropped from external applications as plain text, Visible right margin at column 80, Allow undo after save, Outline current line.

Although all installed fonts are available to you, stick with fonts that can be read easily for a prolonged period. Many developers find that Courier New and Fixedsys are good choices.

Auto Indent

NEW TERM *Auto Indent* is a HomeSite feature that automatically indents your text (if needed) when you press Enter. For example, if you start an unordered list (with the <UL> tag) or a table row (with the <TR> tag), pressing Enter would indent the next line so that your code is formatted properly.

This option is available in the Edit page of the Settings dialog (refer to Figure 4.7), and I highly recommend that you keep it selected at all times.

Allow Undo After Save

The Undo button can be a programmer's best friend. HomeSite features both Undo and Redo buttons (so you can undo your undoings, if needed). By default, you can undo (and redo) as far back as the last time your file was saved. Most programmers like to be able to undo every change from the time the file was opened, and HomeSite supports this feature.

This option also is available in the Edit page of the Settings dialog, and I highly recommend that you keep it checked at all times as well.

Managing Toolbars

HomeSite's toolbars provide single-click access to all sorts of functions, tags, scripts, and wizards. Because toolbars are such an important tool within the editor, HomeSite allows these to be configured to best suit your needs.

Toolbar Placement

HomeSite's 13 standard toolbars (as well as any of your own) can be placed or docked in several ways, as shown in Figure 4.8.

- To float a toolbar, simply drag it to the desired location.
- To dock a toolbar to the top, bottom, or either side of the screen, drag the toolbar to the edge of the HomeSite window and release it.
- To add a toolbar to the Quick Bar, simply drag it to the Quick Bar and release it.

4

Quick Bar

FIGURE 4.8

You can float, dock, or embed HomeSite toolbars in the Quick Bar.

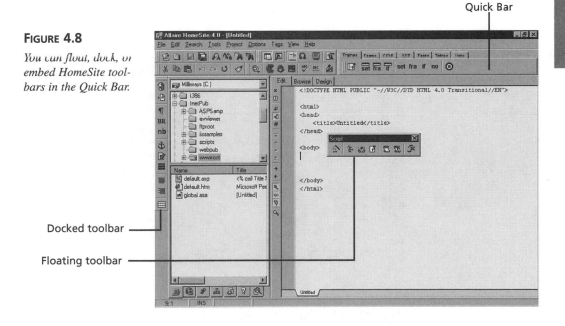

Docked toolbar

Floating toolbar

To drag a toolbar, click the double vertical lines on the left of the toolbar (see Figure 4.9). To drag a toolbar from the Quick Bar, first select it by clicking its tab.

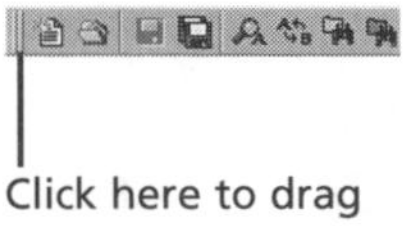

FIGURE 4.9

You move toolbars by dragging the left vertical lines.

Click here to drag

> HomeSite automatically saves the locations and placements of any toolbars, so the next time you start HomeSite, everything will be exactly where you want it to be.

Customizing Toolbars

HomeSite has 13 standard toolbars (Hour 2, "Getting Started," looked at a few of them). You can customize these standard toolbars and even create new ones of your own.

HomeSite toolbars are configured by using the Customize dialog's Toolbars page (see Figure 4.10). The Customize screen is activated by clicking Shift+F8 or by choosing Customize from the Options menu.

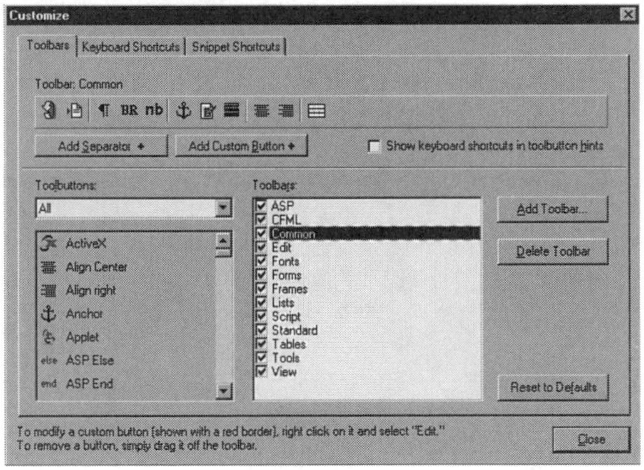

FIGURE 4.10

Use the Customize dialog's Toolbars options to edit or add toolbars.

One popular use for custom toolbars is grouping functions or features that you commonly use in one place. The following steps take you through creating your own toolbar:

1. If you haven't yet opened the Customize screen, do so by choosing Customize from the Options menu.

2. To add a new toolbar, click the Add Toolbar button.

3. At the prompt to name your new toolbar (see Figure 4.11), type any name you like in the pop-up dialog and then click OK.

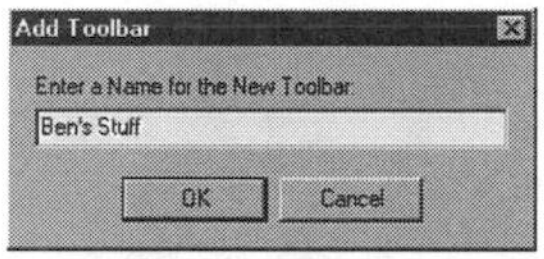

FIGURE 4.11

Every HomeSite tool-bar must have a unique name.

4. Make sure that the new toolbar is listed in the dialog's Toolbars list, and check its box (if it isn't checked, the new toolbar won't be visible). The empty toolbar appears at the top of the dialog.

5. To add items to the toolbar, select and drag a feature from the list under the Toolbuttons drop-down to the toolbar. For example, select and drag the Easter Egg feature to the toolbar.

> The HomeSite Easter Egg is an arcade-style game built right into the product. When you've finished all your work, it's time for some good old-fashioned fun with an HTML twist.

6. Add as many buttons as you need to the toolbar by repeating step 5. You also can add separators between buttons by clicking the Add Separator button.

7. To add a button that's not listed in the Toolbuttons list, click Add Custom Button. You'll be prompted for the type of button to create (see Figure 4.12).

8. When you're done, click Close in the Customize dialog. Your new toolbar will appear floating on the HomeSite screen (of course, you can move and dock it as described earlier).

> Another way to hide or show toolbars is to simply right-click any toolbar. This will display a list of toolbars, and you can check or uncheck them as needed.

4

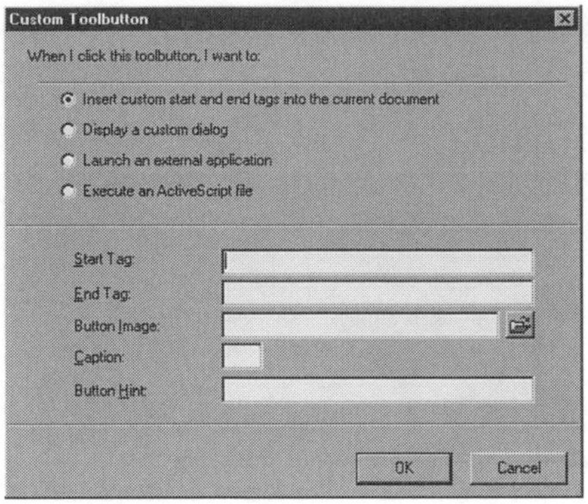

FIGURE 4.12

*HomeSite lets you cre-
ate custom buttons that
can embed text, display
dialogs, execute appli-
cations, and call
scripts.*

Summary

Not only is HomeSite a powerful and flexible editor, it's also highly configurable and
customizable. By using the techniques and features you learned in this hour, you can
adapt HomeSite so that it works the way you work best, rather than have you adapt to it.

Q&A

**Q HomeSite seems like a powerful editor. Can I use it to edit files other than
HTML files?**

A HomeSite is indeed a powerful editor, and yes, you can use it to edit any text files,
not just HTML files. However, by default the HomeSite Resource Tab displays
only Web-related documents in the file list. To display all documents (and files),
right-click in the file list window, select Filter, and then select All Files. Now,
every file is displayed in the file list. Don't try to edit non-text files with
HomeSite—that just won't work.

**Q I want to experiment with creating custom toolbars, but I am scared I'll com-
pletely mess up the standard toolbars, rendering myself editorless. What can I
do to prevent this from happening?**

A It's indeed possible to mess up the standard toolbars, but don't panic. If you create
a mess, just click the Restore to Defaults button in the Customize dialog's Toolbars
page to return to where you started. Of course, you'll lose any changes you've
made to the toolbars, so make sure that that is what you want to do.

Q **You mentioned that scripts can be called by clicking toolbar buttons. Where can I find add-on scripts that I can use within HomeSite?**

A Check out the Allaire Developer's Exchange at `http://www.allaire.com/developer/gallery/`. Select the Visual Tools option to browse through scripts (and other HomeSite extensions) developed by Allaire and third-party developers.

Workshop

The Workshop contains quiz questions and activities to help reinforce what you've learned in this hour. If you get stuck, the answers to the quiz questions can be found in Appendix A, "Answers to Quiz Questions."

Quiz

1. Why does HomeSite provide options that let you control the case of inserted tags?

2. Why is editor color coding so important?

Exercise

Create your own toolbar, and add the buttons you use most frequently into it. You might even want to dock your toolbar to the right of the editor window so that it's always available.

4

PART II
Creating Web Pages

Hour

Hour **5**

Creating a Web Page

You now know how to navigate HomeSite, use menus and toolbars, access the integrated browser and design tools, and get help. Now let's move on to Web page creation.

In this hour you'll learn the following:

- How to create Web pages
- How to use and create templates
- How to use the Web page wizards
- How to save and reopen Web pages

Creating Web Pages

As explained in Hour 1, "Understanding HomeSite," Web sites are simply collections of Web pages (and supporting graphics and other files). A Web page is simply a plain text file that usually contains embedded HTML code—the instructions used by the browser to correctly render the output.

There are basically three ways to create Web pages within HomeSite:

- Manually enter all the HTML
- Use a template to start with a basic predefined page
- Use a wizard to interactively create more complex pages

Using the Default Template

When HomeSite is started, the editor displays a simple Web page for you to start editing (see Figure 5.1). The standard default template contains a <!DOCTYPE> tag, which describes the page type and language; <HTML> and matching </HTML> tags to mark the beginning and end of the page; <HEAD> and </HEAD> tags to create a page header (and empty <TITLE> tags within it); and <BODY> and matching </BODY> tags to mark the page body itself. A default page title also appears in the page header and in the browser title bar. With the basic page shell in place, you can now start placing content in the page body (between the <BODY> and </BODY> tags).

FIGURE 5.1

At startup, HomeSite displays a page by using the default template.

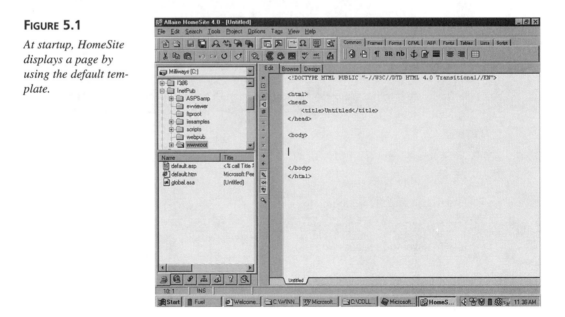

The default template is used every time you create a new file by using the New button on the Standard toolbar.

The <TITLE> tag isn't required in HTML pages and is often omitted. This is a bad practice, however, that should always be avoided. The title is what most search engines use when listing your page within search results. If you omit the title, search engines display some default text, and you lose potential visitors.

HomeSite allows you to change the contents of the standard default template, or even specify a template of your own to be used as the default template. To change the default template, press F8 and then select the Locations tab in the Settings window.

Using Wizards and Templates

In addition to the default template just discussed, HomeSite ships with a set of additional templates and wizards that you can use when creating Web pages. To select a template or wizard, create a new file by selecting New from the File menu. The New Document dialog shown in Figure 5.2 appears.

FIGURE 5.2

The New Document dialog contains templates and wizards that you can use when creating new Web pages.

Templates and wizards are tools used to simplify the creation of new Web pages, but they are very different:

- *Templates* are blocks of text that can be dropped into any empty page. You can edit this text or use it as a starting block for your page. Creating templates is simply a matter of creating new HTML files.

- *Wizards* are sets of interactive screens that prompt you for information step by step so that a page (or set of pages) can be constructed for you. Creating your own wizard is possible, but this involved process is beyond the scope of this book.

To use a template or wizard, simply double-click it (or select it and click OK). To demonstrate this, let's first use a template to create a simple Table of Contents page (like the one shown in Figure 5.3):

1. Select File, New to display the New Document dialog.

2. Double-click the Table of Contents icon to embed the HTML code within your new page.

3. Click the editor Browse tab to browse your new page (it should look like the one in Figure 5.3).

FIGURE 5.3

The Table of Contents template creates a simple Table of Contents using an HTML unordered list.

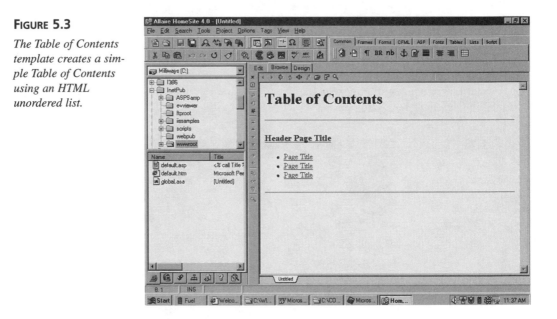

Wizards work much the same way, except you are prompted for information used to create your page. To see how this is done, use the Quick Start Wizard to create a simple home page:

1. Select File, New to display the New Document dialog.

2. Double-click on the Quick Start Wizard icon to display the first wizard screen (see Figure 5.4).

FIGURE 5.4

The Quick Start Wizard can be used to interactively start your new Web page.

3. Type the page title in the Title field (I used Ben's Home Page for mine; you can use your own name or whatever other title you'd like).

4. Select <!DOCTYPE HTML PUBLIC "-//W3C//DTD HTML 3.2 Final//EN"> as the DocType.

5. The next wizard dialog prompts for page headers that you don't need for this page, so click the Finish button.

The wizard creates a new page (similar to the one created by the default template) containing your title text in the header title.

As you can see, templates and wizards both greatly simplify creating new Web pages.

Opening Existing Web Pages

Now you know how to create new Web pages in HomeSite. The next thing to look at is opening existing pages (for viewing or editing).

There are basically three ways HomeSite can open files for viewing or editing:

- Any local files (or files accessed via the Network Neighborhood) can be opened by using standard file open techniques.
- Any Web page that you can access (local, on the Internet, and on intranets or extranets) can be opened directly by simply specifying its URL.
- HomeSite also can read and write files on a remote server directly over an FTP connection. Hour 19, "Working Remotely," looks at this in detail.

5

Opening Local Pages

Local pages are any files that you can access directly from your computer (either on your local drive or on any network drive that you have access to). More often that not you'll be working with local files, so let's start with these.

The simplest way to open files for editing is to select them within the Resource Tab Local Files tab (see Figure 5.5). The Resource Tab lets you select a drive or network server, and then browse through its directories. When you select a directory, its contents are displayed in the bottom pane. You can simply double-click any filename to open that file.

Drive or server

FIGURE 5.5

The Resource Tab provides fast and easy access to all local files.

Directory ———

Files ———

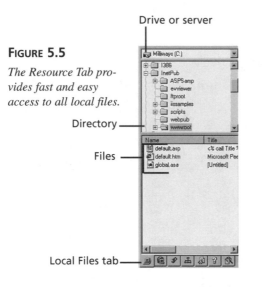

Local Files tab ——

Double-clicking a file that's already open doesn't open a second copy of that file. Instead, it activates the already opened copy, making that the current document.

Files also can be created within the Resource Tab. To create a new file, select the drive (or server) and directory where you'd like the file created, and then right-click in the file window and select File, Create Here.

The other way to open local files is with the Open dialog access via the File Open menu selection (or the Open button on the Standard toolbar). The Open dialog (see Figure 5.6) works just like the Open dialogs in most Windows applications, and should therefore be familiar to you.

FIGURE 5.6

The Open dialog provides access to local files via a dialog similar to the one found in most Windows applications.

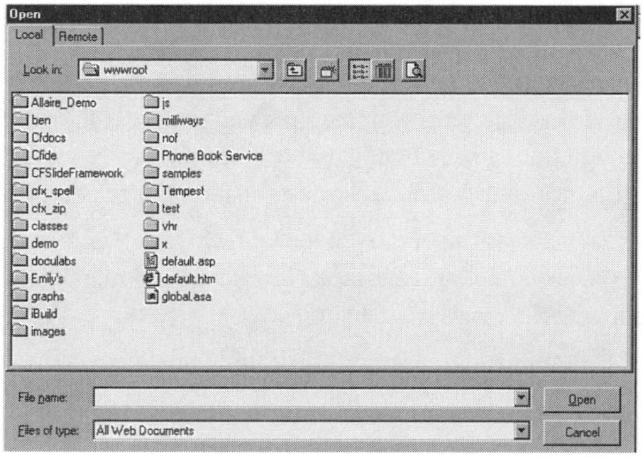

Opening Pages From the Web

HomeSite lets you open files on any server that you have access to simply by specifying its URL. This is useful if you have to access your files being hosted on another server, or simply want to peek at how other Web developers do what they do.

> One of the best ways to learn HTML is to see how other sites did what they did. This practice is legal, allowed, and highly recommended. The HTML code that makes up your Web page isn't secure or hidden. In fact, most Web browsers contain a View Source option that displays the underlying HTML in an integrated or external viewer. Of course, HomeSite makes viewing HTML source even easier, allowing you to open any URL right within your editor.

To open files from the Web, do the following:

1. Select File, Open From Web to display the Open from the Web dialog (see Figure 5.7).

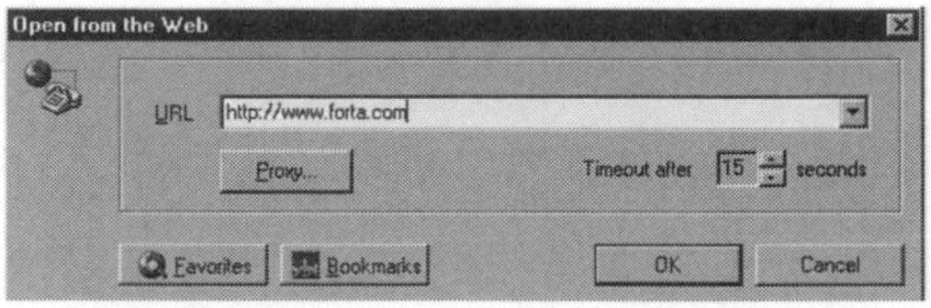

FIGURE 5.7

The Open from the Web dialog allows you to open any Web page directly within HomeSite.

2. Enter the URL to open in the URL field.

3. If you are on a network that requires you to access the public Internet via a proxy server, click the Proxy button and provide the proxy server details (if you are unsure as to what this means, you probably don't need to worry about it).

4. HomeSite lets you select saved URLs from your Microsoft Internet Explorer Favorites list and your Netscape Navigator Bookmarks list. You can access these by clicking the appropriate buttons.

5. Click OK to open the page right within HomeSite.

Although HomeSite lets you open pages from the Web, you won't be able to directly save them back to where you got them from. This would be a serious security breach; besides, this feature isn't supported by HTTP and most Web servers. If you need to save files that you have opened from the Web, you need to save them as local files.

Opening files on the Internet requires that you have Web access. If you connect to the Internet by dialing up an ISP, make sure that you are connected before using this feature.

Saving Web Pages

Now that you know how to create and open Web pages, let's look at saving pages, and how to save pages as templates.

Saving Local Pages

As explained in Hour 2, "Getting Started," the HomeSite editor displays a tab for each open file. Besides being used for switching between open files, this tab lets you know whether a page is saved (it changes color if changes haven't been saved).

To save a Web page, do any of the following:

- Select Save from the File menu
- Click the Save button on the Standard toolbar
- Press Ctrl+S
- Right-click within the editor and select File, Save

If the file is already named, HomeSite saves it without prompting you. If the file isn't yet named, you're prompted for the new filename.

> If you are working on multiple files at once, you can use the Save All option (on the File menu and on the Standard toolbar) to save all unsaved pages with one selection.

Where to Save Your Pages

HomeSite lets you save your Web pages anywhere, in any directory and on any server that you have access to. But not every directory is a suitable location for Web pages. If you are opening files within HomeSite (or even within your Web browser by using its File, Open option), any directory will probably work for you. But when you need to access the pages via a Web server, that likely won't be the case.

As explained in Hour 1, Web pages are returned to visitors by Web servers. Web servers typically don't have access to entire servers or all directories. Rather, they have access to directories beneath a specified document root.

When you create pages for your Web site, they should be saved in a directory beneath the Web server's document root (or a subdirectory somewhere beneath it). This way, you can access your pages via a Web server when you are ready to test them, and the underlying directory structure needed by the hosting Web server will already be in place. Even if you don't have a local Web server and are developing your site on a standalone machine, you should still use proper directory structures for your work.

It is a good idea to lay out your site's directory structure *before* you start creating Web pages. As you'll see in upcoming lessons, file and directory location is very important when creating links between pages (or embedding graphics). HomeSite can completely automate the process of building relative URLs for these links, but only if the directory structure is already in place.

5

Most Web site developers lay out their directory structure in a format similar to this:

- A directory is created beneath the document root to contain the new Web site (this may be a directory directly beneath the document root, or in subdirectories any-where beneath it). This new directory is the Web site root.

- The entire Web site is *not* saved in one mammoth directory. Rather, subdirectories are created for each subject or area (often corresponding directly to home page menu selections).

- The Web site root contains just the home page (and any supporting files).

- Graphics (buttons, logos, toolbars, and so on) are stored in an IMAGES or a GRAPHICS directory (keeping them grouped together makes reusing them simpler).

After you create your Web site and are ready to deploy it to a production Web server, the exact same directory structure (for your own site) should be used. This way, any links and graphic references will work properly the first time.

> Directories (also called *folders*) can be created within the HomeSite Resource Tab. To create a new directory, select the drive (or server) and directory where you'd like the directory created; then right-click in the file window and select Create Folder.

Hours 18, "Managing Your Web Site," and 20, "Managing Your Projects," look at direc-tory structures and site planning in more detail.

Saving Templates

As you saw earlier in this lesson, templates are a valuable tool for creating new Web pages. HomeSite comes with a set of standard templates, and you can create your own too.

> If you are working on a Web site that needs standard page headers, footers, or menus, you can save this basic information as a template for future use. Templates also can be shared between developers.

To create a template, simply create your Web page and save it by choosing File, Save As Template. You are prompted for a template name, as seen in Figure 5.8.

FIGURE 5.8

Every HomeSite template must be uniquely named.

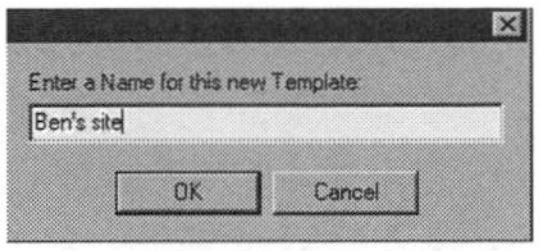

After your template is saved, you can use it by displaying the New Document dialog as explained earlier. Click the Custom tab (see Figure 5.9) to access your new templates.

FIGURE 5.9

The New Document dialog displays your saved templates in the Custom tab.

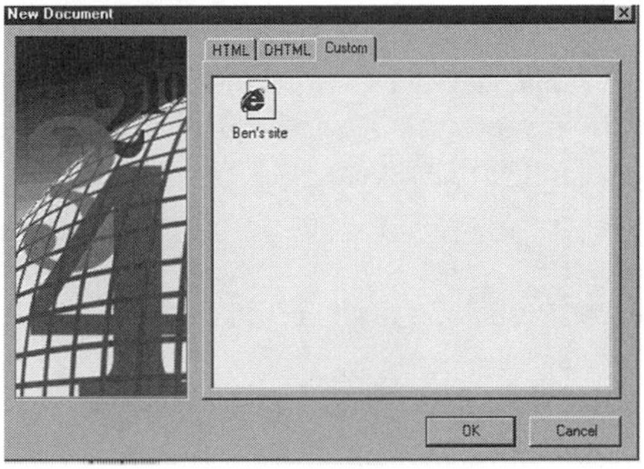

Summary

HomeSite provides multiple ways to create new Web pages, and includes templates and wizards to help you get up and running more quickly. HTML files can be opened locally, and HTML pages can be opened directly from the Web by simply specifying their URLs. Finally, HomeSite allows you to create your own templates if needed.

Q&A

Q **You said that writing wizards is beyond the scope of this book. Where can I go to find information on writing my own wizards?**

A The best resource is right within HomeSite, in the integrated help system. Go to the Resource Tab's Help tab, and open the help branch called Customizing the Development Environment. You'll see a document called Building Custom Wizards that should get you started.

Q Wizards are invaluable shortcut tools. Is there somewhere I can find additional HomeSite wizards?

A The first place to look is the Allaire Developer's Exchange at `http://www.allaire.com/developer/gallery/`. Select the Visual Tools option to browse through wizards (and other HomeSite extensions) developed by Allaire and third-party developers.

Workshop

The Workshop contains quiz questions and activities to help reinforce what you've learned in this hour. If you get stuck, the answers to the quiz questions can be found in Appendix A, "Answers to Quiz Questions."

Quiz

1. True or false: The Resource Tab's Local Files tab provides access only to files on your own computer.

2. True or false: Any Web page can be read into HomeSite by simply specifying its URL.

Exercises

1. Pick a few Web sites that you visit regularly, and peek at how their pages are created. Do this by using HomeSite's Open from the Web feature.

2. Experiment with creating templates for projects you are working on. You can access the templates by choosing New from the File menu.

Hour **6**

Designing a Web Page

Now that you know how to create, open, and save pages, it's time to actually design and create a page from scratch. The first thing you need to learn is how to manage and place text within your page.

To demonstrate this, I'm going to walk you through creating my personal bio page. I'd suggest that you follow all the steps here, replacing my bio with your own.

In this hour you'll learn how to do the following:

- Manage basic page layout
- Create lists
- Format text

Working with Text

More often than not, most Web content is textual. Understanding how Web browsers display text and what you can do to control that display is an important part of learning to create Web pages.

Basic Paragraph Formatting

To see how Web browsers handle simple text, let's start with a demonstration. The following is a text block that I typed into a new HomeSite page. Save this page as BIO.HTM in a directory under your Web server document root (or in any other new directory, if you don't have access to a Web server). Feel free to experiment with your own text; just type it in between the <BODY> and </BODY> tags.

```
I was born in London, England, and lived there until I was
fifteen. I came to the United States when I was eighteen,
and spent four years living on both coasts before I married
and settled in Michigan.
When not working, writing, or spending time with my family,
I enjoy reading, listening to music, watching plays, and
inline skating.
```

To see what this text will look like in a browser, click the editor's Browse tab. You'll see a display similar to the one in Figure 6.1.

FIGURE 6.1

When viewed in a browser, text usually isn't formatted exactly as it was typed.

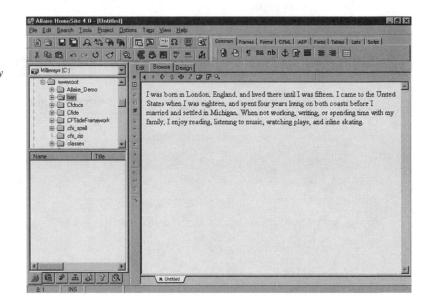

First, notice that the browser lost all formatting. My text was typed into two paragraphs; the browser displayed the text as one long paragraph. Furthermore, any line breaks were ignored; the browser displayed all my text as one long line, wrapping where it thought appropriate.

This is an important rule to remember: Web browsers ignore whitespace—carriage returns, tab characters, and even multiple spaces, which Web browsers will treat as a single space. In other words, the text

```
My name is Ben
```

and the text

```
My   name   is   Ben
```

will be displayed the same as the text

```
My name
is Ben
```

To control paragraph layout, use the HTML <BR> and <P> tags.
 is the line break tag, which instructs the browser to embed a line break, pushing the following text to the next line. <P> is a paragraph break, which instructs the browser to push the following text to the next line and to insert a space before that line, effectively starting a new paragraph.

To display my bio correctly, I inserted a <P> tag after the first paragraph (the sentence ending with the word Michigan). The <P> tag can go on the same line as the text or on a line by itself; it makes no difference because whitespace is ignored. The correctly formatted text is shown in Figure 6.2.

FIGURE 6.2

To check your formatting, view all changes in HomeSite's Browse mode.

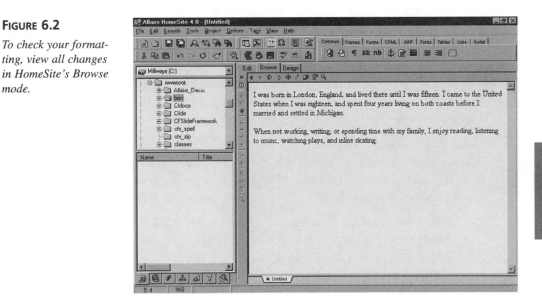

6

Rather than type the <P> and <BR> tags, simply place your cursor at the desired tag location and click the appropriate buttons on the Quick Bar's Common tab.

As you have seen, Web browsers control where text wraps lines. This ensures that text will display correctly on all browsers, regardless of how large the screen or browser window is. Occasionally you'll want to prevent the Web browser from wrapping in the middle of a phrase (maybe a company name or an address). To do this, simply enclose the text within <NOWR> and </NOWR> no-wrap tags. These tags force the browser to wrap before or after the enclosed text, but not in the middle of it.

Using Special Characters

As you have seen, the < character begins a tag, an instruction to the Web browser that's not displayed. So how can you display a < within your page?

Granted, your page probably doesn't include too many less-than characters, but there are many other characters with special meanings within browsers, such as the ampersand (&) and double quotation marks, and these shouldn't be used within Web page text either. So how can you display these characters?

NEW TERM   The answer is the use of entity references, unique names for special characters. The entity reference for < is < and the entity reference for an ampersand is &. An *entity reference* is a special text representation of a character or symbol. Entity references always begin with an & and end with a semicolon. When a Web browser sees an entity reference, it displays the character that it refers to instead of the reference itself.

Before you panic, no, you don't have to remember the entire entity reference table. As a HomeSite user, you can take advantage of HomeSite's Special Characters window. To use this feature, do the following:

1. Place your editor cursor at the location where you want the entity reference inserted.
2. Select Special Characters from the View menu (or click the Special Characters button in View toolbar) to display the Special Characters window (see Figure 6.3).

FIGURE 6.3

The Special Characters window lets you enter entity references by clicking select characters.

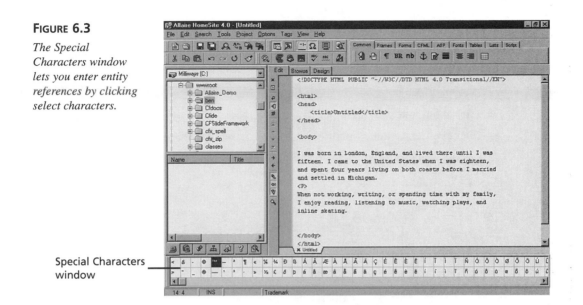

Special Characters window

3. Click the desired character in the Special Characters window to insert its entity reference into your page.

4. Close the Special Characters window by right-clicking it and selecting Close.

Rather than select entity references as you type, HomeSite can analyze your text and replace all illegal characters with their appropriate entity references in one step. To use this feature, choose Replace Special Characters from the Search menu.

Laying Out Your Page

Web pages flow from left to right and then downward. This means that unless you explicitly specify text alignment, format, and dividers, your page will be one large left-aligned paragraph. Fortunately, HTML provides all the tags needed to correctly format your page.

6

Centering and Alignment

I want to add a title above the bio I typed earlier. And so that it stands out as a title, I want it centered above the text. To do this I can simply do the following:

1. Type the title text. I used "About Ben" for mine.
2. Click the title text to highlight it.
3. Click the Center button on the Quick Bar's Common tab (or press Ctrl+Shift+C).
4. Insert a space between the title and the body by using the <P> tag.

Figure 6.4 shows the new bio, complete with centered title.

FIGURE 6.4

Center titles or any text that needs to stand out.

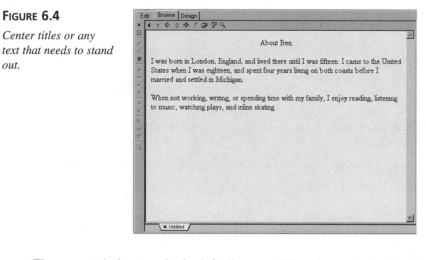

The same technique works for left alignment. There is no shortcut button for creating justified text; instead, use the DIV button on the Quick Bar's Common tab, and select JUSTIFY in the ALIGN field.

By default, HomeSite uses the <DIV> tag for text alignment. Although this is the correct way to do this, some older browsers don't understand the <DIV> tag. As explained in Hour 4, "Customizing HomeSite," you can tell HomeSite to use <CENTER> or <P ALIGN=CENTER> instead of <DIV>.

Creating Lists

The next item I want to add to my bio is the names of the books I have written. The text looks like this:

```
I am the author of:
ColdFusion 4.0 Web Application Construction Kit,
Advanced ColdFusion 4.0 Application Development,
Sams Teach Yourself HomeSite 4 in 24 Hours,
Sams Teach Yourself SQL in 10 Minutes.
```

As you already know, this will be displayed as a simple paragraph—not exactly the ideal formatting for this kind of text. Because the information is a list (of books), I'd be better served by using HTML lists to display the data.

NEW TERM *Lists* are special formatting types used to display information in a sequential, ordered fashion. HTML supports several list types, the most common of which are bulleted lists (known within HTML as *unordered lists*), and numbered lists (known within HTML as *ordered lists*).

Creating lists involves the use of several new tags. The entire list must be enclosed within list designators—<UL> and </UL> for unordered lists, or <OL> and </OL> for ordered lists. Each item within the list must begin with the list item tag <LI>.

To manually create an unordered (bulleted) list containing four items, I could type the following text:

```
I am the author of:
<UL>
 <LI>ColdFusion 4.0 Web Application Construction Kit
 <LI>Advanced ColdFusion 4.0 Application Development
 <LI>Sams Teach Yourself HomeSite 4 in 24 Hours
 <LI>Sams Teach Yourself SQL in 10 Minutes
</UL>
```

As I'm sure you've already guessed, HomeSite provides an easier way to do this. The first button on the Quick Bar's Lists tab is the Quick List function, which we'll use to create the same list:

1. Place the editor cursor at the location where you'd like your list placed.
2. Click the Quick List button to display the List dialog (see Figure 6.5).
3. Specify the number of rows in your list (I chose four for mine).
4. Choose your list style, ordered or unordered (I chose unordered).
5. Type the list contents in each row provided.
6. Click OK to insert the list code into your page.

6

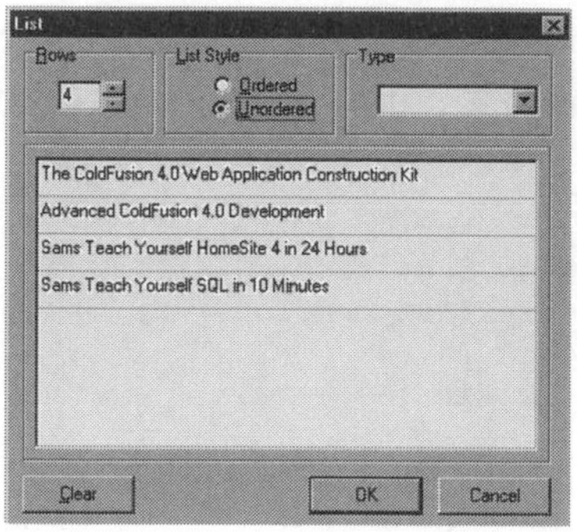

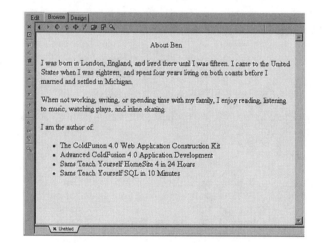

FIGURE 6.5

The Quick List feature can be used to simplify HTML list creation.

After you create your list, switch to Browse mode to view it. It should look similar to the list in Figure 6.6.

FIGURE 6.6

Bulleted lists are an efficient and effective way to display lists of information.

The Quick List feature can only be used to create lists. To edit existing lists you will have to edit the HTML list code manually.

Horizontal Dividers

When Web pages contain blocks of information, it is often useful to separate these blocks with dividers. HTML supports embedded horizontal dividers via the <HR> (horizontal rule) tag.

To display a horizontal rule beneath the title of my bio, I need to add only the <HR> tag after it. Now the page will look like the one in Figure 6.7.

FIGURE 6.7

Horizontal rules divide your page or break up text blocks.

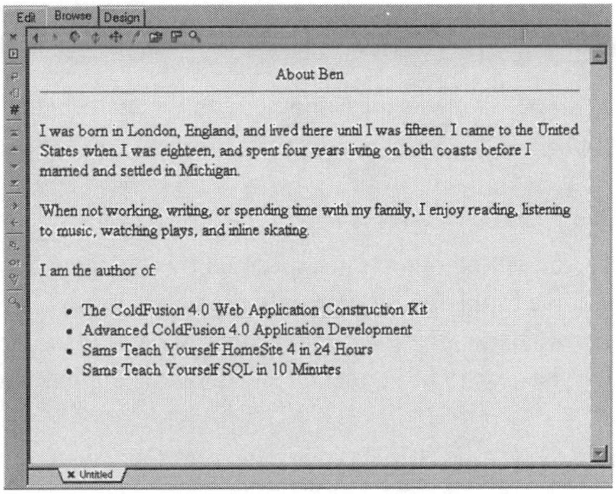

HTML allows you to control the appearance of horizontal rules. The <HR> Tag Editor (see Figure 6.8) prompts you for bar alignment, color, size, width (in pixels or percentages), and other options. You can access the <HR> Tag Editor by clicking the Horizontal Rule button on the Quick Bar's Common toolbar.

FIGURE 6.8

The <HR> Tag Editor provides easy access to horizontal rule configuration.

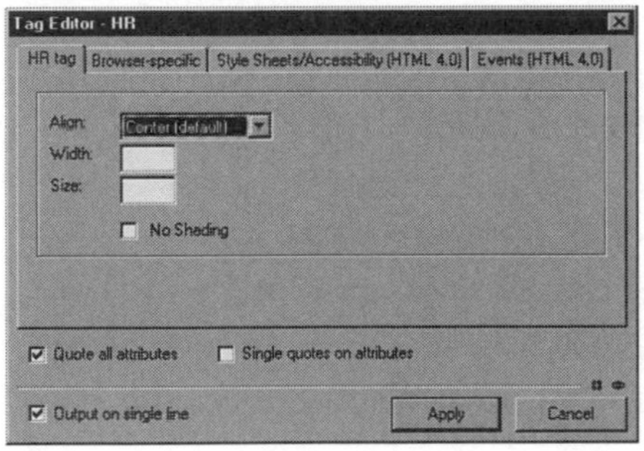

6

If no width is specified, horizontal rules will span the entire width of the browser window (or the space in which they appear). If you need to use specific widths, try using percentages as opposed to fixed widths. Specifying 400 as the width (that's 400 pixels) might look good in your browser, but not in a larger or smaller browser window. If 400 pixels is about 90 percent of the browser width, specifying 90% as the width might ensure correct display on other browsers.

Using Text Formatting and Styles

So far we have used plain text for the entire page. Obviously, a correctly formatted page should use all sorts of formatting and style options to break the monotony of the page, as well as force emphasis where it's needed.

HTML provides extensive text formatting options, some of which we'll look at in the following sections.

Basic Text Formatting

All HTML text formatting options are specified by enclosing text within formatting tags. Table 6.1 lists some of the more commonly used formatting options. Each formatting option has a corresponding button on the Quick Bar's Fonts toolbar. To apply a format, simply highlight the text to be formatted and click the appropriate button.

TABLE 6.1 COMMONLY USED HTML TEXT FORMATTING OPTIONS

Format	Description
Bold	Bold text created by using `<B>` and `</B>`.
Emphasis	Highlight for emphasis, created using `<EM>` and `</EM>`; on most browsers, displayed in italics.
Italic	Italicized text, created by using `<I>` and `</I>`.
Preformatted	A typewriter-style font honoring all whitespace, created by using `<PRE>` and `</PRE>`.
Strikethrough	Strikethrough formatting, created by using `<S>` and `</S>` (some browsers use `<STRIKE>` and `</STRIKE>`).
Strong	Strong formatting, created by using `<STRONG>` and `</STRONG>`; on most browsers, displayed in bold.
Subscript	Displayed below the line, created by using `<SUB>` and `</SUB>`.
Superscript	Displayed above the line, created by using `<SUP>` and `</SUP>`.
Underline	Underlined text, created by using `<U>` and `</U>`.

The following steps demonstrate how to highlight text in bold:

1. Highlight the text to be formatted in your editor window.

2. Click the Bold button (the one with the B on it) on the Quick Bar's Fonts tab (or press Ctrl+B). HomeSite inserts a `<B>` before the highlighted text and a `</B>` after it.

After you format your text, switch to Browse mode to view it. Figure 6.9 shows Browse mode displaying bold text wherever <B> tags were used.

FIGURE 6.9

The <B> tag is used to format text in bold.

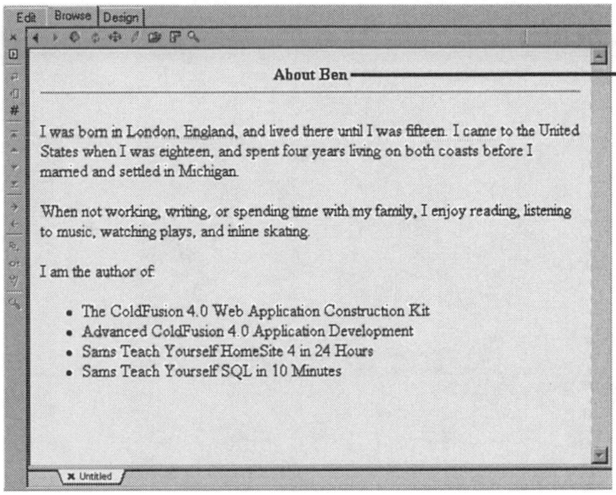

Edit | Browse | Design

About Ben ———————— Bold text

I was born in London, England, and lived there until I was fifteen. I came to the United States when I was eighteen, and spent four years living on both coasts before I married and settled in Michigan.

When not working, writing, or spending time with my family, I enjoy reading, listening to music, watching plays, and inline skating.

I am the author of

- The ColdFusion 4.0 Web Application Construction Kit
- Advanced ColdFusion 4.0 Application Development
- Sams Teach Yourself HomeSite 4 in 24 Hours
- Sams Teach Yourself SQL in 10 Minutes

✕ Untitled

When using HTML formatting tags, be sure not to mismatch tags. Tags must be closed in reverse of the order in which they were opened. For example, <B><I>Hello</I></B> displays the word Hello in bold italic. The bold tag is started first, so it is correctly closed last. However, <B><I>Hello</B></I> is incorrect and won't display correctly on some browsers.

Working with Headers and Other Styles

In addition to text formatting such as bold and italic, HTML supports the use of formatting styles. For example, the text "About Ben" in my bio is a title. To display it as such I could use a header tag. HTML supports six levels of headers from <H1> (the biggest) to <H6> (the smallest).

To format the title as a header, do the following:

1. Highlight the title in your editor window (be sure not to select the centering tags).
2. Click the H1 button on the Quick Bar's Fonts tab. HomeSite will insert an <H1> before the highlighted text and an </H1> after it.

Figure 6.10 shows the updated bio page, complete with the title formatted as a header.

6

FIGURE 6.10

Header tags can be used to attract attention to specific text.

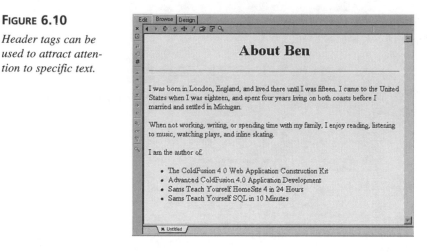

In addition to the headers, Table 6.2 lists some of the other commonly used formatting styles.

TABLE 6.2   COMMONLY USED FORMATTING STYLES

Format	Description
Address	Contact address (usually email) created by using `<ADDRESS>` and `</ADDRESS>`; on most browsers, displayed in italic.
Citation	Citation text created by using `<CITE>` and `</CITE>`; on most browsers, displayed in italic.
Code	Code example created by using `<CODE>` and `</CODE>`; on most browsers, displayed in a typewriter-style font.
Header	Headers created by using `<H`*n*`>` and `</H`*n*`>`, where *n* is a number from 1 to 6.
Keyboard	Keyboard entry created by using `<KEY>` and `</KEY>`; on most browsers, displayed in a typewriter-style font.
Teletype	Display text in a typewriter-style font created by using `<TT>` and `</TT>`.

Different browsers might display styles differently. There is no guarantee that the font and size used by one browser will be the same used by another.

Greater control over formatting styles can be achieved by using style sheets. We'll look at these in Hour 15, "Using Style Sheets."

Summary

We covered a lot of ground in this lesson. You learned how to manage the display of text, use lists to display information in a structured linear format, use horizontal dividers, and format your text. Next we'll look at using fonts and colors. If you haven't already done so, save the page you created this hour; you'll continue using it during the next few hours.

Q&A

Q Can I control the bullet type used in unordered lists?

A Yes. The TYPE attribute lets you specify values like DISC, SQUARE, and CIRCLE. Be warned, however, that many browsers don't support all types. If you select a type that a browser doesn't support, a default bullet will be used instead.

Q Are there any guidelines as to when different header styles should be used?

A There are no real rules or guidelines governing the use of any styles, but it is a good idea to only have one <H1> per page, and more of other headers as needed. The larger the header, the less frequently it should be used within a single page. This will help prevent wasting page space and make your pages easier to read.

Q I've seen some sites use horizontal rules with pictures or designs in them. How is that done?

A The <HR> tag creates a pretty simple horizontal rule. You can control color, size, width, alignment, and whether shading is to be displayed. To create fancier rules, many Web designers use graphics rather than the <HR> tag. Hour 8, "Using Images," looks at using graphics.

6

Workshop

The Workshop contains quiz questions and activities to help reinforce what you've learned in this hour. If you get stuck, the answers to the quiz questions can be found in Appendix A, "Answers to Quiz Questions."

Quiz

1. True or false: Browsers always ignore whitespace such as carriage returns.
2. Why are entity references used?
3. Should horizontal rule widths be specified as fixed values or percentages?
4. True or false: The rendering of styles such as <H1> is rigidly enforced, and the output will be the same in all browsers.

Exercises

1. As explained in this lesson, there is more than one way to center or align text. Try experimenting with the <CENTER>, <P ALIGN=CENTER>, and <DIV ALIGN=CENTER> tags to see which work with which browsers, and to find any subtle differences between them.

2. HTML lists can be nested—that is, a list can contain a list. When creating nested lists, be very careful to correctly match your tags (the inner list must be after a <LI> and must be terminated correctly). Create a list with at least one nested list. If you are more adventurous, try nesting at multiple levels.

3. Create a page that uses all the various styles listed in Tables 6.1 and 6.2, and then view that page in different browsers (at minimum, Microsoft Internet Explorer and Netscape Navigator). See which styles are consistent and which aren't.

HOUR 7

Working with Fonts and Colors

Fonts and colors bring your text alive. You can specify background colors, default text colors, specific colors for blocks of text, and fonts and font sizes anywhere within your page. To demonstrate some of these techniques, let's update the bio page created in the last hour.

In this hour you'll learn the following:

- How to specify page-wide colors
- How to color specific blocks of text
- How to use fonts
- How to specify font sizes

Working with Colors

As explained in Hour 4, "Customizing HomeSite," there are two ways to specify colors within Web pages:

- Color names are plain text strings (such as red, yellow, and cyan). Because these names are highly self-explanatory, many Web developers prefer working with them. The problem with color names is that many colors (particularly subtle changes in color shades) do not have text names. Furthermore, many browsers do not understand these names, or only understand a subset of them.

- Colors can also be specified as RGB values. An RGB value uniquely identifies a color by specifying how the color is created. RGB values are understood by all browsers, but they are not intuitive to work with.

> **NEW TERM** *RGB* is a method for specifying colors by number. RGB stands for red-green-blue, the three colors of light that when mixed in specific combinations can make any other color.
>
> RGB values are specified as three sets of numbers: first the red, then the green, then the blue (and thus RGB). The amount of each color is specified as a number from 0, which means none of that color, to 255, which means all of that color. (For you mathematicians out there, that's 256^3—or 16,777,216—possible combinations.) That's the easy part; the tricky part is that the numbers are represented in hexadecimal notation (from 00 to FF). So every RGB value is made up of six characters: The first two specify the amount of red in the color, the middle two specify the amount of green, and the final two specify the amount of blue.
>
> In other words, the RGB value for red is FF0000 (FF of red, 00 of green, and 00 of blue). Yellow is specified as FFFF00 (FF of red, FF of green, and 00 of blue). Orange is specified as FFA500 (FF of red, A5 of green, and 00 of blue).
>
> As you can imagine, remembering RGB values is not a fun task, which is actually why commonly used colors were assigned names in the first place.

Color names and RGB values can be used interchangeably. Any attribute that accepts colors accepts both color specification formats. To distinguish between color names and RGB values, RGB values are always preceded by a pound sign (the # character).

The following code sample sets the page background to blue:

```
<BODY BGCOLOR="blue">
```

This next code sample does the exact same thing, using the RGB value for blue:

```
<BODY BGCOLOR="#0000FF">
```

Selecting and Specifying Colors

HomeSite provides several ways to select colors. Depending on what operation you are performing, you can use any or all of these tools and techniques:

- The Tag Editors for tags that accept color attributes allow you to select colors from a drop-down list (see Figure 7.1).

- The Tag Inspectors for tags that accept color attributes allow you to select colors from a drop-down list (see Figure 7.2).

- The pop-up Tag Insights for tags that accept color attributes allow you to select colors from a pop-up list (see Figure 7.3).

- The Palette button on the Tools toolbar displays a color palette grid (see Figure 7.4) that can be used for color selection. Clicking any color in the grid inserts that color at the current cursor location in your page.

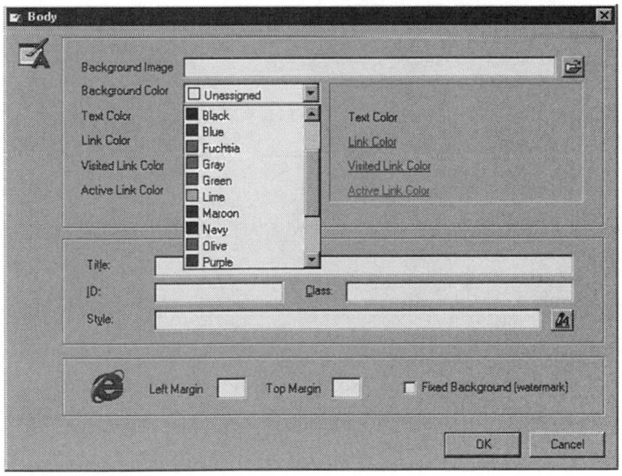

FIGURE 7.1

Tag Editors display color selection lists for all color attributes.

7

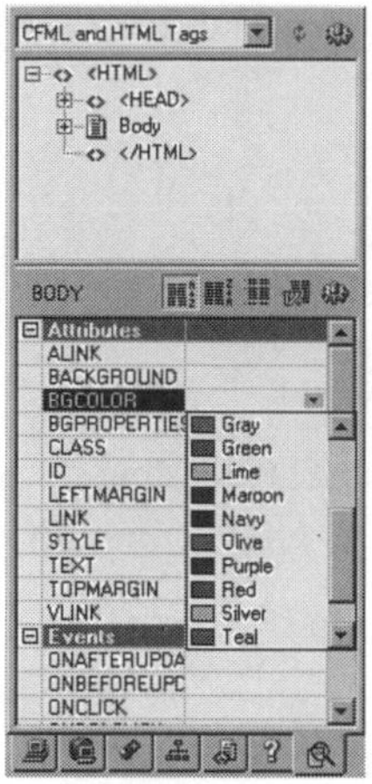

FIGURE 7.2

The Tag Inspector displays a drop-down color list box where appropriate.

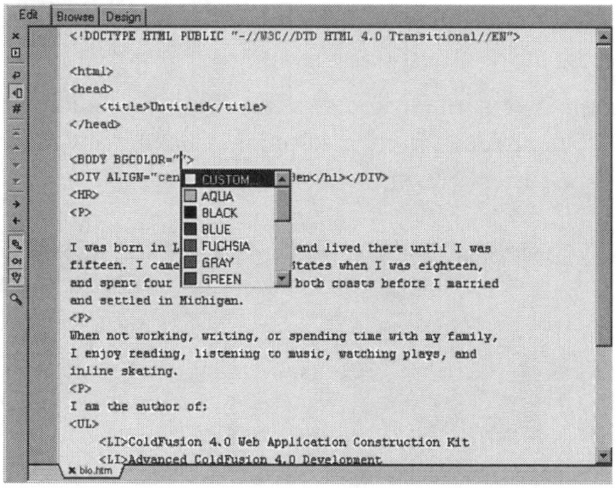

FIGURE 7.3

Tag Insight displays a pop-up color selector for color attributes.

Regardless of how a color is selected, HomeSite intelligently inserts either the color name or the RGB value. Obviously, if you select a color that has no name value, HomeSite always uses the RGB value. But if you select a color that does have a name value (such as RED), then depending on how HomeSite is configured, either the name or RGB value will be inserted. (This configuration option was explained in Hour 4.)

Understanding Palettes

NEW TERM   Before you can actually start playing with colors, one last issue needs to be addressed—that of color *palettes*. Palettes are sets of colors, and picking the right color palette is extremely important. A palette can contain one or more colors, although the smallest commonly used palette has 16 colors in it. HomeSite uses six standard palettes, all providing access to a specific set of colors.

FIGURE 7.4

The color palette grid provides the most flexibility in color selection.

Color palette grid —

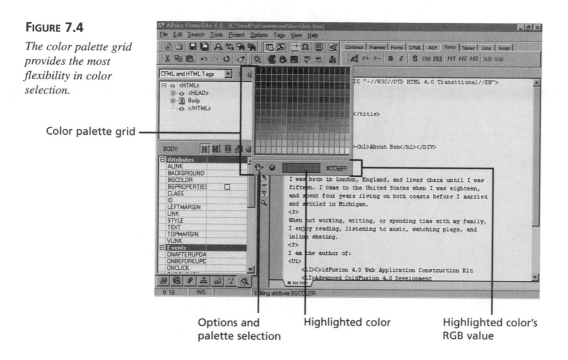

Options and palette selection

Highlighted color

Highlighted color's RGB value

Even though RGB values allow for the specification of more than 16 million colors, not all of those colors will display properly on all computers and in all browsers. The HomeSite standard palettes are color sets that work well in known environments. The most commonly used palette is the Browser Safety Palette, a palette containing 216 colors that all browsers should be able to display without difficulty. (The notable exception is older computer systems with very low-end graphics cards. These computers can often display only 16 standard colors, and yes, there is a special palette for these too.)

The color palette grid (refer to Figure 7.4) displays all the colors within a selected palette. To select a palette, click the Options button at the bottom left of the color palette pop-up window. This displays a list of available palettes (see Figure 7.5), as well as options for editing and creating palettes, and color sorting options. The standard color palettes are listed in Table 7.1.

7

FIGURE 7.5

*The color palette grid
displays the colors
available within a
selected color palette.*

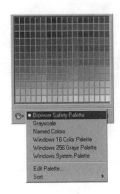

TABLE 7.1 STANDARD COLOR PALETTES

Palette	Description
Browser Safety Palette	The 216 standard colors supported by most browsers. As a rule, try to use only colors within this palette.
Grayscale	256 shades of black, white, and all the grays in between.
Named Colors	The 140 colors that have names. Although most browsers can display these colors as RGB values, many don't support all the text names. (If you use a text name that a browser doesn't understand, the result won't be what you want—and could be something rather bizarre.)
Windows 16 Color Palette	The 16 colors supported by all Windows-based computers, even those with low-end hardware.
Windows 256 Grays Palette	Windows version of 256 shades of black, white, and all grays in between; varies slightly from the Grayscale palette.
Windows System Palette	216 colors that can be correctly displayed by most Windows-based computers.

To ensure maximum compatibility, always try to select colors from the
Browser Safety Palette. The colors in this palette can be correctly displayed
by almost all browsers.

Specifying Page Level Colors

Page-wide color schemes are specified in the <BODY> tag. The BGCOLOR attribute specifies the color to use for the page background; the TEXT attribute specifies the color for the page text.

For my own bio page, I want to use a background color of maroon and a text color of yellow. (You, of course, are free to use colors of your own choice.) The following steps walk you through setting page background and text colors:

1. Open the BIO.HTM page, if you have not already done so.
2. Right-click the <BODY> tag and select Edit Tag to display the <BODY> Tag Editor (refer to Figure 7.1).
3. Select a background color from the Background Color drop-down list (I selected maroon).
4. Select a text color from the Text Color drop-down list (I selected yellow).
5. Click OK to write the new color selections to the page.

To test the new color scheme, click the Browse tab to browse your page. If you are not satisfied with your color choices, go back to the editor and repeat the preceding steps.

Coloring Specific Text

The <BODY> tag is used to specify page-wide color settings. To color specific text, use the <FONT> tag. For example, the following line of code displays the text "Hello Ben" in blue:

```
<FONT COLOR="BLUE">Hello Ben</FONT>
```

Back to my bio page. I want to display the title in white (so that it stands out from the rest of the yellow text). The following steps demonstrate how to do this:

1. Highlight the title text (including the <H1> and </H1> tags).
2. Click the Font button on the Quick Bar's Fonts toolbar (the first button on the left, the one with the 3 A's on it) to display the <FONT> Tag Editor (see Figure 7.6).
3. Select a color from the Color drop-down list (I selected white).
4. Click the Apply button to write the font information to the page.

To test the new color scheme, click the Browse tab to browse your page. If you are not satisfied with your color choices, go back to the editor and repeat the preceding steps.

7

FIGURE 7.6

The <FONT> Tag Editor allows you to specify the text color for selected text.

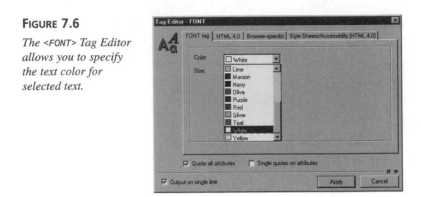

There is no limit to how many times you can use the <FONT> tag in your page to specify text color. Just make sure that you correctly terminate each <FONT> tag with a matching </FONT> tag. (If you use the Tag Editors as we just did, this is done automatically for you.)

Working with Fonts

By default, text on Web pages is displayed in a standard browser font in a standard font size. Let's now look at specifying your own font faces and sizes for a greater degree of control over how your text is displayed.

Specifying Font Faces

Font faces are specified by using the same <FONT> tag that we just used to specify text color. The FACE attribute allows you to specify the name of the font face to use. For example, the following code displays the text "Hello Ben" in the Arial font:

```
<FONT FACE="Arial">Hello Ben</FONT>
```

Of course, to use the font you specify, visitors to your page must have that font installed on their computers. As such, you must be very careful to use only font faces that your visitors are likely to have.

There is no way to know which fonts are installed on the machines of future visitors to your Web site, so there is no way to ensure that any specific fonts will be available. Having said that, most computers have a small number of fonts available, and obviously you should try to use these fonts if possible: Arial, Comic Sans MS, Courier, Times New Roman, Verdana, and Wingdings. As long as you stick with these fonts, you should be okay.

For my bio page, I want to use the Verdana font face. The following steps walk you through setting this up:

1. Highlight the text to be displayed in the font you are selecting. Because we want to format the entire page, select all the text between the <BODY> and </BODY> tags.

2. Click the Font button on the Quick Bar's Fonts toolbar (it's the first button on the left, the one with the 3 A's on it) to display the <FONT> Tag Editor (see Figure 7.7).

3. Click on the HTML 4.0 tab and then select the desired font from the Font drop-down list (I selected Verdana).

4. Click the Apply button to write the font information to the page.

FIGURE 7.7

The <FONT> Tag Editor allows you to select font faces for text display.

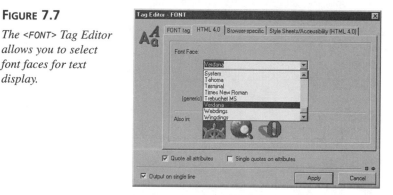

To test the font selection, click the Browse tab to browse your page. Your page should look similar to the one in Figure 7.8. If you are not satisfied with how the font looks, go back to the editor and repeat the preceding steps.

FIGURE 7.8

Font selections should be tested with the integrated browser or any Web browser.

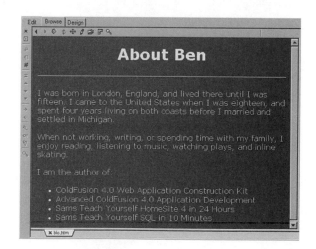

You may have noticed that the page now has two sets of <FONT> tags. The outer set specifies the font face for the entire page; the inner set specifies the text color for the title page. This is perfectly legal, and works because the </FONT> tag does not terminate all formatting—rather, it returns formatting to how it was before the matching <FONT> tag. As such, as long as you make sure you correctly match your <FONT> and </FONT> tags, these tags can be nested as needed.

> The <FONT> FACE attribute can take multiple face names separated by commas. This way, you can specify alternative fonts, so that if your first selection is not available, your second choice will be used (rather than the browser choosing a default font for you). For example, <FONT FACE= "Verdana,Arial"> instructs the browser to use the Verdana font as a first choice, and Arial as a second choice. This way if Verdana isn't present, Arial is used instead. It is a good idea to always provide alternative choices, with the last choice being one of the font faces most likely to be available.

Specifying Font Sizes

The <FONT> tag also can be used to specify font sizes, allowing you to display text in seven possible sizes, from 1 to 7. And although this might sound like a great way to precisely format your text, it isn't.

The exact meaning of a specific size varies from browser to browser, so <FONT SIZE="2"> will not display text in the exact same size on different browsers. The only guarantee is that size 2 is bigger than size 1, size 3 is bigger than size 2, and so on. But the size numbers do not map to point sizes or to any other accurate size measurement. Figure 7.9 shows sample text in sizes 1 through 7.

For this reason, font sizes are almost never specified with fixed sizes. Instead, the <FONT> SIZE attribute is usually used to specify relative sizes, or how much bigger or smaller text should be. For example, the following code specifies that the text "Hello Ben" should be displayed two sizes bigger than the rest of the page:

```
<FONT SIZE="+2">Hello Ben</FONT>
```

Relative sizes are specified by using the + or – prefixes before the value. So –3 decreases the font size by 3, and +1 increases it by 1.

FIGURE 7.9

Most Web browsers support font sizes from 1 to 7.

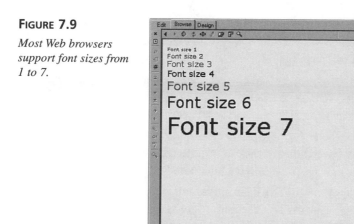

Relative font sizes are not accumulative. This means that if you increase the font size by 2 (using +2) and then increase it again by 1 (using +1), the new size will be 1 higher than the rest of the text, not 3 higher. Every specified relative font size is relative to the default size used for the entire page, not the size used just before the <FONT> tag.

Summary

Colors and fonts are valuable text-formatting tools, but they must be used carefully. You learned about using color names versus RGB values, why using known color palettes is important, and how to use specific font faces and sizes.

Q&A

Q You explained how to specify background colors by using the <BODY> BGCOLOR attribute, but this attribute lets me select only solid colors. I have seen Web sites that use complex color schemes or designs as backgrounds instead of solid colors. How is this done?

A In addition to allowing you to specify background colors, the <BODY> tag also allows you to specify a graphic image to be used for the page background. Using graphics for your page background enables you to create all sorts of special effects. We'll look at working with graphics in detail in the next hour.

7

Q **I want all `<H1>` text in my page to be displayed in blue. Right now I have to use a `<FONT>` tag for each `<H1>`. Is there a way to change the way browsers treat all `<H1>` tags in my page?**

A The formatting of `<H1>` tags, and indeed all tags, can be manipulated by using Cascading Style Sheets. With style sheets, you can manipulate and fine-tune the characteristics of all tags. Hour 15, "Using Style Sheets," looks at style sheets in detail.

Q **The font face drop-down list box in the `<FONT>` Tag Editor lets me select only a single font face. How can I select multiple font faces?**

A Unfortunately, the drop-down list box does indeed allow you to select only a single face. However, you can manually type the names of alternative faces in the Font field, and, of course, you can edit the value in the `FACE` attribute directly in the editor.

Q **What is the default font size used by Web browsers? Is there a way to change this value?**

A The default font size used by all browsers is size 3. Any relative font values are relative to this default base value. The page base value can be changed using the `<BASEFONT>` tag. For example, `<BASEFONT SIZE="2">` changes the base font size to 2, and all relative font values are based on this base value.

Workshop

The Workshop contains quiz questions and activities to help reinforce what you've learned in this hour. If you get stuck, the answers to the quiz questions can be found in Appendix A, "Answers to Quiz Questions."

Quiz

1. True or false: HTML colors should always be specified using color constants such as lime and fuchsia.

2. What is the ideal color palette to use for Web page color selections?

3. True or false: Because there's no guarantee that selected font faces will be available, it is best not to use specific font faces at all.

4. Why should relative font sizes be used instead of actual font sizes?

Exercises

1. The color palette grid provides access to far more colors than the drop-down list boxes in the Tag Editors and Tag Inspector. Experiment with different color selections in the color palette grid, using colors as page background color or font colors.

2. Check to see which fonts are available on your computer (use the Windows Control Panel Fonts applet to do this). Compare the list to the fonts available on other computers you have access to. Are there any fonts other than the ones listed earlier in this lesson that seem safe to use?

7

Hour **8**

Using Images

Up to this point we have worked with Web pages containing only text elements. And although HTML text-formatting features—especially font and color control—can be used to create visually appealing pages for your Web site, an important part of the Web's visual appeal is the use of multimedia elements within pages. The most important (and most used) of these are page graphics.

In this hour, you'll learn the following:

- Which image types are supported by Web browsers and the differences between them
- How to view thumbnail images
- How to embed images within your pages
- How to obtain images

Working with Images

You know that old adage, "A picture is worth a thousand words"? Well, it applies to the Web too, but with some important caveats.

Graphic images are an important part of any Web site. Images attract attention, keep visitor interest, provide visual representation of items or products, and much more. But images must be used carefully, so let's start with some tips on how *not* to use images.

How Not to Use Images

Nothing annoys Web site visitors more than long page download times. Unfortunately, the number one cause for long download times is the use of graphics. That is not to say that graphics should not be used in Web pages—they definitely should, where appropriate.

Here are some guidelines for Web page graphic use:

- Don't overuse graphics; sometimes less is better.
- Make sure that you pick the right graphic file formats (more on that later in this hour).
- Try to reuse images within your site because most browsers cache files for future use. Using the same file (with the same filename) can dramatically improve the performance of subsequent pages.
- The HTML code for text colors and font manipulation downloads far quicker than graphics. Try not to use graphics for displaying text unless absolutely necessary.
- When possible, sacrifice image quality for download time. Shaving 10 percent of the quality of a JPEG file can halve the download time without dramatic quality loss.
- Create graphics with software packages designed especially for the Web. These packages usually are better equipped to play tricks to get the image file size down.

And remember—there's a very fine line between a site that uses graphics and a site that abuses graphics use. The difference is easily measured—if your site is the latter, visitors won't come back.

> To check your page's download time, use the HomeSite Document Weight feature. Document Weight displays your page's approximate download times at various modem speeds and helps you pinpoint potential performance problems. To access this feature, select Document Weight from the Tools menu.

You need to understand how Web browsers handle pages with embedded graphics. When a Web browser requests a page from a Web server, all that gets sent back is the HTML code that makes up the page. The browser then reads through the HTML for references to graphics, and then makes a separate request for each graphic. So to load a page with five graphics, a Web browser must actually make at least six requests: one for the HTML page, and then one for each graphic. (If the visitor is on a bad connection, images might have to be requested several times.)

Web servers call these requests *hits*. A hit is a single request from a client. From a Web server's perspective, a page with five graphics generates a minimum of six hits.

So the next time you see a site boasting about how many hits it receives, don't be so impressed. Hit counts have absolutely nothing to do with how many *visitors* a site gets.

Using Different Image Types

As noted earlier, choosing the right image file format is extremely important. Several different image types are supported on the Web, each with advantages and disadvantages. Table 8.1 describes some of these graphic types and what they should and shouldn't be used for.

TABLE 8.1 IMAGE TYPES USED ON THE WEB

Image Type	Description
BMP	Bitmaps generally shouldn't be used on the Web. They are not supported by all browsers, and are usually much larger than the same image in another format.
GIF	Graphics Interchange Format images are typically smaller than images in other formats because GIF supports only 256 colors. As such, this format is very well suited for small graphics (such as buttons). A more recent version of the GIF format supports animation by allowing multiple images to be stored in a single file, and then played back at timed intervals. Recently the GIF format has been the subject of copyright and patent concerns, so some vendors are looking into alternative graphic formats (such as PNG).

continues

TABLE 8.1   CONTINUED

Image Type	Description
JPEG	Joint Photographic Experts Group images (also referred to as JPG) can contain millions of colors, so they are very well suited for photographs or detailed images. JPEG images also can be compressed (by degrading the image quality slightly), which can help keep the download time down on larger images.
PNG	Portable Network Graphics was created as an alternative to GIF because of the copyright issues involved with that format. PNG is actually similar to GIF, but has been enhanced to overcome some of GIF's technical limitations. PNG is still a relatively new format but is gaining popularity rapidly.

So, which format should you use? Well, there is no hard and fast rule, and PNG is not yet a real contender (although it is fast becoming so), but here is a general guideline. GIF is usually better suited for small images such as buttons, toolbars, and backgrounds, whereas JPEG is better suited for larger, more detailed images such as photographs.

> Many developers save all their graphics in more than one format, and then decide which one to use based on file size. Many factors can affect file size, and often just comparing the two is the simplest way to pick the right one.

Viewing Thumbnails

As you develop your Web site you'll find yourself collecting and saving graphics. Ideally you'll create a directory for them (perhaps called IMAGES) under the Web server root, and possibly create subdirectories within that directory to organize them as you see fit.

But as you collect and save more and more graphics, you'll often find yourself having to browse through file listings to find the file you need. Files used on the Web, including images, cannot have spaces in their filenames, so images often have cryptic-looking names such as bf1cl.gif. The only way to know what is in each of these files is to open them one by one.

NEW TERM   To solve this problem, HomeSite features an integrated thumbnail viewer. *Thumbnails* are miniature versions of images designed to provide a sneak peek at what an image file contains. Thumbnails are useful because they are small enough to allow many images to be displayed at once for you to browse. You do not have to create thumbnails of your image files; thumbnails in HomeSite are created on-the-fly as needed.

8

To use HomeSite's thumbnail feature, do the following:

1. In the Resource Tab Local Files tab, click the directory containing the images to make it the current directory.

2. Click the Thumbnail button in the Tools toolbar (or choose Results from the View menu), and click the Thumbnails tab. Thumbnails for images in the current directory are displayed automatically (see Figure 8.1).

FIGURE 8.1

Thumbnails of all images in the currently selected directory appear in the Results window.

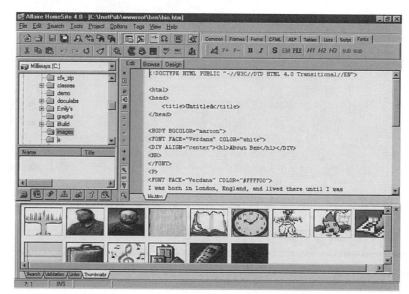

3. Right-click any image and select Properties to display the Image Properties dialog (see Figure 8.2).

4. To close the Results window, click the × button to its right, or choose Results from the View menu.

To quickly see the name, width, and height of a thumbnail image, just place your mouse cursor over it. HomeSite displays a pop-up message containing this information.

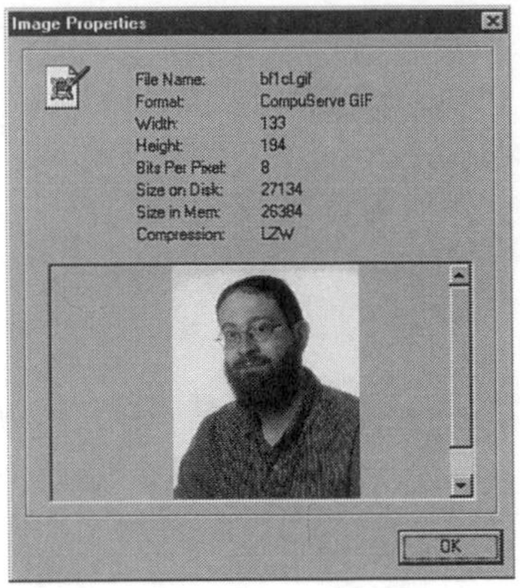

FIGURE 8.2

The Image Properties dialog displays the selected image along with name, format, height, width, size, and compression information.

The list of thumbnails displayed in the Results window is not automatically updated as you change directories in the Resource Tab Local Files tab. To refresh the thumbnails after changing directories, right-click between thumbnails and select Reset to Current Folder (you also can click the Thumbnails button in the Tools toolbar).

Embedding Images

Now that you know all about using images within your Web pages, let's try this out for ourselves.

The `<IMG>` Tag

As with everything else in HTML, images are embedded into pages with a tag—the `<IMG>` tag. `<IMG>` takes an attribute called `SRC`, which specifies the address of the image file. The following code embeds an image in the IMAGES directory beneath the document root:

```
<IMG SRC="/images/bf1cl.gif">
```

If the image was in the same directory as the HTML file itself, the path (/images/) could have been omitted, and the following code could have been used instead:

```
<IMG SRC="bf1cl.gif">
```

File locations also can be complete URLs, so you could embed an image that is on another server altogether simply by specifying its URL.

Of course, if you are using HomeSite, you don't need to worry about constructing SRC attribute paths. HomeSite will do the work for you. To demonstrate embedding images, I'll add my picture to my bio page. Following are the steps to do this:

1. Open the file BIO.HTM in HomeSite.

2. Place the cursor in the editor at the location where you want the image code placed.

3. Click the Image button in the Quick Bar's Common toolbar to display the Image Tag Editor (see Figure 8.3).

FIGURE 8.3

The <IMG> Tag Editor can be used to simplify embedding images.

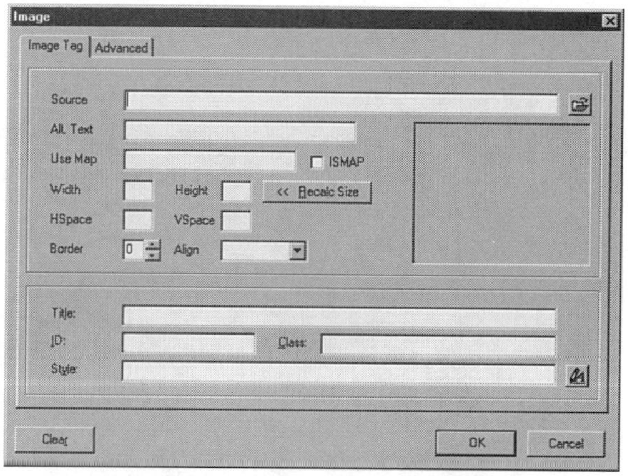

4. Click the browse button to the right of the Source field (the one with the folder on it) to browse and select your image. The Tag Editor populates the SRC attribute as needed, shows the image in the display window, and automatically populates the WIDTH and HEIGHT attributes with the image width and height (see Figure 8.4).

FIGURE 8.4

After you select an image, the <IMG> Tag Editor automatically populates the WIDTH and HEIGHT attributes with their correct values.

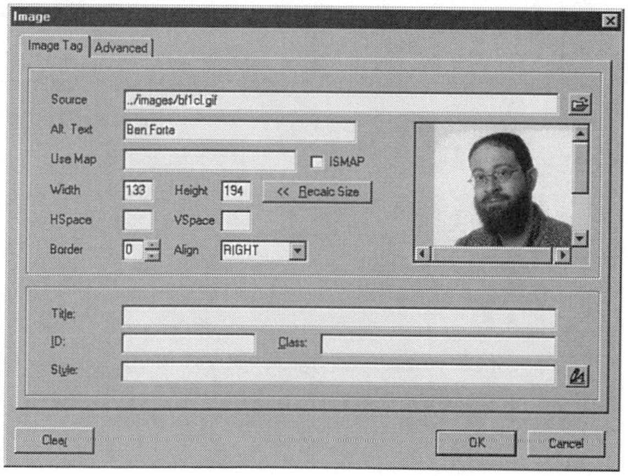

5. Alternative text is displayed in lieu of your image on browsers that cannot display the graphic (or until the graphic is downloaded). Always providing alternative text for your images is a good idea. I used my name (because the picture is a picture of me).

6. The `<IMG>` tag's `ALIGN` attribute lets you specify the position of the image relative to the text next to it. To display the picture to the right of the bio, set `ALIGN` to `RIGHT`.

7. Click OK to insert the tag into your code.

To see how your page looks now, use HomeSite's Browse mode to browse your page. It should look something like the one in Figure 8.5.

FIGURE 8.5

Set image alignment to LEFT or RIGHT to wrap text around it.

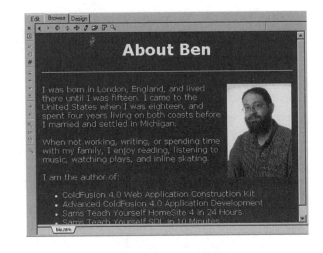

The `<IMG>` `ALT` attribute was originally intended for specifying text to be displayed instead of graphics in browsers that were not graphics-enabled. Although it does serve this purpose, `ALT` is also used by newer browsers as temporary text until graphics are downloaded, or instead of text if automatic graphic download is disabled. As such, it is a good idea to always provide `ALT` text for all images.

The optional <IMG> HEIGHT and WIDTH attributes tell your browser the exact size of an image before it's downloaded. Without these attributes, the browser cannot reserve space for the image, and when the image is eventually downloaded the browser will likely need to reorganize screen elements. With HEIGHT and WIDTH provided, the browser can reserve the screen space for the graphic, preventing annoying repainting. This makes for a much more pleasant user experience, so these attributes should always be used. Of course, if you use HomeSite's image placement tools, the WIDTH and HEIGHT attributes are automatically specified for you.

Using an Image as the Page Background

In addition to being able to embed images within your page, HTML also allows you to use an image for your page's background. This allows you to create more sophisticated backgrounds than what can be achieved by using solid colors and the <BODY> BGCOLOR attribute.

Background images are specified in the <BODY> tag's BACKGROUND attribute, and any image that can be embedded with <IMG> can be used as a background image. The simplest way to specify background images is via the <BODY> Tag Editor. As seen in Figure 8.6, the preview window within the Tag Editor displays a sample of what the page would look like, including the background image.

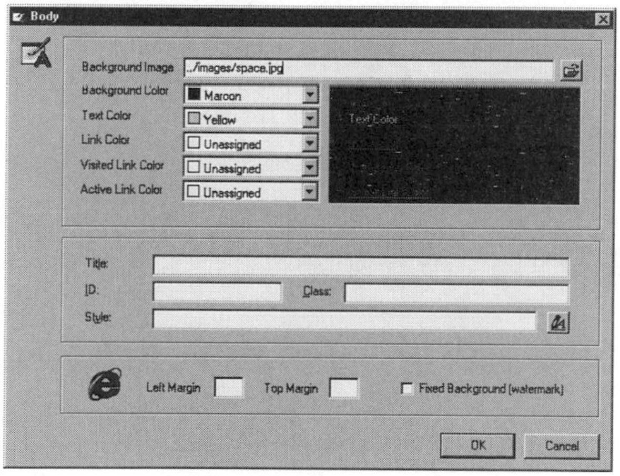

FIGURE 8.6

The <BODY> Tag Editor contains a preview window that displays what the page will look like using the settings specified.

Web browsers handle background images differently than they do embedded images. Background images are automatically tiled so that the image covers the entire page. As such, not all images are suitable for background images, because some won't repeat properly. An ideal background image is small (in both screen coordinates and file size) with a pattern that repeats well.

Simplifying Image Embedding

No discussion on using images within your Web pages would be complete without mentioning some of the shortcuts available to you within HomeSite:

- Any image file in the Resource Tab Local Files tab can be dragged and dropped onto your page. HomeSite will generate a complete <IMG> tag for the selected image.

- Similarly, any thumbnail image can be dragged and dropped onto your page. Again, HomeSite will generate a complete <IMG> tag automatically.

- If you have a graphics editing program installed on your computer (you should have, but I'll get to that soon), you can launch that editor from within HomeSite by simply right-clicking an image within the Resource Tab Local Files tab, and selecting Edit.

Obtaining Images

As explained in Hour 1, "Understanding HomeSite," HomeSite is an editor. It is not a graphic design package, nor does it come bundled with one. To use graphics within your Web pages, you have to download or create them yourself. Here are some suggestions for doing this.

Downloading Images

The Web is full of images that you can download and use. Just make sure that you are not downloading someone else's copyrighted material. To get you started on your graphics hunt, here are some URLs that you can visit:

- At the Allaire Developer's Exchange (http://www.allaire.com/developer/gallery.cfm), select the Web Content option.

8

- The Microsoft Gallery (http://www.microsoft.com/gallery/default.asp) has all sorts of goodies for download (not just graphics).

- Yahoo! (http://www.yahoo.com/Computers_and_Internet/Graphics/Clip_Art/) lists hundreds of Web sites with graphics available for download.

Creating Images

At some point, you most likely will need to create (or edit) your own graphics. The following are the most popular graphics editing packages on the Web, with URLs at which you can obtain product information:

- Adobe Illustrator (http://www.adobe.com/)
- CorelDRAW (http://www.corel.com/)
- Microsoft Image Composer (http://www.microsoft.com/imagecomposer/)
- Paint Shop Pro (http://www.jasc.com/)

Graphic designers make extensive use of scanners. If you intend to create and edit your own images, you might want to invest in one. If you don't have a scanner, try visiting your local Kinko's (or some other copy and printing store); many of these stores can scan images for you or let you use their scanners (for a fee).

Summary

Working with graphics and images is an exciting part of Web page development. There are some issues to be concerned about, particularly as far as bandwidth usage is concerned, but with a little extra effort, graphics can bring your Web site alive. The <IMG> tag is used to embed images into pages; the <BODY> tag's BACKGROUND attribute is used to specify background images. HomeSite provides all sorts of tools and features to simplify working with graphics.

Q&A

Q **I have seen some sites that display a low-resolution black-and-white graphic, and then redisplay a full-color graphic over it. How is this done?**

A That feature is primarily used to ease your visitors' waiting time. Rather than see no image, they see a simple low-resolution image temporarily while the full image is downloaded. To use this feature, simply specify the first image to use in the LOWSRC attribute. But be warned, this feature is supported only by Netscape Navigator. Microsoft Internet Explorer does not support LOWSRC and will ignore that attribute if it's present.

Q **I have seen some sites display transparent graphics. How is this done?**

A Transparency is a feature offered by the GIF format only, and it can be used to create some very dramatic effects. To create a transparent image, you need a graphics editing tool (any of the ones mentioned earlier will work). Basically, one color in the image is specified as the transparent color, and then any pixels in that color are rendered transparent by the browser.

Q **You mentioned using the HEIGHT and WIDTH attributes to reserve Web screen space. Can't these attributes also be used to resize images on-the-fly?**

A Yes, they can, but don't do it. First, some browsers won't honor the sizes you specify if they are smaller than the image, so you really have no idea what the screen will look like. A more important reason not to do this is a bandwidth consideration. If you want your users to see a smaller graphic, make a smaller graphic for them. Client size image resizing might look like you sent a smaller graphic, but in truth the browser has downloaded a large graphic and scaled it on-the-fly. Don't make users wait for downloads of large graphics if you don't intend to show them a large graphic.

Workshop

The Workshop contains quiz questions and activities to help reinforce what you've learned in this hour. If you get stuck, the answers to the quiz questions can be found in Appendix A, "Answers to Quiz Questions."

Quiz

1. What is the number one concern to bear in mind when working with graphics?
2. True or false: Picking the wrong image format can dramatically impact page download time.

3. True or false: `<IMG>` ALT text is not needed anymore now that all browsers can display graphics.

Exercises

1. Exact image placement can be tricky to control. Try embedding images in your page and experimenting with different ALIGN values to see how the various alignment options work.

NEW TERM
2. JPEG images support *lossy compression*, the ability to compress images by reducing image quality. If you have access to a graphics manipulation package, try saving a JPEG image at different compression levels. Try to find a compression ratio that substantially reduces file size without overly compromising image quality.

HOUR 9

Linking Pages

NEW TERM If you've surfed the World Wide Web, you've used links. *Links* are objects within Web pages that, when clicked, take you to other pages. The Web is made up of millions of pages, most of which are somehow linked to each other. In fact, the *Web* in World Wide Web alludes to this feature—linking.

In this hour you learn the following:

- What links are and how they work
- How to use the HTML anchor tags to create links
- How to create text and graphical links
- How to control link color

Understanding Links

Links are integral to the Web. They are the glue that holds Web pages together, allowing visitors to travel from page to page and site to site. Links can be textual or graphical, and can point to servers, directories, pages, and even specific locations within pages.

Most browsers highlight links automatically by changing the mouse pointer when the
mouse moves over them (a hand cursor is most frequently used for this), and by color-
coding links so that they stand out. The default link color in most browsers is blue (or
purple if the link has already been visited).

Links are created by using the HTML <A> (anchor) tag. <A> takes an attribute named
HREF, which must contain the URL to link to. For example, the following link takes a
user to my own Web page:

```
<A HREF="http://www.forta.com">Ben Forta's Homepage</A>
```

The text between the <A> and </A> tags is what is clickable within the browser. So in the
preceding example, clicking "Ben Forta's Homepage" takes the visitor to http://www.
forta.com, the URL specified in the HREF attribute.

> Make sure that every <A> tag has a matching </A> tag, or the rest of your
> page will become one big link. Similarly, make sure that the URL in the HREF
> attribute is enclosed in double quotation marks to prevent the link text (and
> any following text) from becoming part of the URL.

Absolute Versus Relative Links

NEW TERM When linking to specific pages (for example, pages within your own Web site),
you must provide the path to the linked file. There are two ways to provide paths
to pages: absolute paths and relative paths. *Absolute paths* provide the complete path to a
file, using the document root as a base. *Relative paths* provide paths based on where the
current page is.

To understand this distinction, let's look at a typical directory structure (see Figure 9.1).
BEN is a directory beneath the document root, my own Web site's root directory.
Beneath that directory are several subdirectories, FAMILY, FRIENDS, LINKS, and
WORK, each containing pages that are part of my Web site.

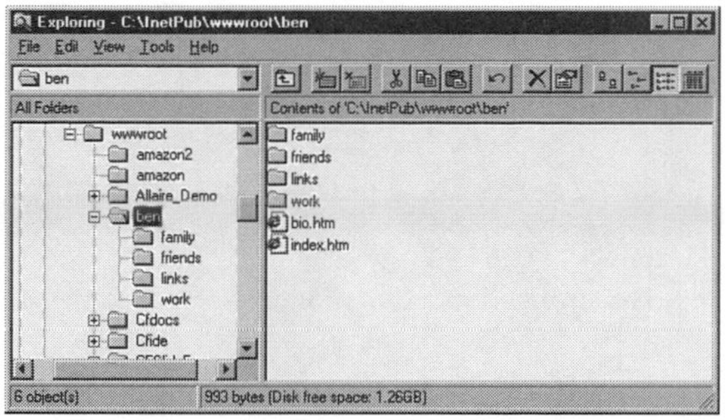

FIGURE 9.1

The files that make up your Web site should be stored in a hierarchical directory structure.

In the LINKS directory is a file named INDEX.HTM, which contains a list of links that I think my visitors might be interested in. Now suppose that I wanted to create a link from this page to the BOOKS.HTM page in the BEN directory. I could do this in two ways:

- The first link uses an absolute path. /ben/ tells the browser to find the file in the ben directory, which is a subdirectory of the document root (the / at the beginning of the path means the document root):

  <A HREF="/ben/books.htm">My books</A>

- The next link points to the same file but makes no reference to directory names. Instead, it uses .., which means go up one directory. Rather than hard-code a file path, this file path is specified based on the current directory. This type of path is a relative path:

  <A HREF="../books.htm">My books</A>

Both paths are valid, and both accomplish the exact same thing. So, what's the difference between the two? Suppose that I had to reorganize my Web site. Perhaps I switched ISPs and now my Web site root is /clients/ben/ instead of /ben/. If my links used absolute paths, the links would be broken because they would point to file paths that didn't exist (there no longer is a file that can be referred to as /ben/books.htm). If, however, I used relative paths, the links would still work correctly, because ../books.htm would now point to /clients/ben/books.htm automatically.

As this example demonstrates, unless you have a compelling reason not to do so, always use relative paths in your URLs.

HomeSite always tries to create links by using relative paths. If you use HomeSite's link-generation features (you'll see some of these in just a moment) rather than code links manually, your links will be relative whenever possible.

Links to External Sites

You can use <A> to link to any page, even a page on another Web server. To link to a page on an external site (a server other than your own), you must always provide a full URL to that page, starting with http://. The following is an example of this kind of link:

```
<A HREF="http://www.forta.com">Ben Forta's Homepage</A>
```

Deciphering Links

To summarize all this information and help you decipher any links that you may come across, here are the key points to bear in mind when reading URLs:

- Any HREF that starts with http:// points to a page using its complete URL. Usually this is used only for links to external pages.
- HREF paths that start with a / are absolute paths that point to files on the same server.
- HREF paths that start with ../ are relative paths. The .. means go up one directory; ../../ means go up two directories.
- If no filename is specified in the path (no file with a . and an extension following it), the URL is pointing to a directory instead of a file. The default document in that directory will be returned.
- File or directory paths that start with an actual name point to files (or directories) in the same directory as the current file.

Using Links

But enough talking about links; let's try some ourselves. The best way to create links within HomeSite is to use the Anchor Tag Editor (see Figure 9.2). To display this Tag Editor, click the Anchor button in the Quick Bar Common toolbar (the one with a picture of an anchor on it).

The Tag Editor prompts you with multiple text boxes, but the only two that you usually need to concern yourself with are the HREF text box, which must contain the link URL, and the Description text box, which contains the clickable text (the information that goes between the <A> and </A> tags).

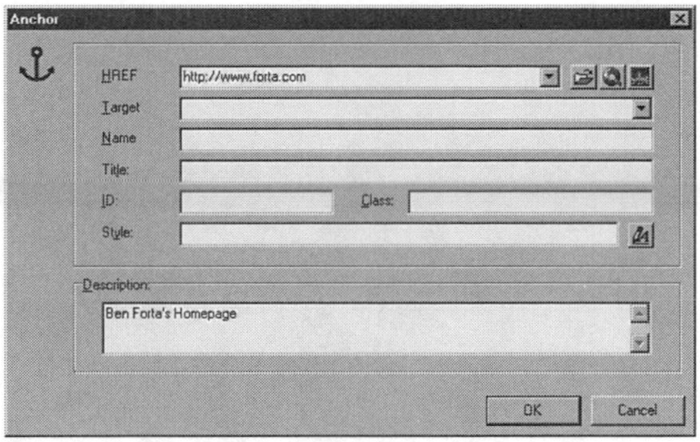

FIGURE 9.2

The <A> Tag Editor greatly simplifies the process of creating relative or absolute links.

If you highlight the text to be linked in the editor before clicking the Anchor button, HomeSite automatically populates the Description text box with the selected text.

Text Links

To demonstrate working with text links, I'm going to create my home page and add a link to the bio page that that we worked on in the past few hours. The following is the HTML for my home page:

```
<!DOCTYPE HTML PUBLIC "-//W3C//DTD HTML 4.0 Transitional//EN">

<HTML>
<HEAD>
    <TITLE>Ben Forta's Homepage</TITLE>
</HEAD>

<BODY BGCOLOR="#800000" TEXT="#FFFF00">
<FONT FACE="Verdana">
<DIV ALIGN="center">
<FONT COLOR="#FFFFFF"><H1>Ben Forta's Homepage</H1></FONT>
</DIV>
<HR>
<P>
Click on any of the links below:
<UL>
    <LI>My Bio
</UL>

</FONT>
</BODY>
</HTML>
```

Figure 9.3 shows you what the page looks like now.

FIGURE **9.3**

HTML lists are a pop-
ular way to organize
links on your page.

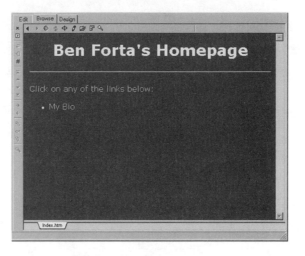

To link the text "My Bio" to the BIO.HTM page, I would do the following:

1. Highlight the words "My Bio" (being careful not to select the <LI> tag).
2. Click the Anchor button on the Quick Bar Common toolbar to display the Anchor Tag Editor (refer to Figure 9.2).
3. Click the folder button to the right of the HREF field to browse for the desired file.
4. Select the BIO.HTM file in the current directory and click the Open button.
5. Click OK to write the tag to the editor.

The list item will now look like this:

```
<LI><A HREF="bio.htm">My Bio</A>
```

Save the page, and switch to Browse mode to test the link. Figure 9.4 shows my updated home page.

Another way to create local text links is to locate the file to be linked within the Resource Tab's Local Files tab, and drag and drop it into the editor. HomeSite creates a complete link (using relative paths) automatically, and can even use the linked page's title as the link text if you want (that option is in the HTML tab in the Settings dialog). To use this feature, be sure to save the file that you are dragging the link into, or HomeSite will display a warning telling you that it can't construct a relative path.

FIGURE 9.4

By default, links in most browsers are displayed in blue, which is difficult to see on a page with a maroon background.

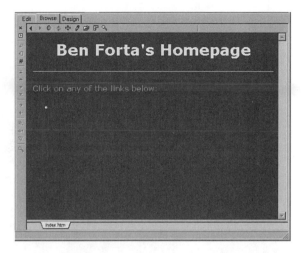

Graphical Links

In addition to letting you link text, HTML lets you link graphics by simply embedding them between the `<A>` and `</A>` tags. For example, the following code embeds an image named refsite.gif and makes it clickable by enclosing it within anchor tags:

```
<A HREF="index.htm"><IMG SRC="../images/refsite.gif"
WIDTH=32 HEIGHT=32></A>
```

I want a Home link on my bio page to return visitors to the home page. To do so, I would do the following:

1. Find the image file in the IMAGES directory and drag it onto the page at the location where I want the link to appear (this creates the `<IMG>` tag for me).

2. Highlight the entire `<IMG>` tag.

3. Click the Anchor button on the Quick Bar Common toolbar to display the Anchor Tag Editor.

4. Click the folder button to the right of the HREF field to browse for the desired file.

5. Select the INDEX.HTM file in the current directory and click the Open button.

6. Click OK to write the tag to the editor.

The link code should now look like the sample I just showed you. Verify that the link works by switching to Browse mode. Figure 9.5 shows my updated page.

FIGURE 9.5

Like all HTML, links can be tested in the integrated browser.

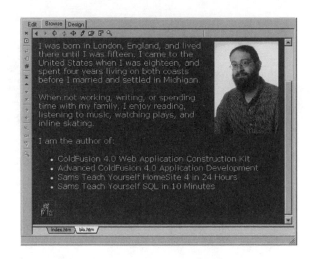

 By default, browsers display a border (in the page link color) around the image to indicate that it's clickable. This border can be turned off or made thicker by using the <IMG> tag's BORDER attribute. Specifying BORDER=0 turns off the border altogether, BORDER=1 is the default border, and values 2 through 10 specify thicker borders (with 10 being the thickest).

Controlling Link Color

I've mentioned link colors several times this hour. By default, most browsers display links in blue and visited links in purple. You can override these defaults using the <BODY> tag link color attributes in Table 9.1.

TABLE 9.1   LINK TYPES THAT CAN BE CONFIGURED VIA THE <BODY> TAG

Link Type	Description
ALINK	The color of active links (the color used when a link is clicked on)
LINK	The color of unvisited links
VLINK	The color of visited links

You can set these three link types to different colors, the same color, or any combination you want.

> The easiest way to manage link colors is by using the <BODY> Tag Editor. See Hour 7, "Working with Fonts and Colors," for instructions on using this Tag Editor.

9

Summary

Links are what makes the Web the Web. Links are used to allow your visitors to travel to pages within your own site or pages on any other Web site. Links are created using the anchor tags, and HomeSite provides Tag Editors and shortcuts to simplify link creation.

Q&A

Q How can I create a link that opens in a different browser window?

A The <A> tag's TARGET attribute lets you specify the target window for opened links. We discuss this in detail in Hour 11, "Working with Frames."

Q Is there any way to link my email address at the bottom of my Web page so that visitors can email me?

NEW TERM **A** Most browsers support a special link type called *mailto* that does exactly what you want. For example, the code <A HREF="mailto:ben@forta.com">ben@forta.com</A> displays my own email address, which, if clicked, lets visitors send me email. Of course, this works only if the visitors have an email program on their computers.

Q I have seen some sites that use a single graphic for multiple links—different regions within the graphic link to different URLs. How is this done?

NEW TERM **A** You are referring to *imagemaps*. These allow you to define regions (squares, circles, and even hand-drawn shapes) with a graphic, and then associate different URLs to each region. HomeSite doesn't include an imagemap editor, but some very good, inexpensive ones are out there. One of the most popular is LiveImage from http://www.liveimage.com.

Workshop

The Workshop contains quiz questions and activities to help reinforce what you've learned in this hour. If you get stuck, the answers to the quiz questions can be found in Appendix A, "Answers to Quiz Questions."

Quiz

1. True or false: Relative URLs should always be used in links whenever possible.

2. Which <A> tag attribute is required for links to work?

3. True or false: Only simple text and embedded graphics can be used as links within your Web page.

4. Which <BODY> attribute is used to set the color of visited links?

Exercises

1. Create a Web page and list your favorite Web sites as links. Use HTML lists to organize the links (using nested lists to sort by category, if appropriate).

2. Try using the drag-and-drop technique I mentioned to create local links within your own site.

PART III

Advanced Web Page Design

Hour

HOUR 10

Working with Tables

Early versions of HTML provided no mechanism with which to control the exact layout of Web pages. All Web pages flowed from left to right, and then downward. This made it impossible to line up objects side by side or place them in specific page locations. For the most part, this problem was resolved with the introduction of HTML tables, and tables remain one of the most important page layout elements within HTML.

In this hour you learn the following:

- What tables are, how they work, and how they are used
- How to use the HTML table tags
- How to use the table wizards and shortcuts

Understanding Tables

The best way to understand tables is to envision a two-dimensional grid, kind of like a spreadsheet grid. The grid is made up of rows, with each row containing cells. Like spreadsheet cells, table cells can contain text, graphics, and other elements. And like spreadsheet cells, table cells can be lined up side by side, one on top of the other, and in other formats too. Figure 10.1 shows a simple HTML table.

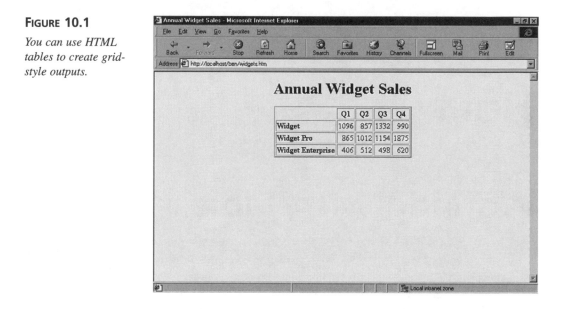

But there's more to HTML tables than simple grids. HTML table cells can contain *any* HTML elements, even other tables. As such, tables aren't just used for displaying grid-like information, but for any page layout that requires more control over element positioning.

Suppose that you wanted to display a text block in two columns (newspaper style). Without tables, your text would flow across the entire width of the page in one wide column. But if you create a table with a single row containing two cells side by side, you could display half the text in the left cell and half in the right cell, thereby creating the desired output (see Figure 10.2).

FIGURE 10.2

*You can use HTML
tables to display pages
in newspaper-style
columns.*

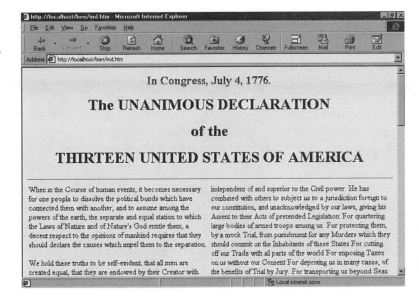

10

Unlike spreadsheets, the table used to create the display in Figure 10.2 has no borders.
HTML table borders are optional and, as you'll see later this hour, you can control borders as well as many other table features and options by using the table tags.

> You also can create columns by using HTML frames. We'll cover frames in
> detail in Hour 11, "Working with Frames."

How Tables Are Used

To better understand how tables are used, look at some examples on the public Internet.

Stoneage Corporation

Stoneage Corporation (http://www.stoneage.com) is one of the largest car-buying (and
selling) sites on the Web. The Stoneage Web site (see Figure 10.3) displays a consistent
set of navigation controls on the left of the screen; as visitors browse through the site, the
buttons remain in the same place. To accomplish this, every page is constructed within a
simple table with a single row containing two cells. The left cell contains the buttons,
and the right cell contains the actual page (including any text, graphics, links, forms, and
even other tables).

FIGURE 10.3

The Stoneage Web site
displays all pages
inside a two-cell table.

FIGURE 10.3

The Stoneage Web site
displays all pages
inside a two-cell table.

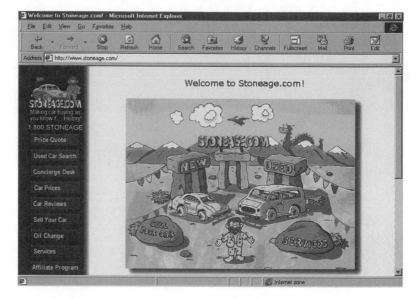

Amazon.com

Amazon.com (http://www.amazon.com) is one of the Internet's major success stories—
the biggest and most popular online book, music, video, and gift store. The Amazon.com
Web site (see Figure 10.4) uses lots of tables in many different ways. The home page is
divided into three columns, each of which is a table cell. The menu bar at the top of the
page is a table row that spans all three columns. Tables also are used to box specific text,
color, and shade backgrounds, and for special announcements.

FIGURE 10.4

Amazon.com uses
tables to divide pages
into columns.

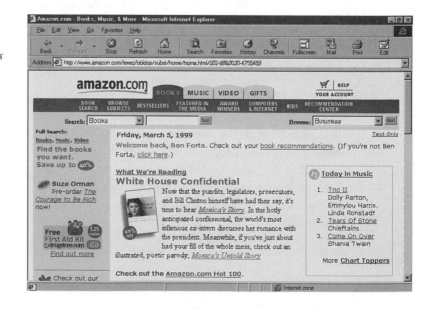

Allaire Corporation

Allaire Corporation (http://www.allaire.com) is a highly successful Internet software development company. Their flagship products are ColdFusion and HomeSite (yep, the same product that this book teaches). The Allaire Web site in Figure 10.5 uses tables to lay out all pages. In fact, the entire page shown is displayed within a fixed-width table so that element placement can be controlled exactly.

FIGURE 10.5

The Allaire Web site uses tables for navigation menus and buttons, columns, text blurbs, and bullet items.

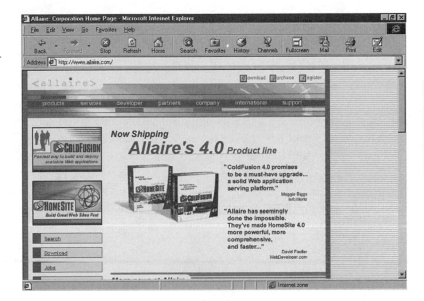

As you can see, there's more to tables than grids containing financial information. Tables are an invaluable page-formatting tool, and their use is limited only by the limits of developer creativity.

> If you want to know how other Web sites use tables, just look. The best way to learn the tips and tricks of fine-tuning page layout is to pick a site that you like, and then view the HTML used to create it. You can do so by using your browser's View Source option, or from within HomeSite directly by choosing Open From Web on the File menu.

Why Not to Use Tables

Now for the obvious question: If tables are so powerful and useful, why do some sites still not use them? There are two primary reasons not to use tables:

- Some older browsers can't display HTML tables. Because browsers ignore tags they don't understand, the table cell contents are displayed but all table formatting is ignored. A visitor using one of these browsers will see a page layout that likely won't be what you intended, and may possibly even be completely unintelligible. Fortunately, very few of these browsers are still in use (most estimates put it at less than 0.1 percent).

- The biggest problem with tables is the time it takes to display them. So as not to make your visitors wait unnecessarily, browsers display data as it's received. If your page contains thousands of lines of text (which it shouldn't), a browser will start displaying the first lines as it receives them so that the visitor can start reading your page even before the entire page is loaded. But tables are more complex. Browsers can't display any part of the table until the entire table is loaded, because rows and cells further down the table could affect the sizing and positioning of the entire table. So although the page takes no longer to load, it takes longer to display initially. From a visitor's perspective, your site will appear slow.

The bottom line is that tables are invaluable to Web-page designers but shouldn't be overused or used unnecessarily.

The Table Tags

HTML tables are created by using four sets of tags:

- The <TABLE> tag creates a new table; </TABLE> terminates a table.

- Table rows are created by using <TR> and </TR>. All tables must contain at least one row; there is no imposed maximum number of rows.

- Within a row, individual cells are created by using the <TD> and </TD> tags (<TD> stands for *table data*). There's no imposed maximum number of cells per row.

- Table cells can be formatted as *headers* by using <TH> and </TH> instead of <TD> and </TD>. However, most tables don't use header cells because the header formatting can also be achieved (with greater control) by using just <TD> tags.

To understand this, look at a few examples. This first block of code creates a simple table with two rows, each containing two cells. Figure 10.6 is the browser output created by this code:

```
<TABLE>
 <TR>
  <TD>First name:</TD>
  <TD>Ben</TD>
 </TR>
 <TR>
  <TD>Last name:</TD>
  <TD>Forta</TD>
 </TR>
</TABLE>
```

FIGURE 10.6

HTML tables are created by using the <TABLE>, <TR>, and <TD> tag sets.

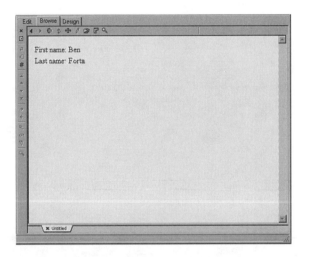

10

When using tables, make sure that text (or HTML code) is placed only within table cells. Text must never be placed outside cells (for example, between a <TR> and a <TD>) because this can distort the table, prevent the table from being displayed, and even cause text to be displayed outside the table.

The next code example creates a larger table, with four rows and two cells each. The <TABLE> BORDER attribute is used to define a border around the table and between the cells. The cells in the top row are formatted as headers (centered and displayed in bold) by using the <TH> tags. Figure 10.7 is the browser output created by this code:

```
<TABLE BORDER="1">
 <TR>
  <TH>Title</TH>
  <TH>ISBN</TH>
 </TR>
 <TR>
  <TD>Advanced ColdFusion 4.0 Development</TD>
```

```
 <TD>0789718103</TD>
</TR>
<TR>
 <TD>ColdFusion 4.0 Web Application Construction Kit</TD>
 <TD>078971809X</TD>
</TR>
<TR>
 <TD>Sams Teach Yourself HomeSite 4 in 24 Hours</TD>
 <TD>0672315602</TD>
</TR>
</TABLE>
```

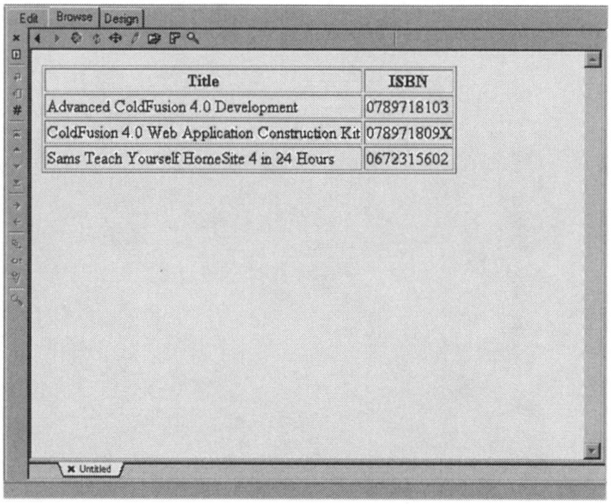

FIGURE 10.7

Table borders are managed by using the <TABLE> BORDER attribute.

Title	ISBN
Advanced ColdFusion 4.0 Development	0789718103
ColdFusion 4.0 Web Application Construction Kit	078971809X
Sams Teach Yourself HomeSite 4 in 24 Hours	0672315602

Notice the indentation in the code examples we just looked at. Indenting code has no impact on how the browser displays the table (remember, browsers ignore whitespace), but it does make the code easier to read and thus easier to troubleshoot. Most table problems are caused by mismatched (or incorrectly nested) tags. Indentation can help pinpoint and even prevent this type of error.

As you can see, with a little care and planning, table tags can be used to format data in ways impossible without them.

Simplifying Table Creation

As the preceding code suggests, creating tables manually isn't impossible, but it can be tedious. As the size and complexity of your tables grow, so does the number of tags needed to create them, and thus so does the chance of making a mistake or typo.

For this reason, HomeSite provides you with tools and shortcuts to simplify table creation.

Using the Table Toolbar Options

HomeSite's table creation and editing features are accessed through 11 buttons in the Quick Bar's Tables toolbar. The nine middle buttons embed tags or display Tag Editors. Each button is named with the tag it corresponds to (*tbl* is short for *table*, *cp* is short for *caption*). The buttons with the blue bar above the text display Tag Editors (see Figure 10.8); the buttons without the blue bars embed tags directly into your editor.

FIGURE 10.8

The <TABLE> Tag Editor provides simple access to all tag attributes (including some advanced and obscure options).

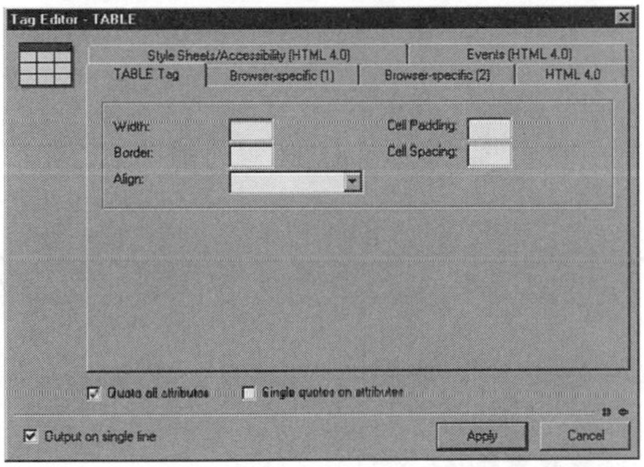

The button on the right of the toolbar is the Table Sizer (also known as Quick Table). This remarkable tool is undoubtedly the fastest way to create HTML tables. To try the Table Sizer, follow these steps:

1. Place your editor cursor at the location on your page where you want the table inserted.
2. Click the Table Sizer button to display the Table Sizer control.
3. Without clicking, move the mouse downward and to the right to select the number of rows and cells you want in your table (see Figure 10.9).

4. After you highlight the number of rows and cells that you need, click to make your selection. HomeSite automatically generates all the HTML code needed to create your table (and even properly indents the code for you).

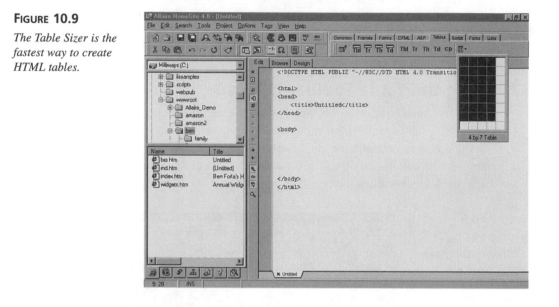

 The Table Sizer can create tables up to 23 rows deep and 14 cells wide, far bigger than most tables you will ever (or should ever) create.

Using the Table Wizard

The leftmost button on the Quick Bar's Table toolbar is the Table Wizard. This wizard isn't that useful for simple tables (use the Table Sizer instead), but for complex tables you'll find it invaluable.

To practice using the Table Wizard, try the following:

1. Place your cursor at the location on your page where you want the table inserted.

2. Click the Table Wizard button to display the first Table Wizard dialog, titled Table Design.

3. In the Table Design dialog, specify the number of rows and columns by clicking the + and – buttons. You also can click specific cells within the preview grid to span rows and columns (see Figure 10.10).

FIGURE 10.10

The Table Wizard Table Design page is used to lay out table rows and columns.

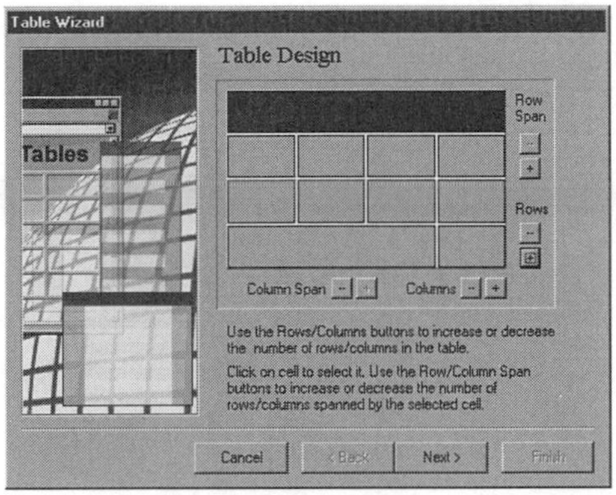

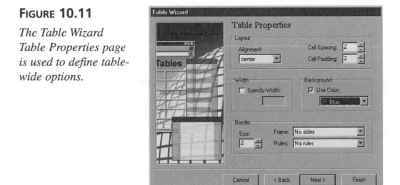

4. After you create the basic table layout, click Next to display the Table Properties dialog. This dialog, shown in Figure 10.11, lets you fine-tune table properties with options including alignment, cell padding and spacing, table width, background color, and borders.

FIGURE 10.11

The Table Wizard Table Properties page is used to define table-wide options.

5. After you set table properties, click Next to display the Cell Properties dialog (see Figure 10.12), in which you fine-tune the properties of specific cells. You can click any cell in the preview grid to set its options, including width, whether it allows text wrapping, displaying the cell as a header, and content alignment.

6. After you set all the cell properties with the desired values, click Finish to write the table code back into your page.

10

FIGURE 10.12

The Table Wizard Cell Properties page is used to define cell-specific options.

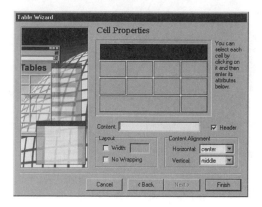

> You also can use the preview grid in the Table Wizard for specifying row height and column width. To do so, click the lines between cells and drag them as needed.

Summary

HTML tables are a powerful and important page-layout tool. Table syntax can get tricky as table complexity grows, so HomeSite provides shortcuts and tools to simplify table creation. The Table Sizer is the fastest way to create tables, and the Table Wizard is useful when creating more complex tables.

Q&A

Q Is there a way to specify the exact width of a table?

A There are several ways to do this. The `<TABLE>` tag's `WIDTH` attribute lets you specify absolute widths in pixels (for example, `WIDTH="400"`) and relative widths as a percentage of browser window width (for example, `WIDTH="100%"`). You also can specify individual cell widths by using the `<TD>` and `<TH>` `WIDTH` attributes. To maximize browser window use, try to use relative widths whenever possible.

Q How can I control the alignment of table cell contents?

A By default, cell contents are left justified, header cell contents are centered, and all cells are centered vertically. You can fine-tune cell alignment by using the `ALIGN` (horizontal alignment) and `VALIGN` (vertical alignment) attributes. These attributes may be used at the `<TABLE>` and `<TR>` levels, as well as for specific cells. Cell-specific settings override table- and row-level settings, and row-level settings override table-wide settings.

Q Some of my tables display correctly in some browsers but incorrectly in others. What could cause this?

A This is almost always caused by mismatched tags, or by specifying text outside tags. Some browsers are more forgiving than others when it comes to invalid tables, so although table problems might not show up in your browser, they could show up in another. This is yet another reason to check all your pages in multiple browsers.

Q I've noticed that sites use tags other than the ones you listed in their tables. Where can I get more information on these tags and what they do?

A There are indeed other table-related tags, including <CAPTION>, <COL>, and <TBODY>, all of which are used very infrequently. Some of these tags aren't supported by all browsers, so use them with caution. For more information on these tags, use HomeSite's help system and select HTML Reference, Tables to display the tags.

10

Workshop

The Workshop contains quiz questions and activities to help reinforce what you've learned in this hour. If you get stuck, the answers to the quiz questions can be found in Appendix A, "Answers to Quiz Questions."

Quiz

1. What is the primary benefit of using tables?

2. What is the fastest way to create tables?

3. True or false: Avoid code indentation because it increases code size and thus download time.

4. What's wrong with the following code snippet?

```
<TABLE>
 <TR>
  First name:
  <TD>Ben</TD>
 </TR>
 <TR>
  Last name:
  <TD>Forta</TD>
 </TR>
</TABLE>
```

Exercises

1. Visit your favorite Web sites and view their HTML source to see how they use tables. Be warned, however, that lots of badly formatted tables are out there. Don't be surprised if you find syntax problems on some very high visibility sites.

2. Nested tables allow you to create one table within a cell of another table. Try creating a nested table, making sure to correctly start and finish the entire inner table within a cell. (Tip: Indenting your code will prove invaluable for this exercise.)

3. Cell spacing and cell padding behave differently in different browsers. Try creating a simple table, experimenting with the CELLPADDING and CELLSPACING attributes to see these differences, and learning how to compensate for them. Use the HomeSite help system to get help on these attributes.

HOUR 11

Working with Frames

NEW TERM Most modern browsers allow you to create screens made up of
multiple windows. These windows, which may be within a single
browser or in separate browsers, are known as *frames*. HTML frames can
be used to create sophisticated multiwindow sites, where one window can
change based on activity in another window.

In this hour you learn the following:

- What frames are, how they work, and how they are used
- Why the use of frames isn't overly popular
- How to use the HTML frame tags
- How to use the Frame Wizard

Understanding Frames

When you browse the Web, you usually browse one page at a time. You load
a page, read it, and click a link; then a new page replaces the page you were
reading in your browser window.

Great. But what if you wanted to go back to the first page and follow another link? You'd have to click your browser's Back button, wait for the first page to redisplay, click the next link, and then wait for that page to load.

Now you want to follow a third link, so click Back again, and...well, you get the picture.

A better interface might be to split your browser into two side-by-side windows. The left window would contain a list of links, and the right window would display the pages that the links point to. Each time you'd click a link in the left window, the right window would display the linked page. This type of multiwindow interface (see Figure 11.1) is an example of HTML frames.

FIGURE 11.1

Frames allow you to split your browser screen into multiple windows.

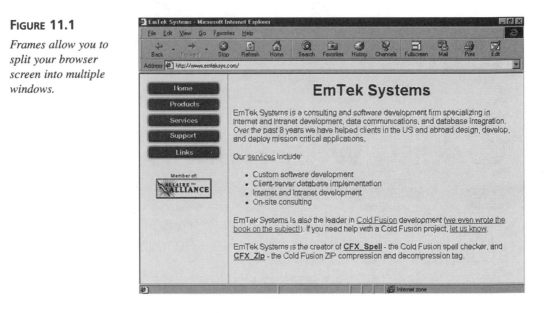

The key here is that by using frames, a single browser can display multiple Web pages at once, one in each frame, and each frame can be updated independently of the others.

How Frames Are Used

To better demonstrate how frames can be used, let's look at some examples on the public Internet.

EmTek Systems

EmTek Systems (http://www.emteksys.com) is a computer consulting firm. Its Web site (see Figure 11.2) is constructed with a simple two-frame screen. The left frame contains navigation buttons; when any button is clicked, the appropriate page is opened in the right frame. Displaying consistent navigation controls is one of the most common uses of frames.

FIGURE 11.2

Displaying navigation controls is a popular use for frames.

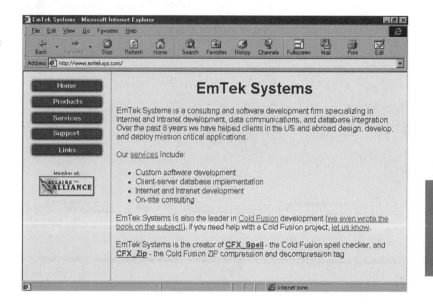

11

Netscape DevEdge Online

Netscape publishes an extensive collection of developer reference material on its DevEdge Online Technologies site at http://developer.netscape.com/tech/javascript/ (see Figure 11.3). The JavaScript section, like many other sections, uses a three-frame display. The top frame contains header information and navigation links. The left frame contains a list of contents in this section. The right frame contains the details for any item clicked in the left frame.

NEW TERM Data drill down is another popular use for frames. The term *data drill down* describes the process of searching for information by successive refinement. Usually this involves selecting a high-level topic, selecting a subtopic within that topic, and then viewing the details for that subtopic. The page-based nature of the Web makes data drill down a very popular user interface.

As you'll see later this hour, the exact layout of your frames can be configured by using the frame tags and their attributes.

FIGURE 11.3

Data drill down inter-faces are well suited for framed environments.

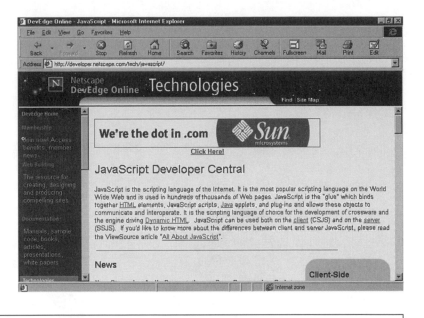

The Netscape DevEdge site is an invaluable resource for information on many Internet-related technologies. Visit `http://developer.netscape.com` to access this site.

Why Not to Use Frames

Before you run off and rewrite your Web site to use frames, take a moment to look at the primary reasons not to use them:

- Some older browsers can't display HTML frames. As you'll soon see, creating frames involves creating multiple Web pages, and the page that creates the frame usually has no other content in it. This means that visitors using browsers that don't support frames might see nothing at all when viewing your site. Fortunately, very few of these browsers are still in use (most estimates put it at less than 0.1 percent). The HTML frame syntax also allows you to specify content to be displayed only by browsers that don't support frames. So with a little extra work, you could create a frameless version of your page to be displayed by older browsers.

- Many of the public search engines won't index framed pages. If search engine indexing is important, you'll definitely want to provide a frameless interface to your site as well.

- The biggest problem with frames, however, is that many users find them very annoying. You want your visitors to enjoy your site (so that they return); you don't want them to get annoyed. The main reasons they get annoyed is that navigating out of a framed site can be tricky (just clicking the Back button is usually not enough), and printing framed pages is particularly difficult. But these problems are not insurmountable; with some extra care, you can work around these limitations.

Many developers get emotional about frames—they either love 'em or hate 'em, and unfortunately, the latter sentiment seems to be the prevalent one. This is primarily the result of having experienced sites with badly implemented frames when this technology was first introduced. But frames have come a long way in a short time. Most browsers now support them, and developers now have extensive control over the exact look and behavior of their frames. As such, I think frames deserve a second chance.

How Frames Are Constructed

Creating frames involves creating multiple HTML files. For example, the EmTek Systems Web site (refer to Figure 11.2) requires three HTML files to display the home page:

- One page (usually the default page) defines the frames. There's no content per se in this page—just the frames definition and the names of the files to load into each frame.
- The left frame contains a simple HTML page that displays the navigation controls. This separate page isn't part of the frame definition page.
- The right frame contains whatever is clicked in the left frame, but a default selection is made so that the page doesn't load initially empty.

These pages are linked by using the HTML frame tags.

The Frame Tags

HTML frames are created by using the following tags:

- The <FRAMESET> tag creates a new set of frames and defines the number of frames in a frame set. </FRAMESET> terminates the set.
- Within a frame set, individual frames are defined with the <FRAME> tag. A <FRAME> tag is specified for each frame in the set.

- The optional <NOFRAMES> and </NOFRAMES> tags may be used to specify text and HTML to be displayed by browsers that don't support frames.
- Microsoft Internet Explorer supports *floating frames*, which can be placed anywhere within the browser screen. These are defined by using the <IFRAME> and </IFRAME> tags.

To demonstrate this, let's look at a few examples. This first block of code creates a simple frame set:

```
<FRAMESET COLS="50%,50%">
 <FRAME NAME="menu" SRC="menu.htm">
 <FRAME NAME="details" SRC="main.htm">
</FRAMESET>
```

The <FRAMESET> tag's COLS attribute lists the size of the columns in a comma-delimited list. COLS="50%,50%" instructs the browser to create two columns (side-by-side frames), each 50 percent of the browser screen's width. To create four columns each a quarter of the browser width, use COLS="25%,25%,25%,25%". Widths can be specified as percentages or in pixels. Wildcards also can be used to specify "the rest of the space," so COLS="250,*" would create a column that was 250 pixels wide and a second column that uses whatever browser width was available.

The two <FRAME> tags in the preceding example specify the names and contents of each of the two frames. <FRAME NAME="menu" SRC="menu.htm"> names the frame "menu" and tells the browser to load the file menu.htm into it. This is the code for page menu.htm:

```
<BODY>
<UL>
 <LI>Menu item 1
 <LI>Menu item 2
 <LI>Menu item 3
</UL>
</BODY>
```

Page main.htm contains the following code:

```
<BODY>
text goes here
text goes here
text goes here
text goes here
text goes here
</BODY>
```

Figure 11.4 shows the output created by these three code files.

FIGURE 11.4

Frames are defined using the <FRAMESET> and <FRAME> tags.

menu.htm ——

main.htm ——

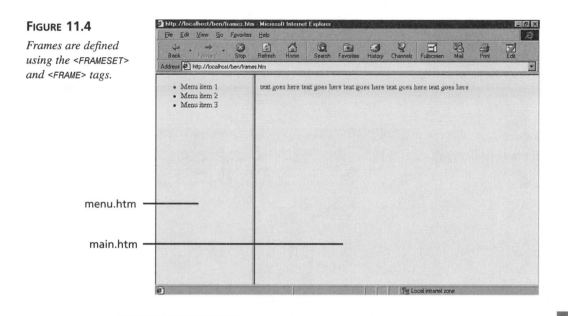

Technically, frame names are optional. In practice, however, frames really aren't useful without unique names, as you'll see later this hour. It's worthwhile to get into the habit of always naming frames with unique names.

11

This next code example creates a more complex set of frames:

```
<FRAMESET ROWS="100,*">
 <FRAME NAME="header" SRC="header.htm">
 <FRAMESET COLS="200,*">
  <FRAME NAME="menu" SRC="menu.htm">
  <FRAME NAME="details" SRC="main.htm">
 </FRAMESET>
</FRAMESET>
```

The code starts with a <FRAMESET> that creates two ROWS (instead of columns). COLS creates side-by-side frames; ROWS creates frames one on top of the other. The first row is 100 pixels high, the second row uses whatever space is left over.

Then a <FRAME> tag names the top frame and tells the browser to display the header.htm page within it. The code for header.htm is as follows:

```
<BODY>
<DIV ALIGN="center"><H1>Header</H1></DIV>
</BODY>
```

The bottom frame isn't defined by using a <FRAME> tag. Rather, a set of <FRAMESET> tags is used to create a new set of frames within the bottom frame. This <FRAMESET> creates two side-by-side frames (using COLS); the left one is 200 pixels wide and the right one uses all remaining space.

Figure 11.5 shows the browser output created by these four files.

FIGURE 11.5

Frames may be nested to created a desired effect.

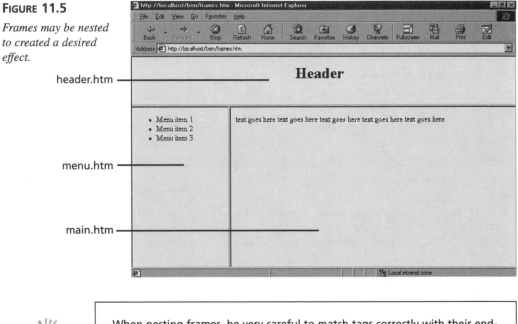

When nesting frames, be very careful to match tags correctly with their ending tags. Most frame-related problems are caused by mismatched tags. Of course, if you use HomeSite to help build your frames, you'll never run into this problem.

Linking Across Frames

Now you know how frames are created. But how do you link across frames? For example, in the Web sites shown in Figures 11.2 and 11.3, clicking a link in the left frame causes a page to be displayed in the right frame.

In Hour 9, "Linking Pages," we looked at creating links using the <A> tag. The default behavior of the <A> tag is that when a link is clicked, the new page replaces the first page in the browser window. But that can be changed. The <A> tag's TARGET attribute allows you to specify the name of a frame in which the link should be opened. The following code displays a link to page main.htm; when the link is clicked, the page is opened in the frame named details:

```
<A HREF="main.htm" TARGET="details">Home</A>
```

Every link that needs to open a page in another frame must use this syntax.

Be careful to correctly specify frame names in the TARGET attribute. If you specify the name of a frame that doesn't exist, a new browser window will open (and will automatically be named with the specified name).

Simplifying Frame Creation

As you've seen until now, the HTML frame syntax can be tricky to work with, particularly when creating complex sets of nested frames (something you shouldn't do too often). As with everything else in HomeSite, there are shortcuts and features built into the product designed to make creating frames much simpler than doing it the manual way.

Using the Frames Toolbar Options

HomeSite's frame creation and editing features are accessed via nine buttons in the Quick Bar's Frames toolbar. The right eight buttons embed tags or display Tag Editors. Each button is named for the tag it corresponds to (*set* is short for *frameset*, *fra* is short for *frame*, *if* is short for *iframe*, and *no* is short for *noframes*). The buttons with the blue bar above the text display Tag Editors (like the one in Figure 11.6); the buttons without the blue bars embed tags directly into your editor.

FIGURE 11.6

The <FRAMESET> Tag Editor provides simple access to all tag attributes.

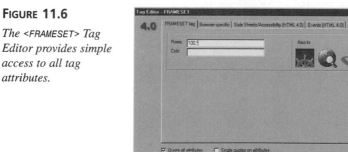

The Frame Wizard

The simplest way to create your frames is by using the Frame Wizard. You can activate this wizard by clicking the leftmost button on the Quick Bar's Frames toolbar, or by selecting Frame Wizard from the New Document dialog.

To see the Frame Wizard in action, try the following:

1. Place your editor cursor at the location on your page where you want the frame definition code inserted (typically this would go into a new empty document). Make sure your frame definition isn't in between <BODY> and </BODY> tags, because frames can't be embedded within a page body.

2. Click the Frame Wizard button to display the first Frame Wizard dialog, titled Frame Design.

3. The Frame Design dialog lets you specify the number of rows and columns by clicking the appropriate + and – buttons (you also can click specific frames within the preview grid to nest frames within frames). Click the Col– button so that you have a simple two-row frame (see Figure 11.7).

FIGURE 11.7

Use the Frame Wizard's Frame Design dialog to lay out horizontal and vertical frames.

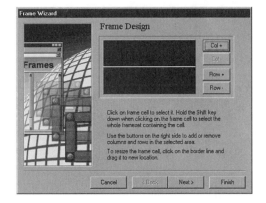

4. To split the bottom frame into two, click the frame to select it, and then click the Col+ button. The preview pane shows two side-by-side frames (see Figure 11.8).

FIGURE 11.8

Selecting a single frame within the Frame Design dialog lets you create frames within frames.

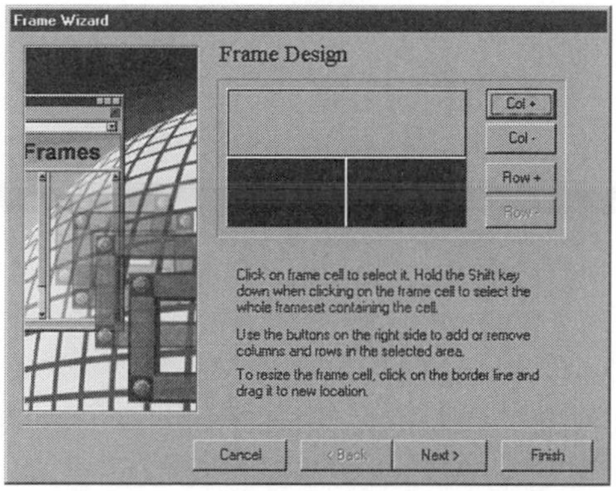

5. Click Next to display the Frame Attributes dialog. This dialog lets you specify frame-specific options and features.

6. Click each frame in the preview grid, and specify a unique name and a source file to be loaded into the frame (see Figure 11.9). You can click any frame in the preview grid to set its options, including height, width, whether it allows scrolling, whether resizing is allowed, and whether to display borders.

7. After you set all the frame properties, click the Finish button to write the frame code back into your page.

FIGURE 11.9

The Frame Wizard's Frame Attributes dialog is used to define frame-specific options.

11

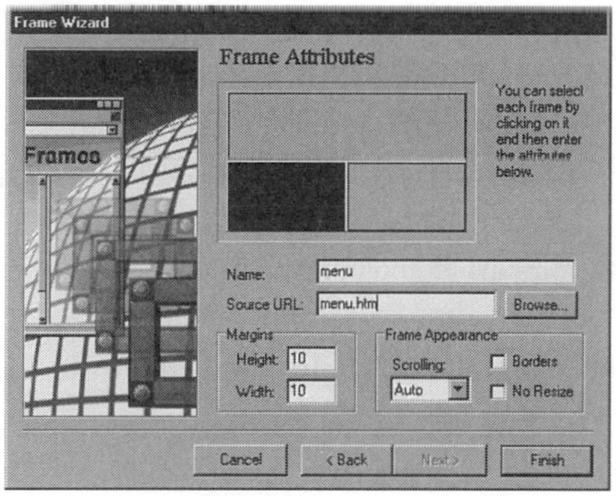

You also can use the preview grid in the Frame Wizard to specify frame height and width. To do so, click the lines in between frames and drag them as needed.

Summary

You can use HTML frames to create sophisticated multiwindow interfaces. The most common uses for frames include providing consistent navigation controls, and creating data drill down interfaces. Frames syntax isn't very intuitive compared to the rest of HTML, so HomeSite provides shortcuts and tools to simplify frames creation.

Q&A

Q You mentioned that when using frames, developers should always provide frameless versions of their pages. What's the best way to do this?

A To do this, use the `<NOFRAMES>` set of tags. Browsers that support frames ignore anything between the `<NOFRAMES>` and `</NOFRAMES>` tags. Browsers that don't support frames ignore those tags, but not the content between them. Therefore, you can (and should) place a `<NOFRAMES>` section on every page that defines a frame set. Browsers that can't display frames will display the `<NOFRAMES>` content instead, and that content may contain text and HTML (including links).

Q Is there a safe way to create frames that may be printed?

A That framed windows don't print well is a fact that you have to work around. Many sites display printable versions of pages on request. You can do this simply by providing a link within your frame that says something like `Display a Printable Copy of This Page`; when clicked, that link opens the page in a new frameless window. The contents of that window can then be printed safely.

Q Why can I resize some frames by dragging their borders, but not others?

A When frames are created, you can tell the browser not to allow resizing. This is done by using the `<FRAME>` tag's `NORESIZE` attribute. Generally, you shouldn't use this option unless you have a good reason to prevent resizing—perhaps to ensure that navigation controls or headers are always displayed.

Q The links you've mentioned this hour allow me to click a link in one frame and display the result in another frame. How can I display the results in a new pop-up window?

A To display the results in a new window, use the special `TARGET` attribute, `new`, which always opens a new window and never reuses it. Another useful `TARGET` attribute is `top`, which allows you to create a link that breaks out of all frames and displays the page in the full browser window.

Workshop

The Workshop contains quiz questions and activities to help reinforce what you've learned in this hour. If you get stuck, the answers to the quiz questions can be found in Appendix A, "Answers to Quiz Questions."

Quiz

1. Why are frames often used for navigation controls?

2. Why should the <NOFRAMES> tag be used with all frames?

3. True or false: Creating frames requires the use of only two tags, <FRAMESET> and <FRAME>.

Exercises

1. Create a simple home page by using two side-by-side frames. Put your links in the left frame and the contents in the right frame. Be sure to use the <A> TARGET attribute to update the right frame when a link is clicked.

2. If you have a copy of Microsoft Internet Explorer installed, try creating a floating frame by using the <IFRAME> tag. You can find information on this tag in the HomeSite help screens.

11

Hour 12

Creating Forms

In the past 11 hours you've learned how to create Web pages and display content in various ways. The next topic that you need to look at is complementing data publishing with data collection. In the HTML world, data is collected through forms. Forms are sets of data input fields that you can use to prompt visitors for information.

During this hour you learn the following:

- What forms are and how they work
- How to use the various form controls
- How to use the Forms toolbar options to simplify form creation

Understanding Forms

If you've surfed the Web, you've seen (and probably used) forms. Forms are used to collect data from visitors to your Web site. Common uses for forms include

- Guest books
- Login screens
- Data entry
- Search screens
- Application forms

And that's just the tip of the iceberg. Anytime you want to collect data from your visitors, you do so by using forms.

HTML provides only the mechanism with which to collect data—it doesn't provide any way to process collected data. This means that by using straight HTML you can create a search screen, but you can't actually perform the search or display search results. Similarly, you can create a guest book form, but you can't save the collected data to a database.

To perform back-end processing on submitted data, you need another product or technology that runs on the Web server. You have many options when it comes to back-end processing, but as a HomeSite user you should look at Allaire's flagship product—ColdFusion. With ColdFusion, you can read and write database records, generate email, process credit-card charges, and much more. You can download an evaluation version of ColdFusion from Allaire's Web site at http://www.allaire.com. You also might want to buy a copy of my *ColdFusion 4.0 Web Application Construction Kit* (ISBN 0-7897-1809-X), published by Que.

Form Controls

HTML forms are made up of form controls, and HTML supports several different control types. Each control has its own syntax and its own set of rules governing its use. To demonstrate the use of these controls, I have added a simple Guest Book page to my Web site (see Figure 12.1).

FIGURE 12.1

HTML supports several different control types for use within forms.

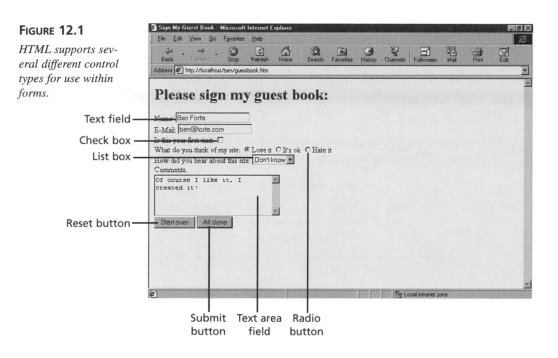

Text field ———
Check box ———
List box ———

Reset button ———

Submit   Text area   Radio
button   field   button

Let's now look at each control type used in Figure 12.1.

Text Fields

NEW TERM *Text fields* collect freeform text. Text boxes allow users to enter a single line of text containing any characters, and whatever the user enters is echoed onscreen. (*Echoing* means that text you type appears onscreen; text that doesn't echo doesn't appear as you type.) You can restrict the maximum number of characters that can be entered, and you also can control the field's width. Text boxes scroll text automatically if more text is entered than can be displayed.

My Guest Book uses two text fields: one for name and one for email address.

HTML also supports a text field that doesn't echo the user's input. This is known as a password field because that's usually what it's used for. Aside from not echoing the input (usually a * is displayed for each character typed), password fields behave just like text fields.

12

Check Boxes

Check boxes are used for on/off fields (also known as *flags* or *true/false fields*). Check boxes have only two possible values: ON and OFF. My Guest Book uses a check box to ask users whether this is their first visit.

Radio Buttons

Radio buttons allow users to select one of a set of mutually exclusive options. My Guest Book uses radio buttons to ask users what they think of my site.

> Although I probably could have used a text field and allowed users to specify whatever they want, collecting structured data is usually preferable if I plan to run statistics or reports on the collected data.

List Boxes

List boxes (or *drop-down list boxes*) are similar to radio buttons in that they usually allow for the selection of one of a set of options. But there are two key differences between list boxes and radio buttons:

- Radio buttons are all displayed onscreen, allowing visitors to see all options before making a selection. List boxes usually display a single selection; visitors must click the down arrow to display the other options. As such, radio buttons take up more screen space and thus aren't well suited for long option lists.

- Radio buttons allow the selection of only a single option. List boxes can be constructed to allow the selection of multiple options, if desired.

My Guest Book uses a list box to prompt visitors for how they found out about my site.

Text Area Fields

Text area fields collect multiline free-form text. Unlike text fields, text area fields allow users to enter as much text as they want on as many lines as they want. You can control the size of the text area box but not the number of lines or characters that may be entered.

My Guest Book uses a text area field for the comments field, allowing visitors to enter any text they want.

By default, text area boxes don't wrap text. This means that the entire box will scroll to the right when the end of a line is reached. Most browsers, however, support optional text area box wrapping. As this makes for a far more pleasant user interface, as a rule you should always use this option in your own forms.

As I just said, HTML enables you to control the size of the text area box. The width of a text area box is specified in columns—the number of columns of text that can be displayed. Unfortunately, different browsers have different ways of interpreting what *columns* are. As such, your text area box will be one size in Netscape Navigator and a different size in Microsoft Internet Explorer. There isn't much you can do about this, but at minimum you should check your forms in multiple browsers to ensure that the controls look right in them all.

Reset Button

The reset button does just that—it resets the form. Any data entered by users is cleared out so that they can start over.

Many Web developers avoid using reset buttons because visitors often click them by mistake when trying to click the submit button. Understandably, users aren't going to like retyping all their text, and omitting the reset button can prevent this from occurring.

12

Submit Button

The submit button submits the form once data entry is complete. Every form is associated with an ACTION—usually a page to which the collected data is sent. When the submit button is clicked, the collected data is sent to the ACTION page, which is displayed in the browser.

Creating a Form

Now that you know all the form controls and how to use them, let's create the Guest Book page. Start by creating a new page in HomeSite called guestbook.htm. Save this file with the files created in the previous hours.

The <FORM> Tag

The first thing you need to do is define the form itself. Forms are defined by using the <FORM> tag:

1. Place your cursor between the page's <BODY> and </BODY> tags.

 2. On the Quick Bar's Forms toolbar, click the Form button to display the <FORM> Tag Editor (see Figure 12.2)

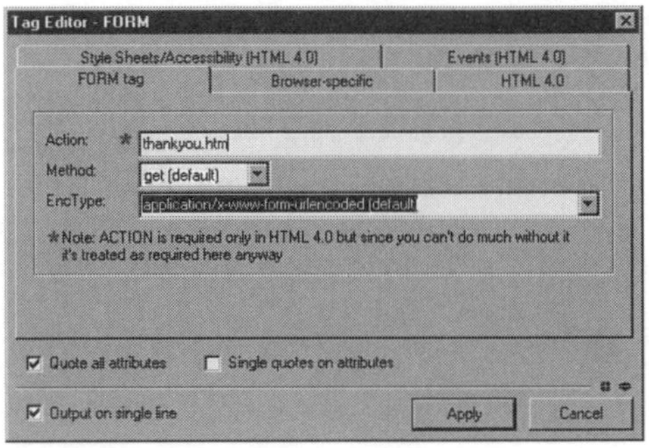

FIGURE 12.2

The <FORM> Tag Editor prompt for the form action, method, and other attributes.

3. Specify the form action in the Action text box. For this example, type **thankyou.htm**. (That file hasn't been created yet; we'll get to that in a few moments.)

4. Leave the default values in the other fields and click the Apply button to generate the form code.

You now have a form in which to embed form controls.

Using Text Controls

All form controls *must* be placed between the <FORM> and </FORM> tags. Almost all controls are created by using the HTML <INPUT> tag, which takes a TYPE attribute that specifies the control type. The exceptions are list boxes (created by using <SELECT>) and text area boxes (created by using <TEXTAREA>).

 By default, the Forms toolbar might not be displayed in ColdFusion Studio. If this is the case, simply right-click the Quick Bar and check the Forms option to display the toolbar.

Let's start by embedding the Name field:

1. Type **Name:** on a new line. This will be the field prompt.

2. Click the Text button on the Quick Bar's Forms toolbar to display the <INPUT> Tag Editor (see Figure 12.3)

FIGURE 12.3

The <INPUT> Tag Editor is a tabbed dialog that's used for all field types other than text area boxes and list boxes.

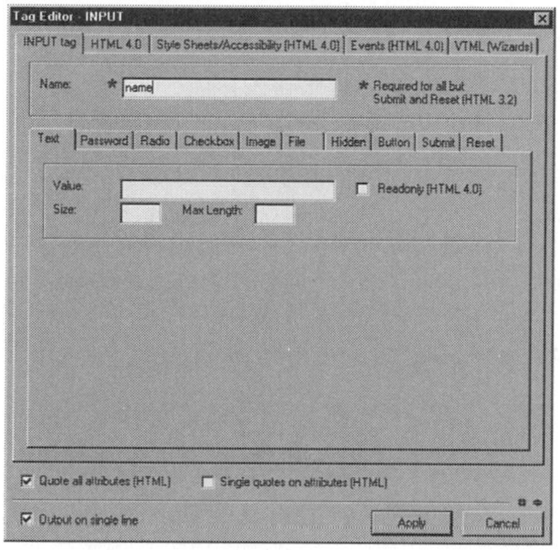

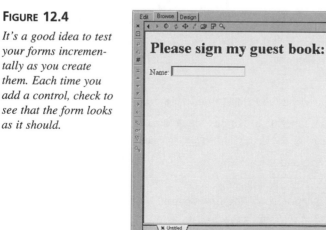

3. Specify the name of this field in the Name text box. Because this field will contain your visitor's name, let's call it "name"; enter **name** in the Name text box.

4. Click the Apply button to write the <INPUT> code into your editor.

5. Save the page and switch to browse mode to see your form. It should look similar to the example in Figure 12.4.

12

FIGURE 12.4

It's a good idea to test your forms incrementally as you create them. Each time you add a control, check to see that the form looks as it should.

Please sign my guest book:

Name:

After you create the Name field, repeat these steps for the E-Mail field. Be sure to insert breaks between the fields; otherwise, they'll all end up on one line.

Using Check Boxes

Next, create the check box field:

1. Type **Is this your first visit:** on a new line. This will be the field prompt.
2. Click the check box button on the Quick Bar's Forms toolbar to display the <INPUT> Tag Editor with the Checkbox page displayed.
3. Specify first_time as the field Name.
4. Click the Apply button to write the <INPUT> code into your editor.

Again, remember to test your form each time you add a control.

Using Radio Buttons

Next comes the radio buttons. These are a little more complicated than the <INPUT> code you have created thus far because each radio button requires its own <INPUT> field.

So how does the browser know to treat these fields as one set? The answer is the field name. A set of radio buttons must all have the same name; they vary not by name but by value. This way, the browser treats them as a set (when one is selected, the others are automatically deselected). When the form is submitted, the value of the selected radio button is submitted.

Follow these steps to add the radio buttons to our Guest Book:

1. Type **What do you think of my site:** on a new line (this will be the field prompt).
2. Click the radio button icon on the Quick Bar's Forms toolbar to display the <INPUT> Tag Editor with the Radio page displayed.
3. Specify rating as the field name.
4. Specify 3 as the value.
5. Click the Apply button to write the <INPUT> code into your editor.
6. Each radio button needs a label (text that describes what it represents), so provide a label by typing **Love it** after the generated <INPUT> code.
7. Repeat steps 2 through 6 to add the next button. Make sure that the name is rating (so that the fields are grouped), and specify a value of 2 and a label of **It's ok**.
8. Repeat steps 2 through 6 again to add the final button. Make sure that the name is rating, and specify a value of 1 and a label of **Hate it**.

When you're done, test your form. Make sure that the radio buttons are displayed correctly, and that selecting one radio button deselects the others.

> Use the <BR> tag to space out form controls on separate lines. Hour 6, "Designing a Web Page," explains the <BR> tag.

Using List Boxes

List boxes aren't created by using the <INPUT> tag. Instead, you need to use two new tags:

- <SELECT> is used to create a list box (HTML calls these *select controls*).
- <OPTION> is used to populate the list box with options.

As you'd expect, HomeSite simplifies creating list boxes as follows:

1. Type **How did you hear about this site:** on a new line.
2. Click the select button on the Quick Bar's Forms toolbar (the one on the far right) to display the <SELECT> Tag Editor (see Figure 12.5)

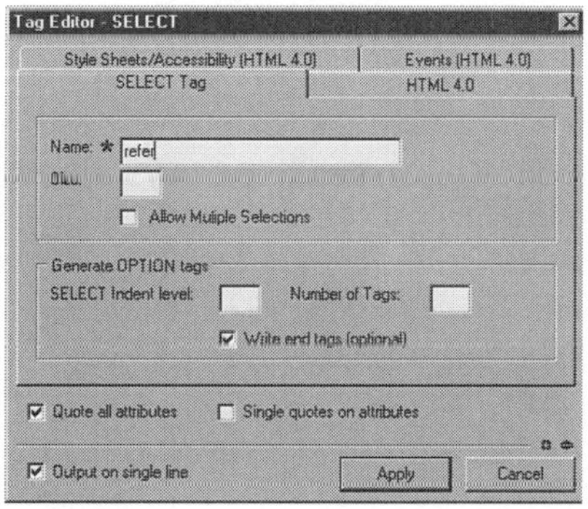

FIGURE 12.5

The <SELECT> Tag Editor is a tabbed dialog that also can create <OPTION> tags, if desired.

3. Set the field name to **refer**.
4. Click the Generate Option Tabs and specify the number of options you want in the field provided (you can add and remove options later if needed).
5. The bottom half of the Tag Editor contains the Generate OPTION Tags pane. Specify the number of options you want in the Number of Tags: field (you can add and remove options later if needed).
6. Populate the options. Each option needs a VALUE (what gets returned when users select the option) and the display text (what users actually see onscreen). The display text is specified between the <OPTION> and </OPTION> tags (for example, I used <OPTION VALUE="yahoo">Yahoo</OPTION> for Yahoo).

After you specify the options, save and test your page.

Using Text Area Boxes

The last field we need is the comments field, a text area box. Follow these steps to add this field:

1. Type the text **Comments:** on a new line (this will be the field prompt) followed by a line break (the <BR> tag).

2. Click the text area button on the Quick Bar's Forms toolbar to display the <TEXTAREA> Tag Editor (see Figure 12.6).

FIGURE 12.6

The <TEXTAREA> Tag Editor is a tabbed dialog that can also be used to populate the field with initial content.

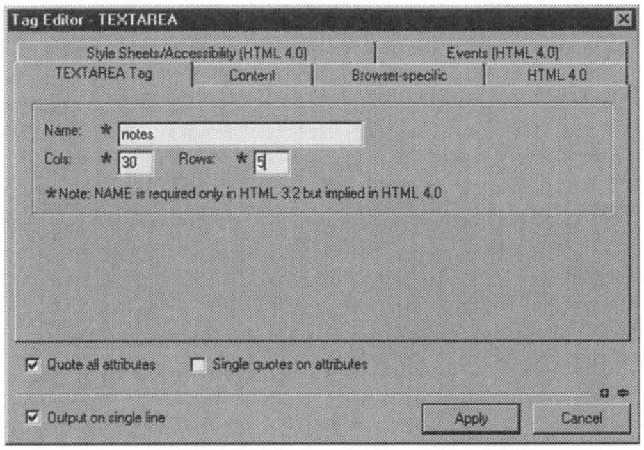

3. Use notes as the field name.

4. Set the control size. I used 30 for the columns and 5 for the rows.

5. Select the Browser-specific tab and set the wrap field to VIRTUAL to make the control behave like most Windows text area boxes.

6. Click the Apply button to write the <TEXTAREA> code into your editor.

Using Buttons

All we need now are the reset and submit buttons. Follow these steps:

1. Place your cursor at the beginning of a new line.

2. Click the Reset button on the Quick Bar's Forms toolbar to embed a Reset button in your code.

3. Right-click the inserted tag and select Edit Tag to display the Tag Editor.

4. Buttons usually don't need names, so leave the Name text box empty.

5. Button text is specified in the VALUE attribute, so set the Value text box to Start over.

6. Click Apply to write the button code to the editor.

7. Place your cursor at the beginning of a new line.

8. Click the Submit button on the Quick Bar's Forms toolbar.

9. Again, leave the Name text box empty, but specify a caption of All done.

10. Click Apply to write the button code to the editor.

Now save and test your form. It should look similar to the one in Figure 12.1 at the beginning of this hour.

> If you don't specify button text, reset buttons will use the default caption of Reset and submit buttons will use Submit Query. Rather than use these default (and not very intuitive) values, always specify your own captions in the button's VALUE attribute.

The Completed Form

Your Guest Book form is now complete. What follows is my own Guest Book code, which you can refer to if yours doesn't look as you'd expect it to:

```
<HTML>
<HEAD>
<TITLE>Sign My Guest Book</TITLE>
</HEAD>

<BODY>

<H1>Please sign my guest book:</H1>

<FORM ACTION="thankyou.htm" METHOD="GET">

Name: <INPUT TYPE="text" NAME="name">
<BR>

E-Mail: <INPUT TYPE="text" NAME="email">
<BR>

Is this your first visit: <INPUT TYPE="checkbox" NAME="first_time">
<BR>

What do you think of my site:
<INPUT TYPE="radio" NAME="rating" VALUE="3">Love it
<INPUT TYPE="radio" NAME="rating" VALUE="2">It's ok
<INPUT TYPE="radio" NAME="rating" VALUE="1">Hate it
<BR>
```

12

```
How did you hear about this site:
<SELECT NAME="refer">
 <OPTION VALUE="altavista">Alta Vista</OPTION>
 <OPTION VALUE="banner">Banner Ad</OPTION>
 <OPTION VALUE="excite">Excite</OPTION>
 <OPTION VALUE="friend">Friend</OPTION>
 <OPTION VALUE="icq">ICQ</OPTION>
 <OPTION VALUE="infoseek">Infoseek</OPTION>
 <OPTION VALUE="yahoo">Yahoo</OPTION>
 <OPTION VALUE="unknown">Don't know</OPTION>
</SELECT>
<BR>

Comments:<BR>
<TEXTAREA NAME="notes" COLS="30" ROWS="5" WRAP="VIRTUAL"></TEXTAREA>
<BR>

<INPUT TYPE="reset" VALUE="Start over">
<INPUT TYPE="submit" VALUE="All done">
</FORM>

</BODY>
</HTML>
```

The form ACTION was set to thankyou.htm. Of course, with straight HTML the action
page doesn't actually do anything with the data—it just displays a thank-you message.
Your own action pages will typically write the collected data to a database table or do
some other processing. Here's the code for my thank-you page:

```
<HTML>
<HEAD>
<TITLE>Sign My Guest Book</TITLE>
</HEAD>

<BODY>

<H1>Thank You</H1>

</BODY>
</HTML>
```

Summary

Forms are used to collect data from visitors. They are created by using the HTML
<FORM> tag and contain one or more form controls. Controls are created by using the
<INPUT>, <SELECT>, and <TEXTAREA> tags. The Quick Bar's Forms toolbar provides
access to Tag Editors that can simplify form creation.

Q&A

Q **The form we created this hour is rather messy. Is there a way to better organize the placement of form controls?**

A The best way to organize form controls is to use HTML tables. You could create a table containing each form element in its own cell, and then place the cells where you want them by using the table tags you saw in Hour 10, "Working with Tables."

Q **Is there any way to validate form submissions (for example, making fields required, or restricting data to specific data types)?**

A HTML itself provides no data validation support (except for a maximum length for text fields). To validate specific field types (date values, numbers, and upper- and lowercase values) and to flag fields as required, you must use client-side scripting. The most popular language for this is JavaScript. Unfortunately, JavaScript validation is beyond the scope of this book. If you're interested in JavaScript client-side scripting, look at another book in this same series, *Sams Teach Yourself JavaScript 1.3 in 24 Hours* (ISBN 0-672-31407-X).

Q **Is there a simple way to send form data to an email address without using back-end processing?**

A Yes, you can use a `mailto` attribute for the form `ACTION`. For example, specifying `<FORM ACTION="mailto:ben@forta.com">` sends the form fields to ben@forta.com via email. But this technique will work *only* if visitors have email clients installed on their computers.

Q **In the code samples in this hour, you instructed me to use a `METHOD` of `GET`. What is the significance of `METHOD`, and what are `GET` and `POST`?**

A `GET` and `POST` are different ways in which the browser can submit form data. The `GET` method appends form information to the end of the `ACTION` URL; the `POST` method sends form fields separately. When using back-end processing, it's preferable to use the `POST` method because `POST` can support a greater number of fields (and larger values) than `GET`. But `POST` requires a back-end script to process the page; `GET` doesn't. Because we were submitting the form to an HTML page (and not a script), we had to use a `METHOD` of `GET`.

Workshop

The Workshop contains quiz questions and activities to help reinforce what you've learned in this hour. If you get stuck, the answers to the quiz questions can be found in Appendix A, "Answers to Quiz Questions."

Quiz

1. True or false: Form controls must be used between <FORM> and </FORM> tags.

2. What's the difference between check boxes and radio buttons?

3. What field type would you use to ask an applicant his or her sex?

Activities

1. Create your Guest Book page and a thank-you page. Then link the Guest Book page to your home page.

2. Look at forms on search engine or e-commerce sites. What controls do they use? Try to determine why they chose the controls they did.

3. If you have access to your own Web server, you might want to download a 30-day evaluation version of ColdFusion from http://www.allaire.com to experiment with back-end processing.

HOUR 13

Using Design Mode

HomeSite is very much a text editor, and HomeSite development involves manually writing HTML code. But HomeSite also features a graphical Design mode for some specific language elements and features. This Design mode isn't a full-blown graphical page layout application, but it does address some very specific needs.

In this hour you'll learn the following:

- When and when not to use Design mode
- How to use Design mode's text formatting features
- How to manipulate tables in Design mode
- How to create forms in Design Mode

Understanding Design Mode

By now, halfway through this book, it should be clear that HTML isn't a difficult language to learn. Indeed, incredible care and attention goes into language changes and enhancements to ensure that HTML remains usable and easy to learn. Having said that, manually coding some HTML elements can be a tedious process and, as such, graphical-based Web page design tools have gained tremendous popularity.

As I explained in Hour 1, "Understanding HomeSite," professional Web developers know that it's impossible to create top-notch Web sites in a purely graphical markup tool. At some point, direct HTML manipulation is needed to fine-tune your page's appearance and elements. But at the same time, there's an advantage to graphically laying out tables or coloring text.

And so HomeSite 4 introduced Design mode. Design mode is *not* a graphical page layout tool. Design mode (see Figure 13.1) is simply a graphical interface that you can use to simplify working with specific language elements.

FIGURE 13.1

Design mode provides a graphical interface for editing specific HTML elements.

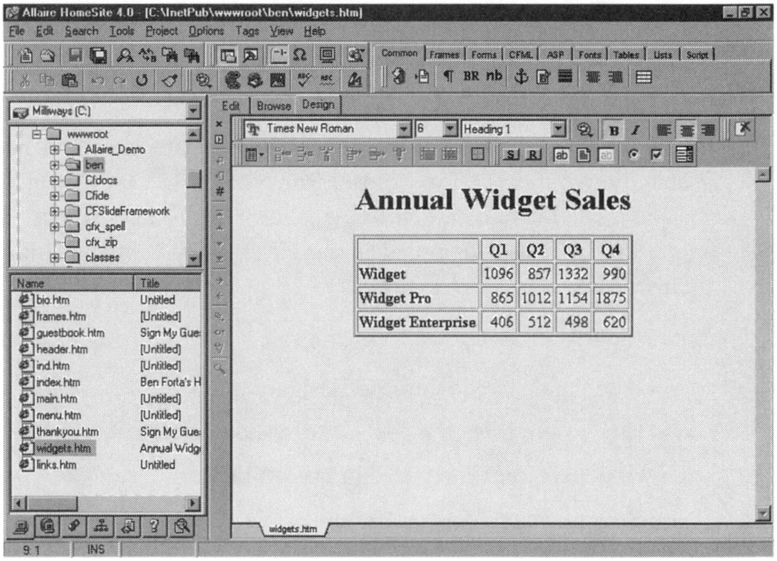

When to Use Design Mode (and When *Not* To)

So, when should you use Design mode? Well, there's no clear-cut answer to this one, but most HomeSite developers find that Design mode is useful in the following situations:

- *Initial page design,* creating a basic page shell in Design mode and then filling in the blanks manually in Edit mode.

- *Fine-tuning table layout,* using Design mode's table manipulation options to manage table width, column spanning, and cell content appearance
- *Resizing form controls*, using the new version 4 browser features

In other words, there *are* legitimate uses for Design mode—especially because in Design mode you are actually editing within a browser, so what you see is truly what you get.

But at the same time, Design mode shouldn't be used to manipulate complex pages that you've already manually edited. Although Design mode makes every effort to keep your formatting and syntax, it is by no means perfect. Also, the code generated by Design mode often uses HTML language features that aren't supported by all browsers.

The bottom line is that Design mode is useful for addressing specific problems in specific scenarios, but it's not intended as a replacement for manual coding.

Alternatives to Design Mode

Graphical page layout tools have their advantages. If you're interested in graphical-based page layout tools, look at Macromedia Dreamweaver. Dreamweaver is a particularly good choice for HomeSite users because

- HomeSite provides built-in support for Dreamweaver, allowing you to use it to edit files right from within HomeSite (see Figure 13.2).
- Of all the graphical tools out there, Dreamweaver does the best job of honoring your own HTML code, keeping it intact and formatted the way you left it.

FIGURE 13.2

If installed, Macromedia Dreamweaver can be invoked right from within HomeSite.

Macromedia Dreamweaver button

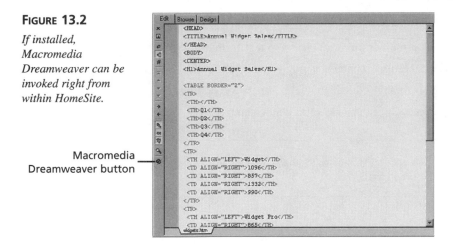

13

If you want to evaluate Macromedia Dreamweaver, visit Macromedia's Web site at http://www.macromedia.com.

Using Design Mode

You can activate Design mode in any of the following ways:

- Click the Design tab above the editor window.
- Select Toggle Edit Design from the View menu.
- Press Shift+F12.

 If Design mode isn't available (or the tab isn't displayed), check the following:

- Microsoft Internet Explorer 4.01 or later must be installed on your system.
- The Design tab may be hidden by checking the Disable Design Tab option in the Settings dialog's Design page.

Now let's look at using specific Design mode features. To get started, create a new empty page and switch to Design mode now.

The Design mode screen (see Figure 13.3) has four toolbars:

- The Format toolbar provides access to text formatting options.
- The Cancel toolbar contains a single button, the cancel button.
- The Tables toolbar contains table manipulation options.
- The Forms toolbar contains form control buttons.

 As with all HomeSite toolbars, the Design mode toolbars can float or be docked as desired.

FIGURE 13.3

*Design mode provides
a graphical interface
for editing specific
HTML elements.*

Format toolbar   Tables toolbar

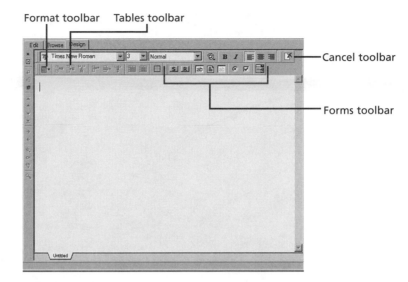

Cancel toolbar

Forms toolbar

Text Manipulation

To demonstrate text manipulation in Design mode, try the following:

1. Type **Please visit these links** and then press Enter to go to a new line.

2. This line of text needs to be formatted as a page header (using the <H1> tag). Click anywhere in the line of text and select Heading 1 from the format list box (the third drop-down list box on the Format toolbar).

3. To center the text, click the Center button on the Format toolbar.

4. Highlight the entire line of text.

5. Apply a font to this text by selecting a font from the font list (I picked Verdana). You also can select a font size or specify bold and italic text by clicking the appropriate controls.

6. To specify text color, choose a color from the color palette (use the Palette button on the standard Tool toolbar or the Design mode Format toolbar).

That's all there is to it. The text you're looking at is displayed exactly as it will appear in a browser because you actually created it in a browser (Microsoft Internet Explorer).

My display is shown in Figure 13.4. Obviously, yours may vary if you selected different fonts or colors.

13

FIGURE 13.4

Design mode lets you develop your page within a real browser, so what you see is truly what you get.

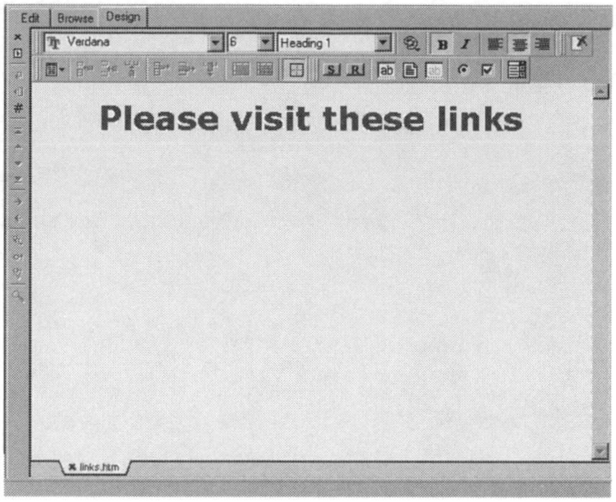

Working with Tables

Where Design mode truly shines is in table design and manipulation. To demonstrate this, let's add a table to this link page. The table will contain two columns: the left will contain the name of a site (which will be linked to the site) and the right will contain a description. Follow these steps:

1. Place the cursor on a new line.

2. Create a table by using the Table Sizer (the same control we saw in Hour 10, "Working with Tables"; refer to that hour if you need help). Your table should be two columns wide; use as many rows as you need (one for each link).

   The initial table will resemble the example in Figure 13.5. Design mode creates the table with cells that are the narrowest width allowed.

FIGURE 13.5

Design mode creates tables with narrow columns, and then grows them as needed.

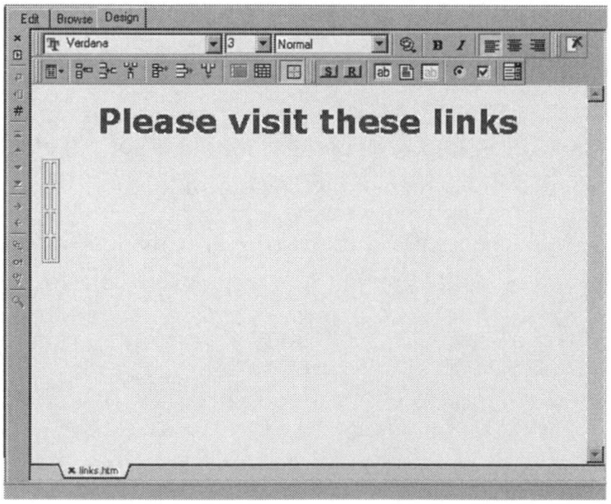

3. Click in the left cell of the first row, and type the name of your first link (I used Allaire Corporation). Notice how the width of the table automatically grows as needed.

4. Click in the right cell of the first row and type the description for your first link (I used The home of HomeSite and ColdFusion. Visit this site to obtain your own evaluation copies of these outstanding software packages.)

5. Repeat steps 3 and 4 to add the rest of your links, one per row (see Figure 13.6). Design mode resizes the table as needed while you type.

FIGURE 13.6

Design mode resizes tables on-the-fly as you type.

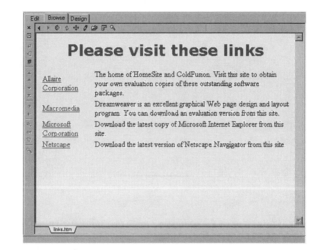

6. You can't actually link the links inside Design mode, so click the Edit mode tab to return to the editor. You'll see the generated HTML code as shown in Figure 13.7.

7. Click each of the site names and link them (refer to Hour 9, "Linking Pages," if you need a reminder on how to do this).

You can use the eight middle buttons on Design mode's Tables toolbar to insert or delete rows and cells, split cells, and merge cells.

13

The rightmost button on the Tables toolbar toggles the display of table borders. This doesn't actually place a border around your table; instead, it helps you see row and cell boundaries. To turn on borders, you must return to Edit mode and use the <TABLE> Tag Editor.

FIGURE 13.7

Switch to Edit mode to view the source code generated by Design mode.

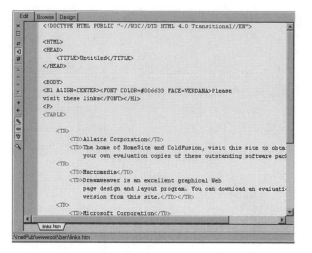

Right-click within any cell to display a shortcut menu that you can use to access table manipulation shortcuts, including inserting and deleting cells.

Form Controls

You also can use Design mode to create forms. The buttons in the Forms toolbar each display the same Tag Editors that we saw in Hour 12, "Creating Forms."

To embed a form control, do the following:

1. Place your cursor where you want the control placed (it can be inside a table cell).
2. Click the appropriate Form toolbar button.
3. Provide control attribute information (as discussed in Hour 12).
4. Click the Apply button.

Design mode generates code for form controls, but not the form itself. You must do that manually in Edit mode.

Summary

HomeSite's Design mode can simplify the manipulation of some HTML elements, particularly text and tables. Design mode isn't intended to be a complete graphical page layout tool; if you want one of those, take a look at Macromedia Dreamweaver.

Q&A

Q Can I disable the Design mode button to prevent developers from using it?

A Many developers disable Design mode because they don't like the code that it generates. To disable Design mode, press F8 to display the Settings dialog, and select the Design tab. The first option can be used to disable (and enable) Design mode.

Q I have installed Macromedia Dreamweaver. How do I use it with HomeSite?

A If you've installed Dreamweaver, press F8 to display the Settings dialog, and select the Dreamweaver tab. This screen lets you enable Dreamweaver support and specify how HomeSite should behave when launching Dreamweaver.

Q Why can't I switch to Design mode to edit pages with frames in them?

A Design mode doesn't support frames. You can use Design mode to edit the pages to be displayed within specific frames, but you can't use it to edit pages containing frame definitions (the <FRAMESET> and <FRAME> tags).

Q I've noticed that Design mode lets me fine-tune the exact sizing of form controls and other elements. How is this done, and is it safe to use?

A Explicit sizing is done by using Styles, which we'll look at in Hour 15, "Using Style Sheets." There's nothing wrong with using styles per se; the only real danger is that most older browsers don't support styles, and many that do don't support the HEIGHT and WIDTH attributes needed to control sizing like this.

Workshop

The Workshop contains quiz questions and activities to help reinforce what you've learned in this hour. If you get stuck, the answers to the quiz questions can be found in Appendix A, "Answers to Quiz Questions."

Quiz

1. True or false: Design mode should never be used and should be disabled.

2. How would you format text as a bulleted list in Design mode?

13

Exercise

Finish the links page that you started in this hour. Add the links to the listed sites, and then link this page to your home page.

HOUR 14

Editing Your Pages

As your Web sites grow in number of pages and complexity, so will your editing needs. HomeSite provides Web developers with all sorts of editing tools designed to simplify the process of developing and deploying professional Web sites.

In this hour you'll learn the following:

- How to use the find-and-replace tools
- How to use the spell-checking features
- How to format and clean up your code

Finding and Replacing Text

All editors provide find-and-replace capabilities, and HomeSite is no exception. In fact, HomeSite provides two distinct forms of find and replace.

Basic Find and Replace

The basic Find and Replace screens are used to perform simple searches (or replacements) within a single file—the currently active file.

 To perform a search, click the Find button, or choose Find from the Search menu. The Find dialog (see Figure 14.1) prompts for the text to search for, as well as other search options. Enter any search text, and then click Find Next to find the next occurrence of the search text. When a match is found, the editor will scroll so that the matching text is visible, and the text will be highlighted.

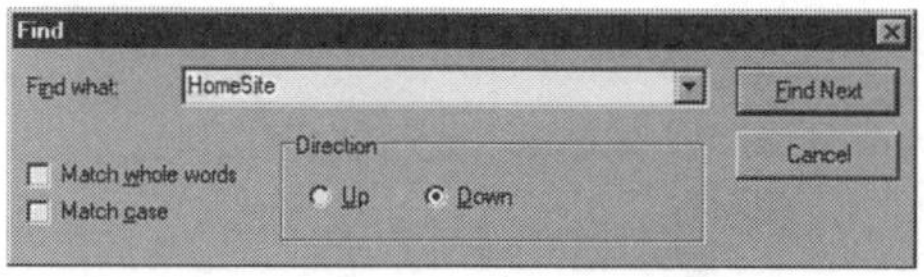

FIGURE 14.1

The Find dialog is used to search for text in the currently selected page.

To perform a replace, click the Replace button, or choose Replace from the Search menu. The Replace dialog (see Figure 14.2) works just like the Find dialog, except that it also prompts for text to replace the search text with. Replace also lets you choose whether to replace just the first match or all matches.

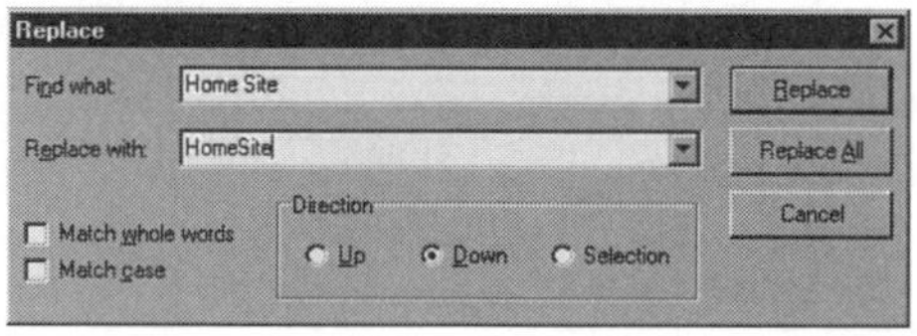

FIGURE 14.2

The Replace dialog performs text replacements on the currently selected page.

> The Find and Replace dialogs keep track of prior searches. Click the down arrow next to the Find What and Replace With text boxes to display (and select) previously used search text. The Find What text boxes in both the Find and Replace dialogs also share listings, so if you search for text in the Search dialog, it will be available as a previously used search in the Replace dialog.

Extended Find and Replace

Every word processor and editor offers basic find-and-replace capabilities. The Extended Find and Extended Replace options make HomeSite stand out from the crowd. Features supported by these extended functions include the following:

- Searching for (and replacing with) long blocks of text (which can be saved and reused)
- Performing searches and replacements on all open documents
- Performing searches and replacements on entire folders (and even subfolders)
- Performing searches and replacements on projects (we look at projects in Hour 20, "Managing Your Projects")
- Enabling support for regular expressions
- Making file backups before performing mass replacements

To perform an extended search, do the following:

1. Click the Extended Find button or choose Extended Find from the Search menu to display the Extended Find dialog (see Figure 14.3).

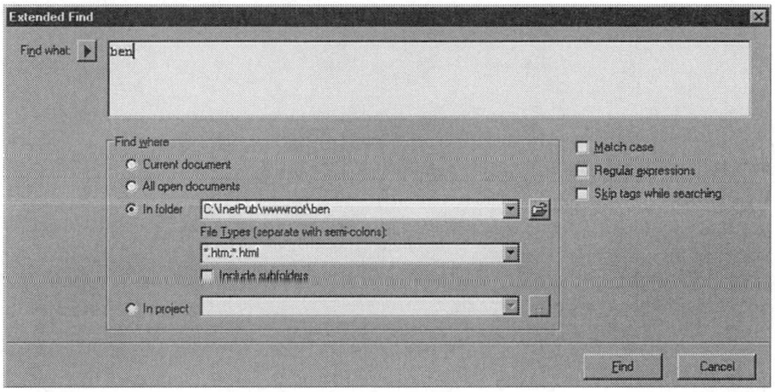

FIGURE 14.3

The Extended Find dialog performs sophisticated search operations on one or more files, and the large Find What field enables you to search for larger blocks of text too.

2. Enter the search text in the Find What text box.
3. Select where to search. You can choose the current document, all open documents, a folder, or a project.
4. Select any of the options to the right of the dialog if needed.
5. Click Find to perform your search.

Search results are displayed in the Results pane (see Figure 14.4). Double-click any listed result to open (or activate) that file and highlight the match.

14

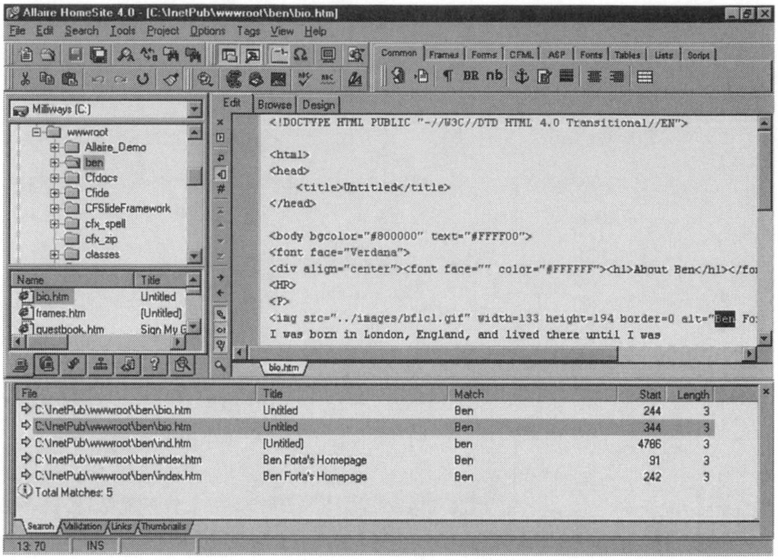

FIGURE 14.4

Extended Search and Replace results are displayed in the Results pane at the bottom of the HomeSite screen.

Extended Replace works much like Extended Find, except that you must provide Replace With text as well. Follow these steps to perform an Extended Replace:

1. Click the Extended Replace button or choose Extended Replace from the Search menu to display the Extended Replace dialog (see Figure 14.5).

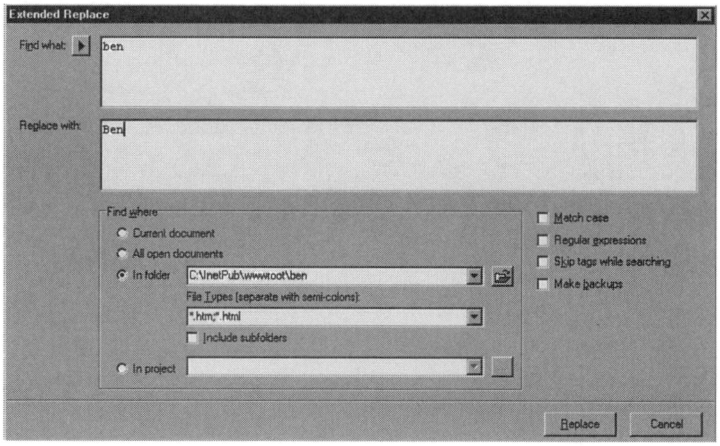

FIGURE 14.5

The Extended Replace dialog performs sophisticated search-and-replace operations on one or more files.

2. Enter the search text in the Find What text box.

3. Enter the replace text in the Replace With text box.

4. Select where to search. You can choose the current document, all open documents, a folder, or a project.

5. Select any of the options to the right of the dialog if needed. If you want backups made of any changed files, for example, check the Make Backups check box.

6. Click Replace to perform your search.

As with Extended Find, results are displayed in the Results pane.

> To reuse search text for subsequent searches, click the button to the left of the Find What text box. You'll be prompted to Open a saved search or to Save a search for future reuse.

Checking Spelling

Your Web site is designed to create a presence on the World Wide Web, and you want that presence to be portrayed professionally. Nothing will tarnish that portrayal as quickly as spelling-mistake–ridden pages. To help you avoid potentially embarrassing typos and spelling mistakes, HomeSite incorporates spell checking right into the editor. The spell checker can be used in two ways:

- On-demand spell checking functions like the spell checker in most applications.
- Background spell checking checks spelling as you work, underlining errors as they occur.

On-Demand Spell Checking

On-demand spell checking is initiated in one of the following ways:

- Click the Spell Check button.

- Choose Spell Check from the Tools menu.
- Press F7.

Any of these display the spell check dialog (see Figure 14.6). This dialog functions much like the spell-checking feature on most Windows applications. Errors are highlighted and underlined, and you can specify corrections or select suggested spellings.

14

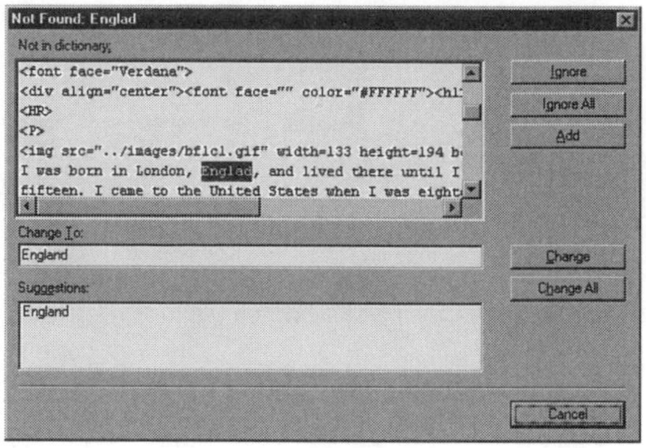

FIGURE 14.6

The HomeSite spell checker should be used to ensure that your pages have no typos.

Background Spell Checking

The background spell-checking feature identifies typos right within the editor. It can be left enabled so that errors are identified as they occur, or turned on as needed so that you can make corrections without using a separate spell-checking dialog. Background spell checking is initiated in one of the following ways:

- Click the Mark Spelling Errors button.

- Choose Mark Spelling Errors from the Tools menu.
- Press Ctrl+F7.

When this option is enabled, errors are underlined with a red wavy line inside the editor. To correct an underlined error, simply right-click it and select the Spelling option. You can select from a list of suggestions (if available), or add the word to the dictionary (see Figure 14.7).

> The HomeSite spell checkers can be configured using the Settings dialog Spelling tab. The configuration options allow you to specify the dictionaries to be used, and how to handle tags within text to be checked. To access this dialog select Settings from the Options menu.

FIGURE 14.7

With background spell checking, you can identify and correct typos right inside the editor.

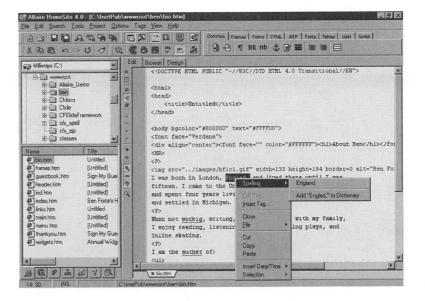

Formatting Your Code

As I explained in Hour 1, "Understanding HomeSite," browsers ignore whitespace. The text on your Web pages can be typed, spaced, and indented, or it can be typed on one long line. From the browser's perspective, there's no difference. But from a developer's perspective, there's a *big* difference. This first code sample is broken up over multiple lines and indented properly:

```
<TR>
 <TH ALIGN="LEFT">Widget</TH>
 <TD ALIGN="RIGHT">1096</TH>
 <TD ALIGN="RIGHT">857</TH>
 <TD ALIGN="RIGHT">1332</TH>
 <TD ALIGN="RIGHT">990</TH>
</TR>
```

This next code sample is the exact same code that creates the exact same table row. But because the code is typed as one long line, it is difficult to read and close to impossible to edit.

```
<TR><TH ALIGN="LEFT">Widget</TH><TD ALIGN="RIGHT">1096</TH>
<TD ALIGN="RIGHT">857</TH><TD ALIGN="RIGHT">1332</TH>
<TD ALIGN="RIGHT">990</TH></TR>
```

Obviously, cleanly formatted code makes a developer's job easier. As such, HomeSite provides a range of tools designed to help you format your code properly.

14

Using Indentation

I've mentioned code indentation several times in the past 13 hours, and I'll mention it again: Indentation allows you to see the logical relationship of tag sets quickly and easily. If you're missing a table row end tag or have a badly nested list, indentation helps you pinpoint the problem code quickly and easily.

Of course, you can indent code manually by entering tabs or spaces, but here's a better way to do it:

1. Highlight the code to be indented.

2. Click the indent button on the Editor toolbar.

   To unindent your code, click the unindent button.

> Many developers avoid using tabs in their code, opting to use spaces instead. HomeSite can use spaces or tabs for indentation—the choice is yours. To configure this setting, press F8 to display the Settings dialog. The setting you want is ìInsert tabs as spacesî on the Edit tab.

> HomeSite features automatic indentation. When enabled, HomeSite automatically indents new lines to match the indentation of the previous line whenever you press Enter. To enable and disable this option, press F8 to display the Settings dialog, and then select Auto Indent on the Edit page.
>
> You can also force outdents and indents as needed by pressing Ctrl-Shift-, and Ctrl-Shift-., respectively.

Line Spacing

Many developers space their code during development, and then remove some of the spacing before deployment. This can reduce the file size slightly, which in turn can reduce page download time.

Indentation should really *never* be removed (the time you'll waste troubleshooting later isn't worth the marginal download time savings), but extra line spaces can be. To do this, choose Replace Double Spacing With Single Spacing from the Search menu. A dialog like the one in Figure 14.8 prompts you before the replacement is made. If you want to proceed, click Yes.

FIGURE 14.8

HomeSite can replace double spacing with single spacing to reduce file download time.

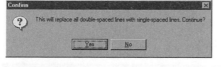

Unlike most operations in HomeSite, line spacing replacement *can't* be undone with the Undo button.

Tag Case Conversion

Hour 4, "Customizing HomeSite," talked briefly about using consistent tag case. HTML is not case sensitive—you can use uppercase, lowercase, or a mixture of the two. But you shouldn't. Web developers usually pick a scheme and stick with it.

To help you convert HTML tags (and their attributes) to a specific case, use the Convert Tag Case option by choosing it from the Edit menu. The dialog in Figure 14.9 prompts you for the case to convert to. Select uppercase or lowercase, and then click OK.

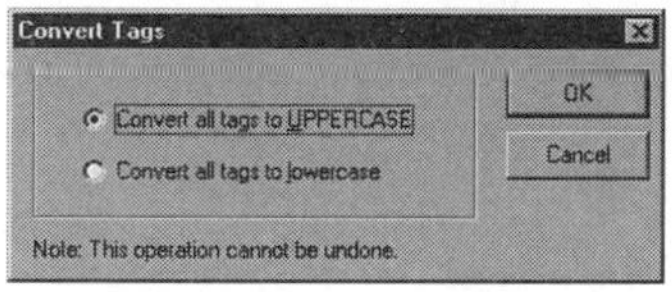

FIGURE 14.9

Use the Convert Tags dialog to convert all tags and attributes to uppercase or lower-case.

Unlike most operations in HomeSite, tag case conversion *can't* be undone with the Undo button.

To control the case of tags inserted by the Tag Editors, Tag Insight, and the Tag Inspector, press F8 to display the Settings dialog, and then select the HTML tab. The first checkbox lets you specify the case to be used.

14

To convert the case of specific text, highlight the text, right-click, choose the Selection option, and then select Uppercase or Lowercase as needed.

Using CodeSweeper

CodeSweeper is a sophisticated tool that can apply formatting rules to your pages. When you run CodeSweeper, your code is reformatted with the settings specified. Lines can be added or removed, indentation can be adjusted, tag case can be converted, and quotes can be inserted or removed. The end result will be code formatted exactly to your specifications.

CodeSweeper is a sophisticated and powerful tool, and full coverage of all its features are beyond the scope of this book. I'll cover the basics here, and I encourage you to experiment with CodeSweeper yourself to learn what it can do for you. Of course, experiment with it by using test pages, not live Web pages that you're working on.

Among the options that can be specified are the following:

- Whether to insert a new line before or after a tag
- Indentation for specific tags (including sub-tag indentation)
- Whether to trim whitespaces within tags
- Case conversions
- Attribute value quoting

You can specify these options for all tags or for specific tags.

To activate CodeSweeper, click the CodeSweeper button in the Edit toolbar. You are presented with a dialog like the one in Figure 14.10. To execute CodeSweeper, click the Run CodeSweeper button; to configure CodeSweeper, click the Configure CodeSweeper button.

You should configure CodeSweeper before using it (most developers don't like the default configuration). CodeSweeper is configured by using the CodeSweeper Settings dialog (see Figure 14.11).

FIGURE 14.10

When you click the CodeSweeper button, you are asked whether you want to run or configure CodeSweeper.

FIGURE 14.11

The CodeSweeper Settings dialog configures CodeSweeper and its formatting options.

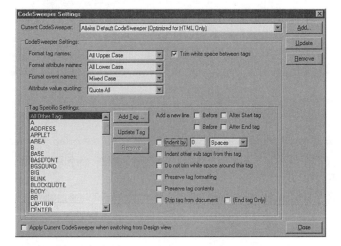

You can create multiple CodeSweeper configurations. You select a configuration from the drop-down list box at the top of the CodeSweeper Settings dialog. Configurations are added, updated, or removed using the buttons on the left. The configuration that's selected when the dialog is closed is the one that will be used when CodeSweeper is run.

Configurations are made up of two types of options:

- Five global options govern the formatting of all tags: Format Tag Names, Format Attribute Names, Format Event Names, Attribute Value Quoting, and Trim White Space Between Tags.
- In addition to global options, individual tags can be configured. To do this, select a tag from the Tag Specific Settings list and use any of the options to the right of the list.

After you make your changes, click Update to save the configuration, and then Close to close the dialog.

14

Unlike most operations in HomeSite, CodeSweeper changes *can't* be undone with the Undo button.

Summary

HomeSite is a powerful editor, providing developers with all the tools they need to edit and maintain growing and evolving Web sites. In addition to standard search-and-replace functions, HomeSite supports powerful Extended Find and Extended Replace functions. HomeSite also features two ways to spell check your pages, and a whole set of page-formatting capabilities that ensure that code remains readable and manageable.

Q&A

Q You mentioned that Extended Find and Extended Replace support regular expressions. What are regular expressions, and how can I find out more about them?

A Regular expressions are special forms of search patterns that you can use to pre-cisely control sophisticated search-and-replace operations. By using regular expres-sions, you can search for sets of characters, one of a set, wildcards, new line characters, digits, spaces, and much more. Unfortunately, full coverage of regular expressions is beyond the scope of this book. But you can get all the information you need to get started right in HomeSite's integrated help system. Select the Resource Tab's Help tab (the one with the yellow question mark), and then select Using HomeSite, Maintaining Web Sites, Using Search and Replace.

Q I have already customized the spell-check engine in Microsoft Office. Can HomeSite use that spell-check engine and my own modifications instead of its own?

A Yes, it can. HomeSite comes with its own spell-checking engine. But if you have Microsoft Office (version 95 or later) installed, HomeSite can use this spell-checking engine instead. The advantage of doing this is that any dictionary changes (that is, words added to the dictionary) made in Word, Excel, Access, or other Office applications are available to HomeSite as well. As such, if you have Office installed, you should use this option. You can select which engine to use by press-ing F8 and selecting the Spelling tab.

Q **CodeSweeper looks like an invaluable tool, but the configuration of profiles looks complex. Is there anywhere I can get already written profiles?**

A You can download additional profiles from the Allaire Developer's Exchange at `http://www.allaire.com/developer/gallery.cfm`. Select Visual Tools, CodeSweeper Scripts.

Workshop

The Workshop contains quiz questions and activities to help reinforce what you've learned in this hour. If you get stuck, the answers to the quiz questions can be found in Appendix A, "Answers to Quiz Questions."

Quiz

1. You need to replace all occurrences of the words "Home Site" with the word "HomeSite" in every single page in your Web site. What feature would you use to do this?

2. Why do many developers remove blank lines and whitespace from their Web pages?

3. True or false: Code indentation is an important debugging tool.

Exercises

1. Look at the formatting used in pages on some of your favorite sites. You can use HomeSite's Open From the Web feature for this if you want.

2. Experiment with CodeSweeper. Try setting the tag and attribute case options to uppercase or lowercase (whatever standard you prefer) and then use CodeSweeper to format the code for you.

14

Using Style Sheets

HTML style sheets are a relatively recent phenomenon (even by Internet time standards). Style sheets simplify page formatting, as well as give you a greater level of control over page layout and formatting. Indeed, some Web page layout and formatting options are available *only* via style sheets. And as you'd expect by now, HomeSite provides all the tools needed to simplify style sheet creation and manipulation.

In this hour you'll learn the following:

- What style sheets are and why they are used
- How to read and write HTML style sheets
- How to use the style sheet editor

Understanding Style Sheets

To understand what style sheets are, look at an application that you are undoubtedly familiar with—your word processor.

Imagine that you're working on a long document with multiple levels of headers, bullets, and footnotes, as well as lots of text. Each element needs to be formatted specifically. All top-level headers have the same font face, font size, and spacing. Similarly, all second-level headers are formatted alike, again with consistent fonts, sizes, and spacing. And so on.

Rather than apply all this formatting manually, most word processors let you create style sheets (most also provide default styles). Each style sheet has an assigned format and name, and applying that style to a block of text applies that formatting to it.

As such, style sheets (or styles) offer the following benefits:

- *Simplified formatting.* Rather than apply multiple formatting options to your text, you simply apply a style to it.

- *Consistent formatting.* If all you have to do to format text is apply a style, it's less likely that you'll omit part of your formatting. Remembering to apply a style (a single step) is less error prone than remembering to apply individual formatting options (multiple steps).

- *Synchronized formatting.* To ensure that any changes to formatting are applied consistently, rather than change every occurrence of specific formatting options, you need to modify just the style. Any text that it has been applied to is updated automatically.

 Style sheets are not an HTML creation. Most major word-processing and desktop-publishing applications have supported style sheets in some form or another for many years. In fact, Microsoft Word for DOS (back before Windows days) already supported the use of style sheets.

Why Use HTML Style Sheets?

NEW TERM Don't be confused by the term *cascading style sheets* (or its abbreviation *CSS*). Cascading style sheets is actually the correct full name for HTML style sheets. Most developers simply use the shorter *style sheets* instead, and they are one and the same.

So, now that you know what style sheets are, what benefits do they offer HTML developers in particular? Here's a partial list:

- Simplify consistent formatting (the advantages discussed in the preceding section)

- Create consistent formatting throughout an entire site, spanning as many pages as needed

- Provide a level of control over elements that's *impossible* when using tag-based formatting
- Separate page content from page layout

These benefits all add up to make learning style sheets a very worthwhile exercise.

The last bullet item (separate page content from page layout) is extremely important. You must remember that HTML was originally intended to be a content-publishing language—a simple way to create output. As HTML evolved, formatting options were added to the language. Although sophisticated and detailed formatting support is useful in page layout, it introduces a new problem. By so closely intertwining content and its presentation, content becomes extremely difficult to reuse. If you've ever tried to copy the text in a Web page to another document, you have experienced this problem. Because the content is chock-full of formatting tags, extracting just the information you want is extremely difficult.

Before you run off to redesign your site by using style sheets exclusively, be warned that not all browsers support style sheets, and even those that do support them inconsistently. Version 4 browsers or later (both Microsoft and Netscape browsers) provide the best CSS support.

Style Sheet Syntax

To understand how style sheets are created, look at a simple example. Suppose that I wanted all <H1> and <H2> headers to be displayed in the Verdana font face, <H1> centered and displayed in blue, and <H2> left justified and displayed in green. The following syntax defines these styles:

```
H1   {
     color : Blue;
     font-family : Verdana;
     text-align : center;
}
H2   {
     color : Green;
     font-family : Verdana;
     text-align : left;
}
```

Each style definition starts with the tag to be defined (specified *without* the < and > symbols), so H1 defines the appearance of any text formatted with the <H1> tag, and H2 defines the appearance of any text formatted with the <H2> tag.

The definition itself is placed within braces ({ and }), with each property formatted as *property* : *value*;. So the following defines the text color as Blue:

```
color : Blue;
```

You can define multiple properties for any style, each separated by a semicolon. There are properties that control every aspect of every element, including font control, exact element height and width, foreground and background colors, relative placement, and element visibility.

And it gets even better. Not only can you redefine the built-in tags (such as the <H1> and <H2> I just showed you), you can also define your own tags and associate styles with them. This gives you the greatest degree of flexibility in style sheet usage.

Style sheets support *inheritance*. As this suggests, tags that are children of parent tags inherit their parents' definitions. For example, if you defined font information for the <TABLE> tag, any table cells (the <TD> tag) and table headers (the <TH> tag) inherit this formatting. Well, at least they're *supposed* to. Unfortunately, some browsers (Netscape Navigator is a prime culprit) don't always pass inherited values to child tags as they should. This means that for maximum browser compatibility, you yourself must assign the formatting information to the child tag as well use additional style definitions.

Linking Style Sheets to Web Pages

Now that you know how to define styles, all that's left is associating them to your pages. There are several ways to do this:

- Styles can be specified right within your page between <STYLE> and </STYLE> tags. By using this method, the style definitions should appear at the very top of the page, before any body text.
- Individual occurrences of tags can be manipulated by using an embedded STYLE attribute (this is *not* recommended, however, because you want to try to separate content from its presentation, not embed it directly within it).

- Styles can be saved in an external file that's called by your page using a <LINK> tag, which must be placed within the page header block (between the <HEAD> and </HEAD> tags). This method allows you to share styles with other pages as all those pages may link to the same style file.

The third method described, using <LINK>, is the preferred method because it lets you share style definitions among multiple Web pages.

Using Style Sheets in HomeSite

I'll be the first to admit that the syntax used to define and manipulate style sheets is neither intuitive nor easy to remember. Thankfully, as a HomeSite user this won't be a problem for you because HomeSite includes a powerful style sheet editor.

 To launch the style sheet editor, click the Style Sheet Editor button on the Tools toolbar. The style sheet editor appears (see Figure 15.1).

FIGURE 15.1

The style sheet editor greatly simplifies HTML style sheet creation and manipulation.

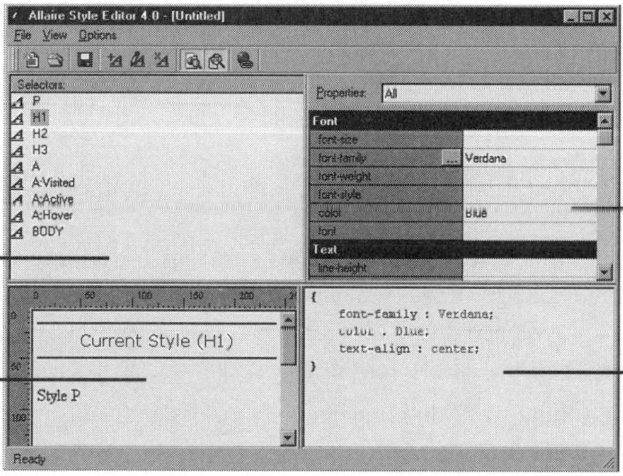

Tag selector list pane ——

Preview pane ——

Tag properties pane

Source pane

NEW TERM When working with style sheets you'll see two terms often used interchangeably: *attributes* and *properties*. The difference is simple—tags have attributes, styles have properties. Because most tag attributes can also be manipulated within style definitions, many tag attributes are in fact properties too.

The style sheet editor is divided into four panes:

- The top-left pane displays a list of tags that can be defined. Click any tag to edit its definition (you also can add and remove tags from this list by clicking the buttons in the toolbar).

- The upper-right pane displays the properties for a selected tag. This is where you edit property values.

- The bottom-left pane is the preview pane, which gives you an idea as to what your tag definition will actually look like in a browser (this pane can be optionally closed).

- The bottom-right pane is the source pane. Here you'll see the CSS source generated for your tag definition (this pane can be optionally closed).

> The style sheet editor is actually a standalone program that's executed by HomeSite when needed. You can run the editor directly yourself—there's a shortcut to it in the HomeSite submenu under your Windows Start menu.

Using the Style Sheet Editor

To demonstrate the style sheet editor, I'll create a style sheet for my own Web site. I'll use the same color schemes, fonts, and layouts defined earlier in this book (of course, you can use your own colors, fonts, and so forth), but this time the styles will be applied globally. Follow these steps:

 1. Launch the style sheet editor by clicking its button in the Tools toolbar.

2. The default new style sheet contains nine tags for editing already selected text. The ones we need are already selected, so there's no need to add any manually. (Although you can delete all but BODY and H1 if you want by selecting them and clicking the Delete Selector button; it's the one with the red X next to a blue A.)

3. The first thing we'll do is assign body colors and fonts, so click the BODY tag in the tag selector list.

 4. The page background I used was maroon, so scroll down to the background-color attribute (in the Background section), click the attribute, and type **maroon** (you also can select a color by clicking the button with the ... on it).

5. The font I used was Verdana, so scroll back up to font-family (in the Fonts section), and specify Verdana as the font face (again, you also can select the font by clicking the ... button).

6. The font color I used was yellow, so set color (also in the Fonts section) to yellow.

7. Now I need to define the appearance of my <H1> tags, so select H1 in the tag selector list.

8. Set the font-family to Verdana.

9. Set the `color` to white.

10. I also centered all my `<H1>` tags, so set `text-align` (in the Text section) to center. Notice how the preview window shows you what the style will look like (see Figure 15.2).

FIGURE 15.2

The style sheet editor preview pane shows you what effect property changes have.

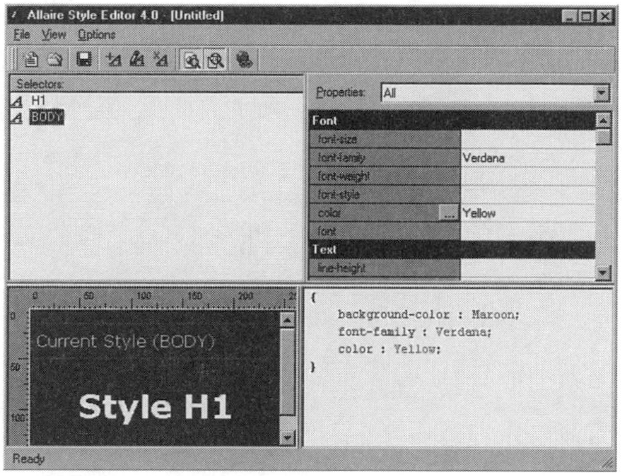

11. Save the styles by clicking the Save button. You're prompted for the filename and directory (see Figure 15.3). Save it with any name you want (I called mine ben.css) in the same directory as your Web pages.

FIGURE 15.3

Style sheet files must be saved beneath the Web server root.

12. Next, you need to link the style file (the file just created) to the Web site pages by using `<LINK>` tags. Click the Link button to display Style Link dialog (see Figure 15.4).

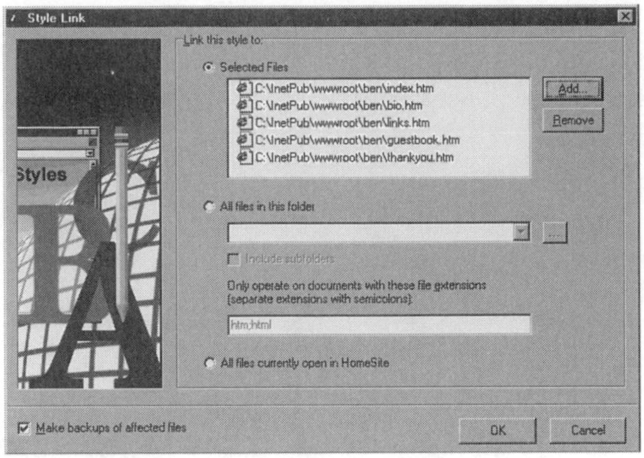

FIGURE 15.4

*Use the Style Link dia-
log to link a style
sheet file with one or
more Web pages.*

13. Click the Add button to add all the files to be linked to the Selected Files list. (If
    you make a mistake, use the Remove button to remove files from the list.)

14. After you select all the files, click OK to write the <LINK> tag to each of them.
    HomeSite notifies you when this process is complete (see Figure 15.5).

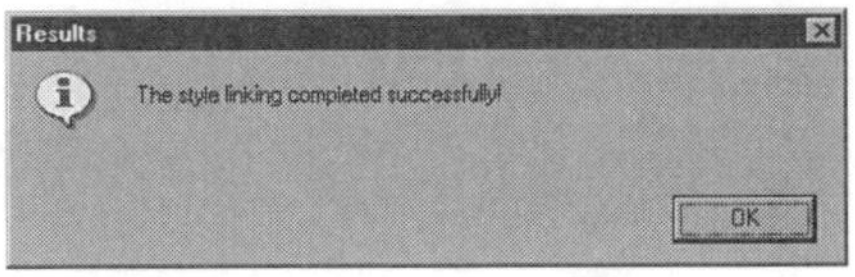

FIGURE 15.5

*The Style Link dialog
can automatically
insert <LINK> tags into
files linking them to
your style file.*

Now that style sheets are being used, there's no need to specify font and color information within the actual pages. Open each page that was linked to the style file and remove
all color, font, and alignment attributes (the <BODY> BGCOLOR and TEXT attributes, the
<FONT> tags, and the centering and coloring tags around the <H1> tag).

Save all the modified pages and test them to make sure that the specified style sheet formatting works properly. The pages should look exactly as they did before.

If you open any of the linked files, notice that the following line was added to them (of
course, your code will be different if you used a different filename):

```
<LINK REL=STYLESHEET TYPE="text/css" HREF="ben.css">
```

As you can see, the style sheet editor not only simplifies style sheet creation, but also
simplifies linking the style file to your Web site pages.

The Style Link dialog lets you specify the files to be linked to a style file, and pages can be specified individually or by folder. If you're linking an entire Web site, use the linking by folder option so that you don't have to select each individual file manually.

Tag-Level Styles

As mentioned earlier, styles also can be applied to specific occurrences of tags. Although this practice isn't recommended, HomeSite does simplify tag-specific style creation too.

To use this feature, click the Style button found in many Tag Editors to display a slightly different style sheet editor (see Figure 15.6). Unlike the style sheet editor used earlier, this editor lets you manipulate the style of a single tag only.

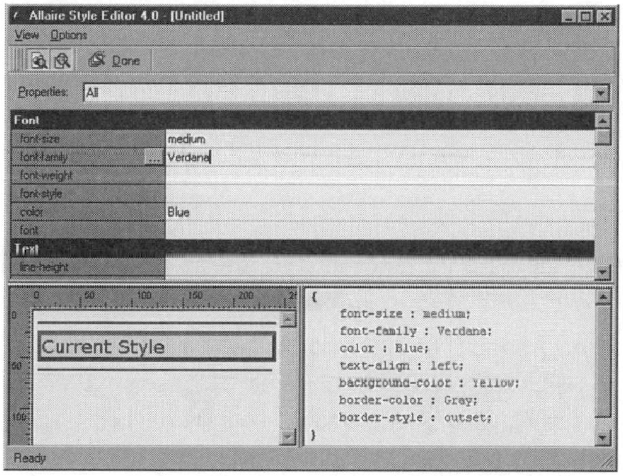
Allaire Style Editor 4.0 - [Untitled]
View Options
Done
Properties: All
Font
font-size
medium
font-family
Verdana
font-weight
font-style
color
Blue
font
Text
line-height
Current Style
{
font-size : medium;
font-family : Verdana;
color : Blue;
text-align : left;
background-color : Yellow;
border-color : Gray;
border-style : outset;
}
Ready

FIGURE 15.6

You also can use the style sheet editor to edit tag-specific styles.

You can edit any of the style properties here. When you click Done, the selected style information is embedded back in the Tag Editor (see Figure 15.7).

Although tag-specific style manipulation is perfectly valid and legal, its use isn't recommended at all. Remember, style sheets are designed to separate content from presentation. Embedding style sheets into tags completely violates this goal.

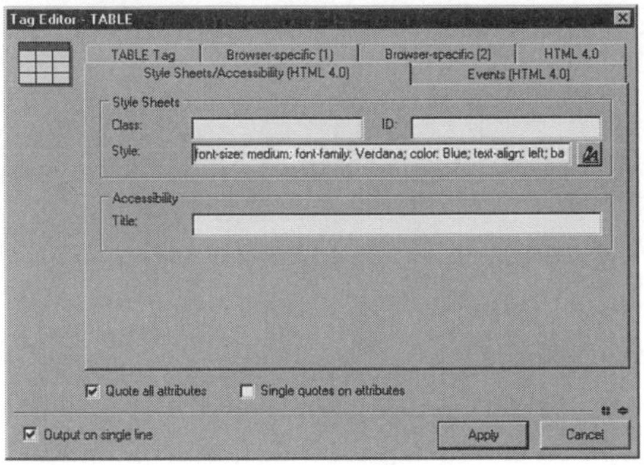

FIGURE 15.7

*Many Tag Editors fea-
ture an Edit Style but-
ton that allows you to
embed* STYLE *attributes
directly into your tags.*

Summary

Style sheets are an important page-layout tool and will continue to be so. Although style
sheet support is still evolving, the major browsers already support enough of the basic
functionality to make them a viable option. HomeSite's style sheet editor greatly simplifies style sheet creation and page linking.

Q&A

Q **I assume there's a lot more to style sheets than what you covered this hour.
Where can I obtain more information on style sheets and their use?**

A The primary source for information about style sheets is the w3.org site (the home
of all Web-related specifications). The URL for style sheet information is
`http://www.w3.org/pub/WWW/StyleSheets/`. There's also extensive coverage of
style sheets right within the HomeSite help system; see HTML Reference, Style
Sheets (start with the Style Sheets Overview page).

Q **Which browsers support style sheets?**

A Style sheets are supported by Microsoft Internet Explorer version 3 or later, and
Netscape Navigator version 4 or later. Microsoft's style sheet support is a little
more extensive than Netscape's at this time.

Q **I've noticed that some sites using style sheets embed the style definitions
within HTML comments. Why is this done?**

A Recall that Web browsers are supposed to ignore tags they don't understand. If a
browser that doesn't support style sheets encountered a page with embedded styles
(using the <STYLE> and </STYLE> tags), it would ignore the tags themselves, but

15

not the text between them. In other words, because the browser doesn't know what to do with the `<STYLE>` and `</STYLE>` tags, the text between the tags will be displayed as page text. Obviously, this isn't what you want. If you place the entire style definition within comment tags (`<!—` and `—>`), older browsers think the entire style definition is a comment and ignore it. This is a good practice; if you do use the `<STYLE>` tag, place the entire style block within comment tags.

Workshop

The Workshop contains quiz questions and activities to help reinforce what you've learned in this hour. If you get stuck, the answers to the quiz questions can be found in Appendix A, "Answers to Quiz Questions."

Quiz

1. What's the difference between the `<STYLE>` tag and the `STYLE` attribute supported by most tags?

2. True or false: Tag-level styles are preferred over page-wide style because they provide a greater degree of element control.

3. What's the recommended way to embed style sheets into your pages?

Exercises

1. Not all style properties are supported by all browsers. Try creating simple styles and viewing their results in multiple browsers. Can you identify properties supported by one browser but not by another?

2. I mentioned earlier that styles let you control elements in ways impossible using simple tags. Try to find examples of this.

PART IV
Managing Your Web Site

Hour

Validating and Testing Your Pages

HTML is a powerful language. Fortunately, introducing HTML elements into your Web pages is easy; unfortunately, introducing errors is easy too. HTML errors can be hard to find, particularly because badly formatted HTML might in fact display perfectly in some browsers, but not in others. Testing your pages in some browsers doesn't guarantee that the pages will display correctly in other browsers.

To ensure that your pages are displayed as intended, you need two things: validation that your HTML is correct and a visual test in multiple browsers. HomeSite provides you with the tools to do both.

In this hour you'll learn the following:

- How to perform tag validation
- How to configure tag validation
- Hot to configure external browsers
- How to use external browsers

Validating Your Code

HTML tags and attributes have rules that govern their usage. Tag validation is a test to ensure that these rules are abided by. Rules that tag validators check for include the following:

- Invalid tag names (often indicative of typos)
- Invalid attributes
- Invalid attribute values
- Start tags without matching end tags
- Mismatched nesting
- Version violations (for example, you want your site to be HTML 3.2–compliant, but you're using HTML 4 tags)
- Browser incompatibility issues

As you can see, tag validators do more than pinpoint bad code. They also try to inform you of any potential trouble spots, even within valid and legal code.

> Most developers complain that tag validators are too strict and that they provide so many warnings and notifications that finding real errors is like looking for a needle in a haystack. Unfortunately, for the most part they are right, which is why HomeSite lets you configure exactly what information the validator returns to you.

HomeSite provides two forms of tag validation:

- *Tag-level validation* checks a single tag on demand or in the background as you type.
- *Document validation* checks an entire document in one step.

We'll look at both of these during this hour.

> HomeSite's document validation is far more thorough than tag-level validation. This is deliberate and by design. Tag-level validation is designed to run in the background as you type. Thorough validation is a time-consuming process (one that would slow down the editor), and so only minimal validation is done at the tag level. For this reason, you should never rely purely on tag-level validation.

Tag Validation

Tag validation is designed to validate two things:

- *Tag name validity.* If you make a typo, you'll be notified immediately.
- *Version incompatibilities.* If you use a tag that's valid only in HTML 4, you'll be notified that it's not supported by HTML 3.2.

Tag validation messages (both error messages and success notifications) are reported on the status line at the bottom of the HomeSite screen (see Figure 16.1).

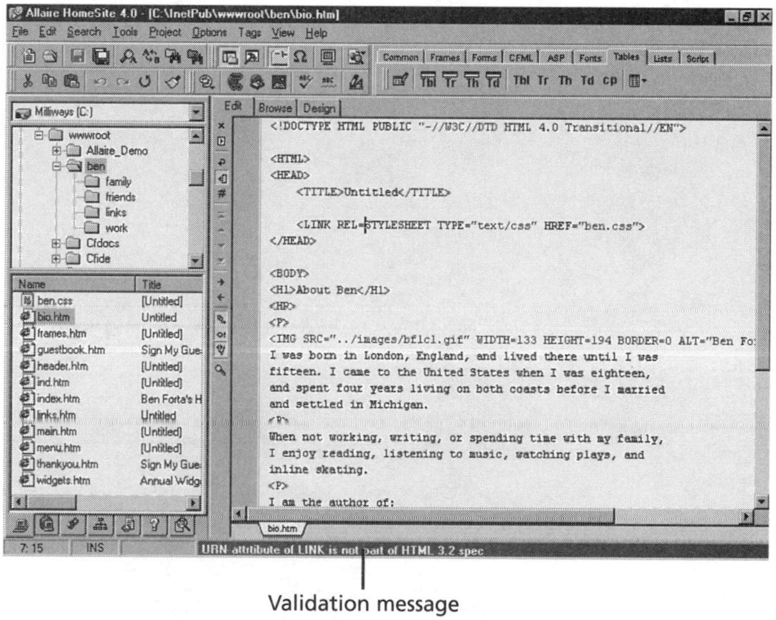

16

FIGURE 16.1

Tag validation messages are displayed on the HomeSite status bar.

Validation message

Tag validation occurs automatically as you type, but you also can validate any specific tag by selecting it and pressing F6.

By default, HomeSite performs tag validation in the background as you type. To turn background validation off, click the Tag Validation button in Editor toolbar.

Document Validation

Unlike tag validation, document validation doesn't occur automatically. To explicitly activate document validation, press Shift+F6 (or choose Validate Document from the Tools menu).

To demonstrate document validation, let's try the following:

1. Open a Web page (I'll use my BIO.HTM page).

2. Press Shift+F6 to validate the document. Validation messages appear in the results window (see Figure 16.2).

3. Double-click any message to go to that line of code.

FIGURE 16.2

The results window displays document-validation messages.

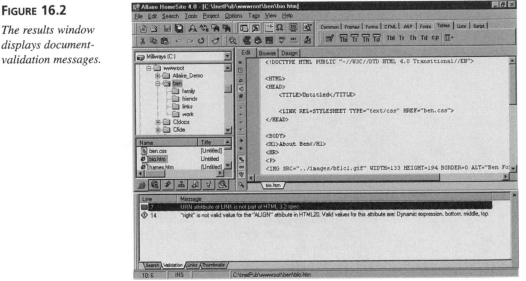

The validation of my own page in Figure 16.2 reports two problems:

- The <LINK> tag that I'm using to embed my style sheet isn't supported by HTML 3.2.

- My <IMG> tag specifies ALIGN="RIGHT" to place my picture to the right of the bio text, but ALIGN="RIGHT" isn't supported by HTML 2.

In other words, my page had no errors in it, but there were two warnings about browser compatibility issues.

If you need more room to see your validation messages, right-click any message and select Browse. This will open a browser window displaying the validation messages in a neatly formatted HTML table, a format well suited for printing.

Configuring the Validator

The validator is configured by using the Settings dialog's Validation page (see Figure 16.3). To display the Settings dialog press F8 or select Settings from the Options menu. This page lists versions that you can validate against (including versions of ColdFusion). This way, you can validate that your code is compatible with specific HTML versions—for example, to ensure that your pages are HTML 3.2–compatible (without any HTML 4 features), turn off HTML 4.0 and any browser-specific extensions.

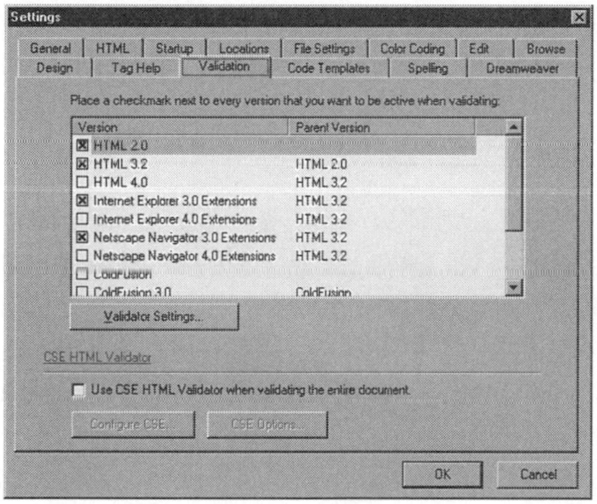

FIGURE 16.3

To validate for specific HTML versions, activate or deactivate versions as needed on the Settings dialog's Validation page.

16

By default, 4.0 browser extensions aren't activated. If you're using any 4.0 browser features, turn on these versions.

To fine-tune the validator settings, click the Validator Settings button to display the Validator Configuration dialog (see Figure 16.4). Use the Options page to specify exactly what the validator should check for. I strongly recommend that you keep all these options selected unless you have compelling reasons not to.

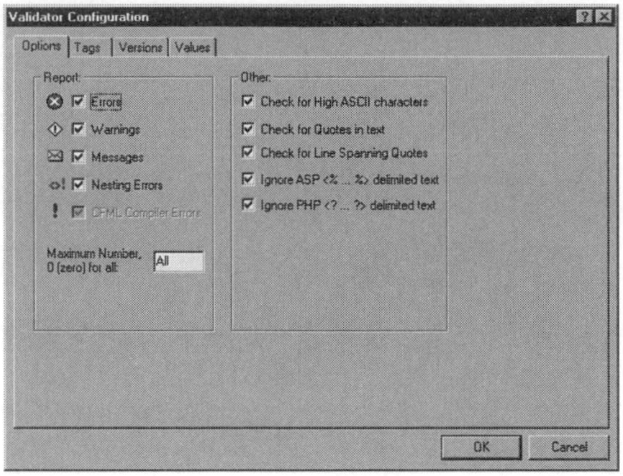

FIGURE 16.4

The Validator Configuration dialog's Options page lets you specify what information the validator should report.

Testing Your Pages

After you validate your pages, the next thing to do is to check how they appear in various browsers. This can be a time-consuming process, but it's an extremely important one. You'd be amazed at the number of high-visibility Web sites that have obviously failed to do this (just surf with a version 3 browser to see this for yourself).

Ideally, you should test your pages by using the following:

- Current versions of the major browsers (Microsoft Internet Explorer and Netscape Navigator)
- Prior versions of major browsers, at least as far back as version 3
- Browsers used by the major online services (such as America Online and CompuServe)
- 16- and 32-bit versions of browsers (never assume that Netscape Navigator 3 running under Windows 3.x will behave the same as Netscape Navigator 3 running under Windows 98)
- Browsers on other operating systems (Macintosh and popular UNIX flavors)

The testing level isn't trivial, particularly as most developers don't have access to all the platforms and operating systems they need to test with. You might want to enlist the help of friends or co-workers using other computers or operating systems. The more diverse the environments you test in, the more compatible your pages will be.

The Internal Browser

By now you should be very familiar with HomeSite's internal browser. As I explained early on in this book, this browser is actually Microsoft Internet Explorer. This means that testing your pages with the internal browser at least ensures that the pages will display correctly within Internet Explorer.

But that's not enough.

Configuring External Browsers

Because testing in multiple browsers is so important, HomeSite provides support for external browsers. These are simply shortcuts to other browsers installed on your computer (you should always have multiple browsers installed on your computer) that you can use to test selected pages.

To configure external browsers, follow these steps:

1. Choose Configure External Browsers from HomeSite's Options menu to display the External Browsers dialog (see Figure 16.5).

FIGURE 16.5

The External Browsers screen is used to add, edit, and delete external browser listings.

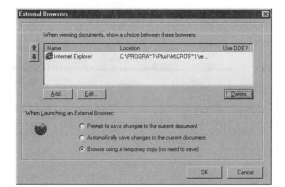

2. To add a new browser, click the Add button to display the Browser dialog (see Figure 16.6).

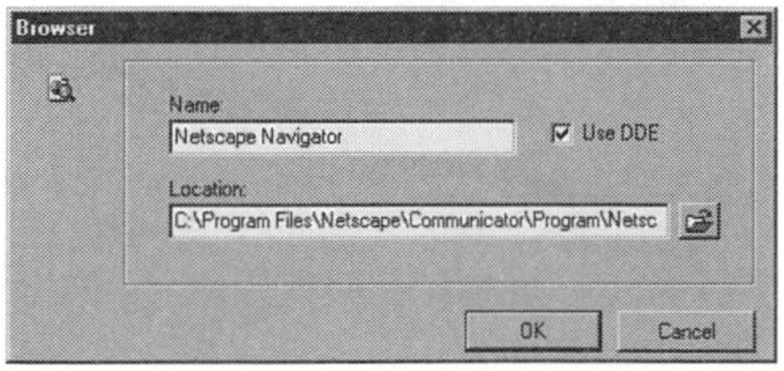

FIGURE 16.6

HomeSite can use any installed browser as an external browser; all it needs is the executable path.

3. Enter a name for the browser (the name that HomeSite will refer to the browser as). Select the path to the browser, and click OK to save the browser.

4. You also can edit or delete browsers from the external browsers list, as well as manipulate the order in which browsers are listed.

5. After you make all your changes, click OK.

Using External Browsers

After you configure external browsers, you can test your pages with them as follows:

1. Open the page to be tested.

2. Click the External Browser List button to display a list of configured external browsers (see Figure 16.7).

External browsers

FIGURE 16.7

HomeSite lists all configured external browsers.

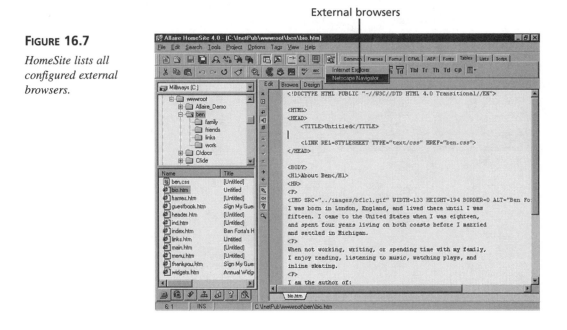

3. Select a browser from the list. The page is displayed in it (see Figure 16.8).

> If you edit a page that's open in an external browser, it's quicker to reload the page by using the browser's reload (or refresh) button instead of selecting the external browser again in HomeSite.

FIGURE 16.8

The selected external browser is opened, and the currently active page is displayed.

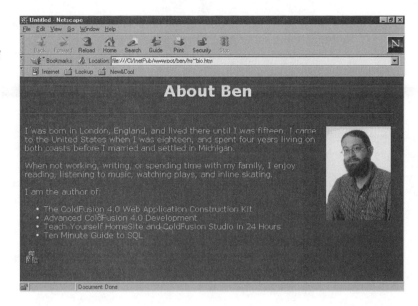

16

Summary

Web pages must be tested thoroughly. Tag validation is used to ensure the validity of your HTML code. HomeSite supports two forms of tag validation. Pages should be viewed in multiple browsers to ensure that pages look correct in as many different browsers as possible. HomeSite's External Browser support can simplify this process.

Q&A

Q Is there any way to add additional tags (and attributes) to the tag validator?

A The Validator Configuration dialog's Tags page displays a tree control containing all the tags known to the validator, along with all attributes (and optional value rules). Right-click anywhere within this tree control to add (or edit) tags and attributes.

Q What is CSE HTML Validator?

A The Settings dialogís Validation tab contains a check box that enables support for a third-party validation product called CSE HTML Validator. This product doesn't come with HomeSite, but if it's installed HomeSite can use it and returns its validation messages. The CSE Validator is extremely thorough, although some developers think it's *too* thorough. If you want more information on this product, click the link in the tab dialog.

Q I can't seem to install multiple versions of some browsers on my computer. Am I doing something wrong??

A Unfortunately, not all versions of browsers can coexist. For example, if you install Microsoft Internet Explorer 4 on your computer, version 3 will automatically be removed—the two just cannot coexist. Netscape is better about allowing coexistence than Microsoft is. There's really not much you can do about this.

Workshop

The Workshop contains quiz questions and activities to help reinforce what you've learned in this hour. If you get stuck, the answers to the quiz questions can be found in Appendix A, "Answers to Quiz Questions."

Quiz

1. True or false: If my page looks fine in the HomeSite integrated browser, it'll look fine in all browsers.

2. What validation checks are performed by background tag validation?

3. How many different browsers should you test your pages with?

Exercises

1. Validate all the pages we created thus far. Fix any errors that are reported to you.

2. Validate the HTML used in Web pages that you visit frequently. The simplest way to do this is by using HomeSite's Open From Web feature. What percentage of pages actually validate without any errors at all?

HOUR 17

Using Snippets and Templates

As your Web site grows in size, and its number of pages grows proportionally, you'll often find yourself copying or retyping the exact same blocks of text over and over. To simplify working with commonly used text blocks, HomeSite supports two forms of code reuse: snippets and code templates.

In this hour you'll learn the following:

- Why to use snippets and code templates
- How to create and use snippets
- How to create and use code templates

Why Use Snippets and Templates?

As you develop your Web sites, you'll find yourself reusing blocks of text repeatedly. These might be menus, logos, headers and footers, disclaimers, contact information, and more. Rather than force you to retype these text blocks each time they are needed, HomeSite provides two code reuse options:

- Snippets can be inserted into any page with a single mouse click. A snippet can contain multiple lines of text as well as starting and ending text blocks.

- Code templates are usually used for single tags (or tag sets) and are inserted by using keyboard abbreviations or pop-up menu selections.

There are advantages to each option, as you'll soon see.

NEW TERM Don't confuse code templates with templates (I know, it *is* confusing). *Templates*, used as starting points for new pages, are accessed by choosing New from the File menu (and are created by choosing Save As Template from the File menu). *Code templates* are typing shortcuts, as you'll soon see.

Working with Snippets

Snippets are text blocks that can include plain text and HTML tags on one or more lines. You can construct snippets of a single block of text or two blocks of text (a starting block and an ending block).

Snippets are accessed via the Snippets tab on the Resource Tab. This tab (see Figure 17.1) lets you create, edit, delete, and browse snippets.

FIGURE 17.1

HomeSite code snippets are managed and selected by using the Snippets tab in the Resource Tab.

Snippets can be made up of just starting code, or both starting and ending code. Your entire code snippet can be specified as a starting block. So why use ending blocks at all? The difference actually isn't in the snippet, but in where your cursor is placed after insertion. If you specify only a start block (or enter the entire snippet in the Start Text box), your cursor will be placed after the inserted snippet. If you specify both start and end text, after snippet insertion the cursor will be placed between the two blocks, ready for you to type any additional text between them.

Creating Snippets

To create a new snippet, do the following:

1. Switch to the Resource Tab's Snippets tab (if it isn't already open).

2. Snippets are stored in folders. Click the folder in which to save your new snippet (if the folder doesn't exist, right-click the top level folder and select Create Folder to create it). Folders may be created within other folders if desired.

3. Right-click and select Add Snippet to display the Snippet dialog (see Figure 17.2).

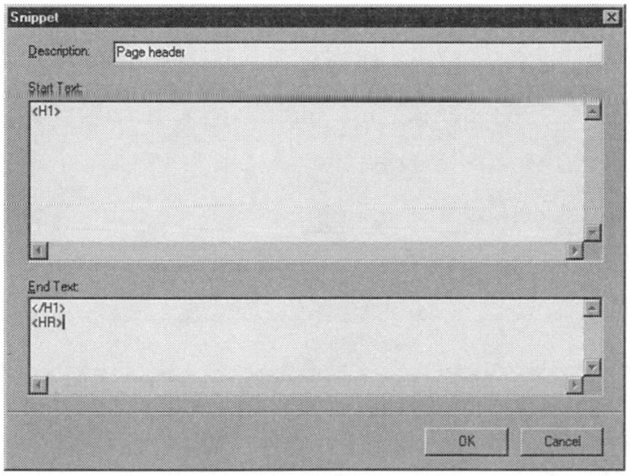

FIGURE 17.2

Snippets are added (and edited) through the Snippet dialog.

4. Specify a snippet description in the Description text box. You'll click this description when selecting the snippet, so make it very descriptive.

5. Enter the snippet text in the Start Text box. You can enter as many lines of text as you need.

6. If your snippet has ending text, enter it in the End Text box.

7. Click OK to save your snippet.

Your new snippet will be listed on the Snippets tab, ready for selection.

 There's no limit to the number of snippets you can create.

Using Snippets

Using snippets is even easier than creating them. To insert a snippet on your page, do the following:

1. Place your editor cursor at the location to insert the snippet.
2. Switch to the Resource Tab's Snippets tab (if it's not already open).
3. Browse the snippet tree to find the snippet to insert.
4. Double-click the snippet.

That's all there is to it. Your snippet text is inserted onto your page for you.

Working with Code Templates

Code templates are similar to snippets in that they allow you to insert blocks of text without retyping them. However, there are important but subtle differences between the two:

- Code templates are made up of a single block of text.
- Code templates can be inserted by using only keystrokes (no mouse intervention).
- Code templates can be selected right within the editor window, without requiring you to switch panes or tabs.

 Most HomeSite developers find that code templates are better suited for single tags (with already populated attributes and values), and snippets are better suited for longer blocks of code often made up of many different tags.

Using Code Templates

The best way to understand code templates is to see them used. HomeSite comes with a series of basic code templates already defined, one of which is basic <LINK> tag used to associate pages with external style sheets (covered in Hour 15, "Using Style Sheets"). The keyword for this code template is *linkrels*.

NEW TERM *Keywords* are code template text shortcuts. To insert a code template, you must type (or select) its keyword.

There are two ways to insert the linkrels code template. Here's the first:

1. Type the keyword **linkrels**.

2. With the cursor immediately after the last character of the keyword (the s), press Ctrl+J. HomeSite replaces the keyword with the complete code template text.

The other way to insert a code template is as follows:

1. Place your cursor where you want the code template inserted.

2. Press Ctrl+J to display a pop-up menu of all available code templates (see Figure 17.3).

3. Select any listed code template (using your keyboard or mouse) to insert it onto your page.

17

FIGURE 17.3

Code templates can be selected from an inline pop-up menu right inside the editor.

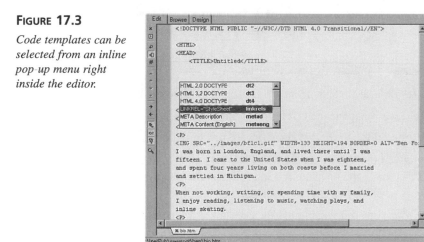

Creating Code Templates

Code templates are created by using the Settings dialog's Code Templates page (see Figure 17.4). Each code template consists of three parts:

- *A description of the code template.* This should be spelled out so as to be completely legible.

- *A keyword.* This is the abbreviated text that you can type in your editor (the abbreviated text gets expanded into the full code template value).

- *A value.* This is the actual code to be inserted when the code template is selected.

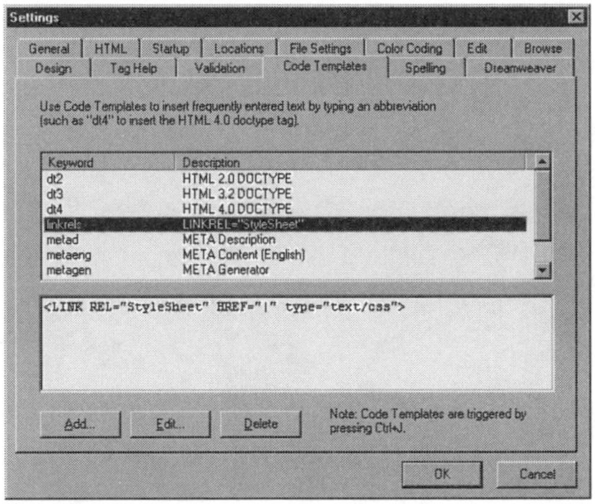

FIGURE 17.4

Code templates are created by using the Settings dialog.

To create a new code template, do the following:

1. Press F8 (or choose Settings from the Options menu) to display the Settings dialog.

2. Select the Code Templates tab (refer to Figure 17.4).

3. Click the Add button to display the Code Template dialog (see Figure 17.5).

4. Enter a unique keyword in the Keyword text box (don't use any spaces in the keyword). Don't make the keyword too long; this is the text you type in the editor, and the object is to reduce typing, not increase it.

5. Describe your code template in the Description text box. Use a detailed description if appropriate (this is displayed in the pop-up menu seen earlier in Figure 17.3).

6. Enter the value (the code to be inserted) in the Value box. You can embed a single pipe character (¦) in your code to indicate the cursor position after code insertion.

7. Click OK to save the code template.

FIGURE 17.5

New code templates are defined in the Code Template dialog.

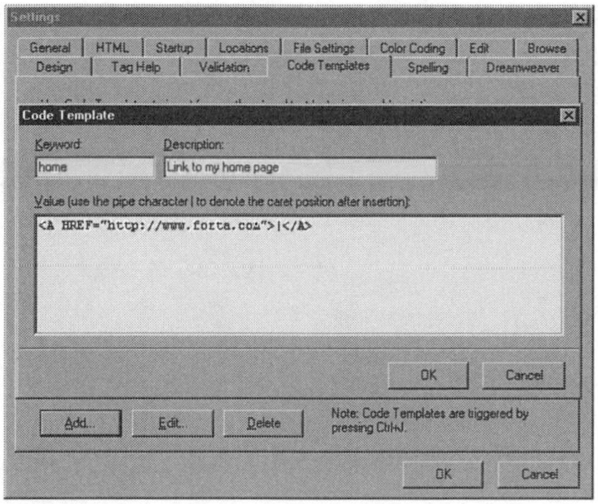

Your new code template will now be listed on the Code Templates tab, as well as in the pop-up menu displayed when you press Ctrl+J.

There's no limit to the number of code templates you can create.

Summary

You can use code templates and snippets to facilitate code reuse. There's a lot of overlap between the functionality offered by these two tools, and it's up to you to choose which to use for which situations.

Q&A

Q I want to create a whole set of snippets to be used by my development team. Is there any way to share HomeSite snippets among developers?

A HomeSite has no built-in method for sharing snippets, but you can share them manually if you want. Snippets are saved in the UserData\Snippets directory beneath the application root directory (usually C:\Program Files\Allaire\HomeSite4 or C:\Program Files\Allaire\ColdFusion Studio4). You can copy files into and out of this directory as needed to share snippet files.

17

Q **Snippets and code templates let me insert code blocks onto my pages. Is there any way to dynamically include pages on-the-fly at runtime without hard coding inserted text?**

A Dynamic inclusion at runtime requires that your Web server support this functionality. If you are a ColdFusion user, you can use the ColdFusion `<CFINCLUDE>` tag to accomplish this.

Workshop

The Workshop contains quiz questions and activities to help reinforce what you've learned in this hour. If you get stuck, the answers to the quiz questions can be found in Appendix A, "Answers to Quiz Questions."

Quiz

1. Which code reuse mechanism is better suited for keyboard-oriented developers?
2. What is the ¦ character used for in a code template value?

Exercises

1. HomeSite comes with nine built-in code templates. Experiment with them and then try adding a few of your own.
2. Look through the Web pages you've created thus far. Try to find reused code blocks and create snippets for them.

Hour **18**

Managing Your Web Site

A Web site is a living entity—it evolves constantly and changes continuously. Links that work one day might not work the next, and subtle changes to a graphic in one page might affect how another page is displayed. Because Web sites are simply collections of files held together by links, Web developers must rely on tools to provide them with a view of the bigger picture and the wherewithal to fix problems should they occur.

In this hour you'll learn the following:

- What the Site View is and how to use it
- How to verify links
- How to monitor page download time

Seeing the Bigger Picture

Your Web pages, and how they relate to each other, change all the time. Because Web sites are simply collections of linked pages, changes to one page often affect many other pages.

The kinds of things that developers need to be concerned about include the following:

- *Navigation*—What pages link to what pages, and how users can get back to main menus and home pages.

- *Site depth*—How many links a user must follow to reach a specific page. The deeper a page is buried, the less likely it'll be found.

- *Site complexity*—How many ways there are to get to a single page and how many ways there are to leave that page.

- *Component reuse*—Which images and backgrounds are shared between pages. Sharing images can dramatically improve download time, but it does create file dependencies—you can't safely change an image without knowing how it will affect every page that uses that image.

All these are important issues, and ones that developers must pay attention to. Alas, these issues surface only when a Web site is visualized as a complete site, and Web developers spend most of their time working in a very page-centric mindset. Because sites are usually developed as sets of pages, we tend to visualize pages and page content, not entire sites.

Of course, reading the HTML code within pages reveals the entire site relationship, but manually reading files is time-consuming and error-prone.

Using the Site View

The HomeSite solution is the Site View, a dynamic tool that displays page and element relationships from a Web site perspective. To use the Site View, do the following:

1. Open the Web page to be used as your browsing starting point (ideally this should be a home page or the top-level page within a section).

2. Click the Site View button in the Resource Tab to switch to the Site View. The Site View tab (see Figure 18.1) displays a chart representation of your page. The page title is displayed at the top, and any images and links are graphically represented.

3. Click any link or graphic to highlight its HTML code within the editor (see Figure 18.2).

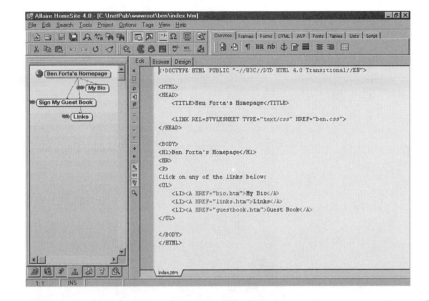

FIGURE 18.1

By default, the Site View is displayed within the HomeSite Resource Tab.

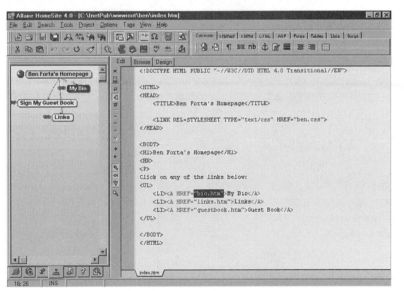

FIGURE 18.2

Clicking any link or graphic highlights its HTML code within the editor.

18

4. Any linked pages are displayed with a link symbol. Click a link symbol to expand the link, showing images and links contained within that page (see Figure 18.3).

FIGURE **18.3**

Site View lets you expand links to other pages to create an ever-growing site tree.

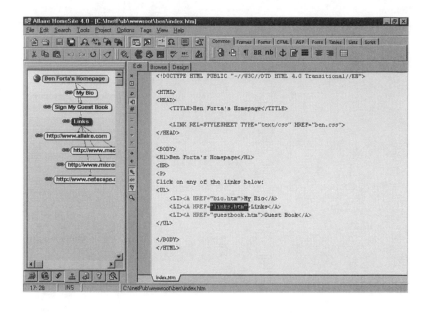

 You can use Site View to expand links in pages on external sites as well.

If the display gets too cluttered, consider switching it from Chart view to Tree view. To do this, right-click in the Site View, select View Style, and then select Tree. Tree view (see Figure 18.4) uses a more structured interface, somewhat similar to that of the Windows Explorer.

FIGURE **18.4**

Site View can optionally be displayed in Tree view.

The Resource Tab isn't very wide, and you might find yourself quickly running out of room while in Site View. Unlike most other tabs in the Resource Tab, the Site View tab can be undocked (see Figure 18.5). To do this, simply drag the tab by the double bar at the top of it (just like you drag a toolbar). To reattach Site View to the Resource Tab, simply close it.

FIGURE 18.5

If you need more room to browse your Site View, try undocking the Site View tab.

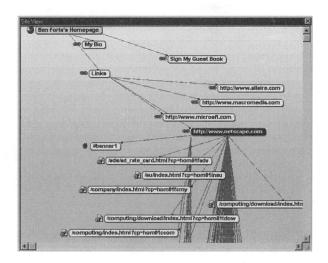

As you can see, Site View provides developers with a different perspective, one that can greatly ease the process of creating professional-quality Web sites.

Site View doesn't automatically update itself if your code changes. If you make code changes while in Site View, you must manually refresh the view by right-clicking and selecting Refresh.

Verifying Links

If you've ever browsed the Web, you've undoubtedly come across the infamous 404 error messages (like the one in Figure 18.6). Although different Web Servers display the 404 error in different ways, the meaning is always the same. 404 is the Web's very non-intuitive way of saying that you requested a file that doesn't exist.

FIGURE 18.6

Web servers display 404 when a request is made for a page that doesn't exist.

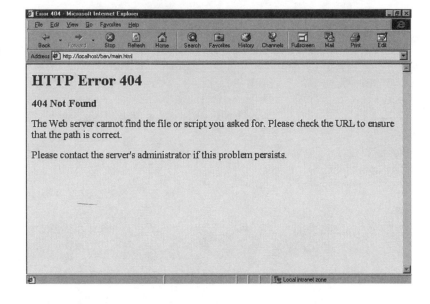

404 is one of many status codes returned by Web servers. In fact, every request made by a Web browser generates a status code. Status code 200 means that the request was successful. We've already seen status code 404, and there are many others. For a full list of status codes, see the HTTP specifications at `http://www.w3.org`.

404 errors are usually caused by one of two occurrences:

- A link that never worked because it contained a typo, and thus pointed to a nonexistent page
- A working link that stopped working because the linked page was changed (perhaps moved or renamed)

Site View can help somewhat when it comes to finding broken links, but there is a better way.

Using the Link Verifier

HomeSite comes with an integrated link verifier that you can use to test all links—links to pages within your own site as well as links to external sites. The following steps walk you through using the link verifier:

1. Open the page containing the links to be verified.

2. To launch the link verifier, click the Verify Links button in the Tools toolbar or choose Verify Links from the Tools menu.

3. The Results window at the bottom of the screen opens (with the Links page displayed), and all your page links are listed with a status of "untested" (see Figure 18.7).

FIGURE 18.7

The Results window's Links page automatically displays a list of all links on your page.

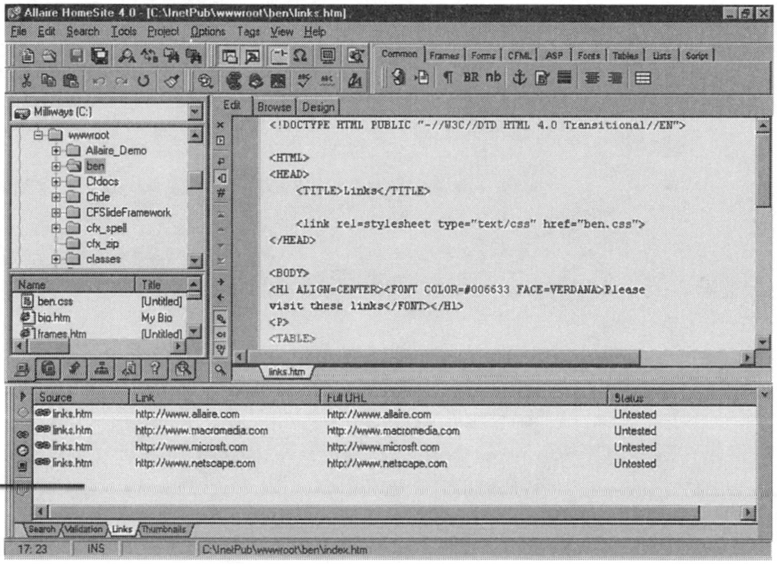

Results window

4. To test the links, click the Start Link Verification button at the left of the Results window. HomeSite tests each link and reports the results in each link's Status column (see Figure 18.8).

As Figure 18.8 shows, the link verifier makes it easy to locate broken links. After you find a broken link, you can simply double-click it to highlight its code in the editor, and make whatever necessary changes to fix it.

> Testing internal links (to pages within your own site) is a quick operation, but testing external links can take a long time. Rather than test all links, you can test individual links by right-clicking the link and selecting Verify This Link.

FIGURE **18.8**

*The link verifier tests
each link and reports
the test results in the
Status column.*

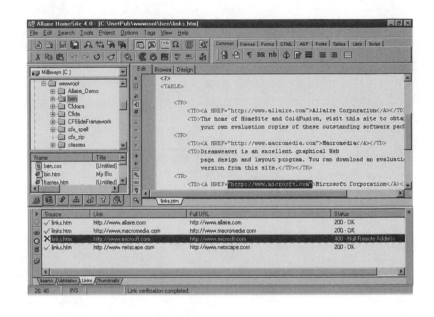

FIGURE **18.8**

*The link verifier tests
each link and reports
the test results in the
Status column.*

You can print a list of failed links by clicking the Print button to the
left of the Results window. This button, however, is available only if
one or more links failed validation. If all your links pass validation, the button is grayed out.

Monitoring Download Time

Now your site is organized properly, and all links work. The final issue to worry about is
download time—the amount of time visitors have to wait while their browsers download
your page and all its elements.

Working out download time involves checking the size of the HTML file itself, adding to
it the total size of all graphics contained within the page, and then dividing that number
by the average number of bytes per second that popular modem speeds are capable of.

There is an easier alternative, however.

Checking Document Weight

HomeSite users are fortunate in that they have a far simpler way to check document
download time. The HomeSite Document Weight feature can perform all the calculations
for you and present you with the estimated download times in seconds.

To use the Document Weight feature, follow these steps:

1. Open the document to be weighed (make sure that all images are embedded and that the file has been saved).

2. Choose Document Weight from the Tools menu to display the Document Weight dialog (see Figure 18.9).

FIGURE 18.9

The Document Weight screen provides estimated download times for Web pages and their embedded graphical elements.

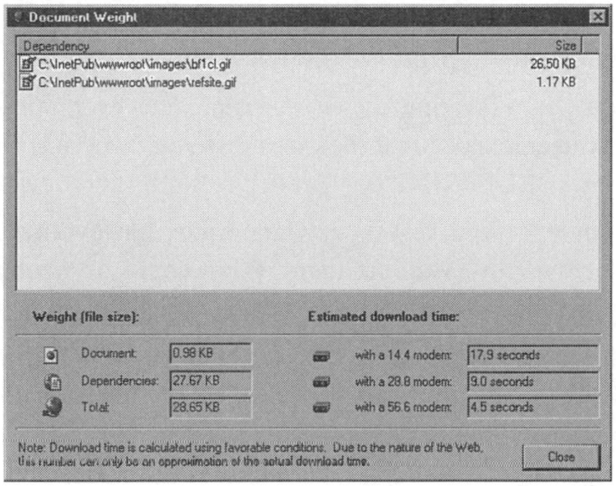

Document Weight	
Dependency	Size
C:\InetPub\wwwroot\images\bf1cl.gif	26.50 KB
C:\InetPub\wwwroot\images\refsite.gif	1.17 KB

Weight (file size):		Estimated download time:	
Document:	0.98 KB	with a 14.4 modem:	17.9 seconds
Dependencies:	27.67 KB	with a 28.8 modem:	9.0 seconds
Total:	28.65 KB	with a 56.6 modem:	4.5 seconds

Note: Download time is calculated using favorable conditions. Due to the nature of the Web, this number can only be an approximation of the actual download time.

[Close]

18

3. The Document Weight dialog automatically calculates page and component sizes, and reports estimated download times at the bottom. Click the Size column header to sort the elements by size (allowing you to pinpoint which graphics are the largest).

The download times presented in the Document Weight dialog are only estimates. Many factors can affect actual download times, including caching (which can dramatically improve download time) and bad connections (which can dramatically degrade download time).

The Document Weight feature takes into account many embedded images, but not all. For example, if you are loading any images dynamically by using DHTML, those dynamic images won't be calculated into the Document Weight formula.

Summary

Site management involves many different things: monitoring page relationships, validating links to internal and external pages, and ensuring acceptable page download speeds. As you'd expect, HomeSite provides tools to simplify all these tasks.

Q&A

Q Is there any way to print the Site View map?

A Unfortunately, at this time the answer is no. However, third-party site-mapping products can create detailed site maps that you can print. One good site-mapping program is <BLUEPRINT> by Brooklyn North (http://www.brooknorth.com).

Q I'm having problems testing external links. I know these URLs are correct, but HomeSite can't validate them. What could be wrong?

A The primary cause for this is performing validations from a network where Internet access is gained via a proxy server. If you must use a proxy server to connect to external sites, click the Set Proxy button on the left of the Results window to provide HomeSite with proxy server information.

Q Is there any way to check a page's weight on another Web server?

A HomeSite's Document Weight feature can be used only with local files. To check the weight of a page on another server, you have to save that page (and its graphics) locally.

Workshop

The Workshop contains quiz questions and activities to help reinforce what you've learned in this hour. If you get stuck, the answers to the quiz questions can be found in Appendix A, "Answers to Quiz Questions."

Quiz

1. What are the two views supported by Site View?

2. True or false: Link verification can be performed only on links to pages within your own Web site.

3. What factors can affect the estimated download times reported by Document Weight?

Exercises

1. Try validating the links in all the pages you've created thus far. If you're validating relative links, you need to notify HomeSite of the base URL to use (there's a button for this in the Results window).

2. Use Document Weight to test the download times of sites you visit regularly (you need to copy HTML and image files locally). Based on the results you obtain, try to determine what download time (and thus file size) is acceptable, and what isn't.

18

Hour 19

Working Remotely

Deploying a Web site to a server that you host is a simple process. Unfortunately, we don't all host our own Web sites on our own Web servers. Most developers have to work remotely—developing their sites locally, and then transferring them to the server when they're complete. As you'd expect from a professional-strength editor, HomeSite provides integrated support for remote development.

In this hour you'll learn the following:

- How remote development works
- What FTP is and what FTP servers are
- How to configure HomeSite for remote development
- How to work with remote pages

Understanding Remote Development

As I explained way back in the first hour of this book, Web sites are collections of pages that are served up by Web servers on request. A Web server is nothing more than a computer running special software, and almost any computer can be turned into a Web server.

So why do most developers not host their own sites on their own servers? Well, unfortunately, there's more to hosting Web sites than just plugging in a computer and installing software:

- For Web servers to be available all the time (as Web servers should be), they must be connected to connections that are active 24 hours a day. Obviously, that precludes the use of dial-up connections.

- To handle multiple, simultaneous visitors, a high-speed connection is needed. Currently, the cost of these connections makes owning your own difficult.

- Although it's true that a Web server is software that runs on any computer, hosting sites usually involves hosting other services too (DNS, email, and more), and those services need computers, software, and someone to run them.

- Web servers must be secure. Ensuring system security (to prevent unauthorized access) is a complicated job—not one you'd want.

For all these reasons and more, most Web sites are hosted by ISPs or hosting providers, companies that specialize in hosting sites and ensuring that they stay up and running.

Of course, hosted sites are typically not hosted where you do your page development. This means that after you create your pages locally, you must find a way to transfer those files to the hosted Web server.

 Even if your site is hosted, you should still have a local Web server installed just for testing. Although it's indeed possible to test your site without a local server, you'll often find that pages and links that work when accessed locally don't work when accessed via a Web server. As such, testing with a real Web server is highly recommended. Web server software is available for almost every operating system, including Windows 95 and 98, and Windows NT, all flavors of UNIX, and Macintosh.

Just What Is FTP Anyway?

There are many ways to transfer files back and forth between hosts. Files can be sent as email attachments, transmitted via HTTP file upload, or copied to a floppy drive and hand delivered. But by far the most popular form of file transfer is FTP.

NEW TERM   FTP stands for *File Transfer Protocol*. As its name suggests, FTP is a mechanism that transfers files between hosts. (In the Internet world, *hosts* refers to computers.) By using FTP, remote users can copy files back and forth between hosts, obtain remote directory lists, and even rename, move, and delete remote files.

> FTP isn't a software program, but a protocol (or standard) that computer programs use to transfer files.

To use FTP, you need several things:

- An FTP program—a simple text-based one is installed with Windows (see Figure 19.1). More powerful third-party graphical FTP programs can be used, too (see Figure 19.2).

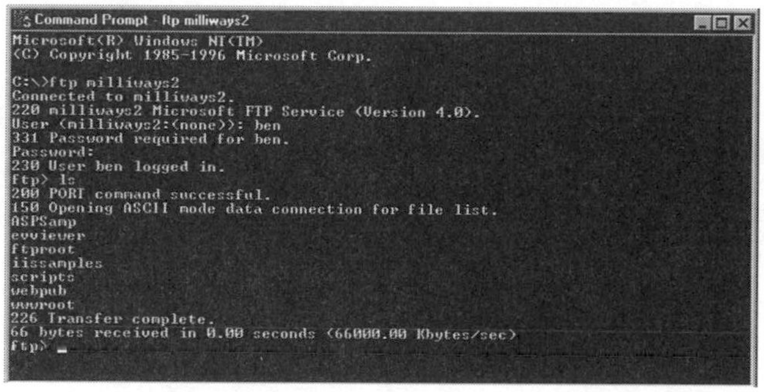

FIGURE 19.1

A text-based FTP program is installed on most Windows computers.

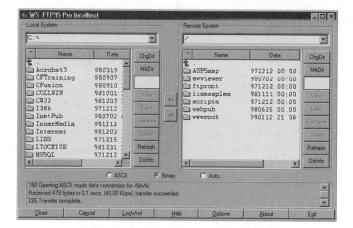

FIGURE 19.2

WS_FTP from Ipswitch is a popular graphical FTP application.

19

- The name (or IP address) of the FTP server to connect to.
- An account on the FTP server (a logon name and a password).

FTP has been around for a long time, long before the Web was created. FTP was designed to be powerful; it was never designed to be intuitive. As such, learning how to access and manipulate files via FTP can be a tedious and annoying process.

The Remote Development Process

Assume that your Web site was hosted by an ISP that allowed you to update your site via FTP. Here's what you would have to do:

1. Create your Web pages and test them locally.
2. Run your FTP program and connect to the FTP server (which is usually running on the same host as the Web server), using the logon name and password provided.
3. Create any directories needed on the Web server (FTP allows you to manipulate directories, too).
4. One by one, copy each file from your computer to the Web server via the FTP connection.
5. Log off the FTP connection and quit the FTP program.
6. Test your site by using a Web browser to request pages from the hosted Web server.

I know that sounds like a lot of work, and indeed it is. Yet this is how *most* developers create and deploy their Web sites. But with HomeSite's ever-growing popularity, that is changing.

When Web sites are created locally and deployed to a remote server, you actually have two entire copies of your Web site. Be careful not to make changes on the hosted site directly; otherwise, the next time you upload your pages, you'll overwrite those changes. All updates and edits should be made locally, and then the edited files should be deployed.

Working Remotely with HomeSite

To simplify working with remote servers, HomeSite has an integrated FTP application. This means that you can open remote files directly from within HomeSite, and save them back to the remote server. Each time you open and close remote files, HomeSite *automatically* transfers the files via FTP, and you don't have to do a thing.

ColdFusion Studio supports another remote server type—the RDS server. We'll discuss this in Hour 22, "Developing Against Remote ColdFusion Servers."

Setting Up Remote Servers

Of course, before you can access a remote server, you need to configure that server in HomeSite. Remote servers are configured (and accessed) via the Remote Files tab in the Resource Tab.

To configure a remote server, follow these steps:

1. Contact your hosting company and have them give you the FTP server hostname and logon information.
2. Open the Resource Tab's Remote Files tab.
3. Right-click in the tab and select Add FTP Server to display the Configure FTP Server dialog (see Figure 19.3).

FIGURE 19.3

The Configure FTP Server dialog adds FTP servers to HomeSite.

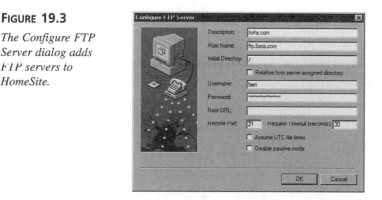

19

4. Specify a unique name for your configuration in the Description text box (you might want to use the name of the site it'll be used for).
5. In the Host Name text box, specify the address of the FTP server. This can be specified as a hostname or an IP address.
6. Enter your assigned logon name in the Username text box.
7. Enter your assigned logon password in the Password text box.
8. If your hosting company gave you a port number, enter it in the Remote Port text box; otherwise, leave this text box empty.

9. The default values can be used in all other text boxes, so click OK to save the configuration.

The new server will be listed at the top of the Remote Files tab ready for use.

There's no limit to the number of FTP servers that can be configured in HomeSite. If you work on multiple sites hosted on multiple servers, you can create an FTP configuration for each of them.

To edit or delete FTP server configurations, right-click the server name and select the appropriate option from the pop-up menu.

Remote Development

Now that your remote server is configured, you can use it as you would any other drive list:

1. Click the server name to connect to it. HomeSite uses the configuration information you provided to log on to the remote server.

2. Click the + icon to expand the server and display a list of directories (the – will close a branch).

3. Click any directory to display the files stored in that directory (see Figure 19.4).

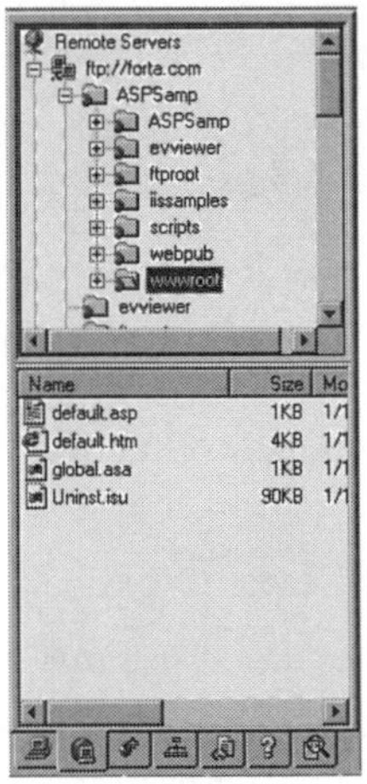

FIGURE 19.4

As you click a remote directory, HomeSite will retrieve and display a listing of that directory's contents.

4. Double-click any file to open it. HomeSite will retrieve the file over an FTP connection automatically (see Figure 19.5).

FIGURE 19.5

HomeSite transparently opens files over an FTP connection, freeing you from having to deal with FTP programs.

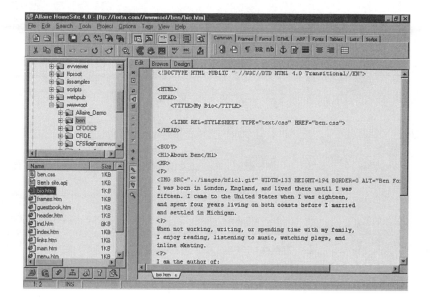

You can tell if an opened file was retrieved over a remote connection by looking at its editor tab. HomeSite displays a green dot after the filename if the file was retrieved from a remote server.

19

To save a new file on an FTP server, do the following:

1. Create the file as you would any other HomeSite file.
2. Click the Save button to display the Save As dialog, and click the Remote tab to display a list of available remote servers (see Figure 19.6).
3. Browse the available servers and directories to locate the directory to save the file in.
4. Name the file in the File Name text box.
5. Click the Save button (HomeSite automatically opens an FTP connection and saves the file over it).

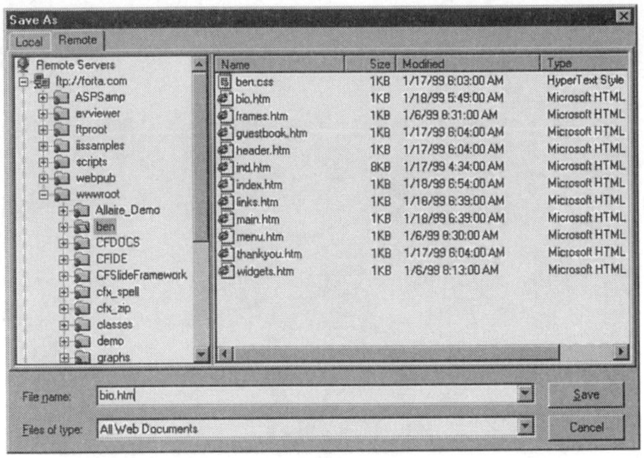

FIGURE 19.6

New files are saved to remote servers by using the Save As dialog's Remote tab.

> File lists displayed in the Remote Files tab aren't automatically updated if files are added or deleted (automatic updates would be terribly slow over slower connections). To update the file list, right-click in the tab and select Refresh.

Summary

FTP is the primary page deployment method used by hosting companies. Rather than require you to work in external FTP programs, HomeSite integrates FTP functionality right within the editor. After remote servers are configured, all FTP transfers occur seamlessly and automatically.

Q&A

Q My hosting company uses UNIX servers. Will this be a problem?

A The FTP protocol is supported in the same way by all major operating systems. Your HomeSite running on Windows won't have a problem connecting to a UNIX-hosted FTP server (or servers on any other platform, for that matter). But remember that most UNIX file systems are case sensitive, so you might need to use the Force File and Folder Names to Lowercase option when deploying your site (your hosting company can tell you whether you need to do this).

Q My hosting company offer Telnet access. What is that used for?

A Telnet is a protocol used to log on to hosts remotely. With Telnet, you're presented with a command prompt at which you type operating system commands. Unlike FTP, which is used to transfer files between hosts, Telnet is used to execute commands on a remote host.

Workshop

The Workshop contains quiz questions and activities to help reinforce what you've learned in this hour. If you get stuck, the answers to the quiz questions can be found in Appendix A, "Answers to Quiz Questions."

Quiz

1. What three pieces of information are needed to log on to an FTP server?
2. What types of operations can be performed over an FTP connection?
3. True or false: FTP servers can be referred to by their hostnames or their IP addresses.

Exercises

1. If your Web site is hosted by a provider offering FTP access, configure an FTP server to connect to the provider's servers.
2. If you're feeling particularly adventuresome, try using the FTP program that comes with Windows (go to a command prompt and type **FTP**). Although this FTP program is far from friendly, it's worth getting to know because you never know what computer you'll one day be working on, and often this is the only FTP client available on a machine.

19

Hour **20**

Managing Your Projects

Web sites are made up of many different files, all of which must be present to edit or deploy your site. HomeSite supports the use of projects to group together related files.

In this hour you'll learn the following:

- What projects are and when to use them
- How to create and manage projects
- How to create and deploy projects on remote servers

Understanding Projects

By now you've learned that Web sites are made up of sets of files of many different types. As the complexity and depth of your site grows, so will the number of files that you'll regularly find yourself working with. Some of the most common types of files are

- Web pages (usually .HTM or .HTML files)
- Images (that is, GIF and JPEG files)

- Style sheet definitions (.CSS files)
- Imagemaps

More often than not, when working on your Web site you'll find yourself having to read, edit, update, and manipulate more than one file at a time. This typically requires opening multiple files and manually determining which files belong with which so as to open the correct set of files.

Introducing HomeSite Projects

NEW TERM　HomeSite allows you to group sets of files in a single unit called a *project*. A project is simply a container for one or more files. You can add files (or entire directories) into a project, open and close entire projects with one selection, and even upload projects to remote servers in one step.

Project support is fully integrated into HomeSite. All of HomeSite's standard development and editing features can be used with project files. The only difference is that, instead of working with individual files, you'll be working with sets of files.

Where to Use Projects

How projects are defined, and what files are put into them, is entirely up to you. You can create projects that contain entire Web sites, small subsets of a site, or any combination thereof.

You can use these guidelines to determine how to define your projects:

- Start off with one project for your entire Web site (including all subdirectories). This project might be too big to use most of the time, but it will still be useful for making global changes or searches.
- Create multiple projects for logical subsets of the site. These subsets can be directories, specific menu options and associated files, or any other grouping that makes sense to you.
- A single file can be included in multiple projects. You therefore can create multiple projects for your site with overlapping files, if needed.

Using Projects

HomeSite projects are created and maintained within HomeSite. The actual projects themselves are stored as plain text files within the directory in which the project was created. These files have an .APJ extension; double-clicking them (in Windows Explorer, for example) directly opens HomeSite with the entire project loaded.

There are two ways to access projects within HomeSite:

- Most project manipulation occurs in the Projects tab in the Resource Tab.

- Specific project-manipulation functions are accessible via the Project menu.

The HomeSite Project Tab

The Project tab (see Figure 20.1) is one of the HomeSite Resource Tabs. It's split into two panes: The upper pane shows directories within a project, whereas the lower pane shows files within a selected directory. Above the upper pane are a series of controls. These can be used as shortcut options to open a recent project, create a new project, or upload a project to a remote server.

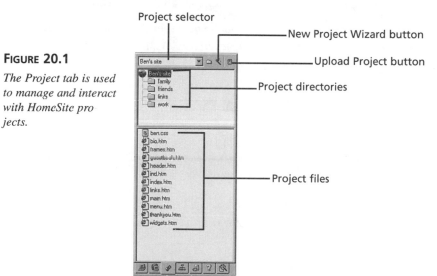

FIGURE 20.1

The Project tab is used to manage and interact with HomeSite projects.

Creating Projects

There are several ways to create a new project:

- Select New Project from the Project menu.

- Click the New Project button at the top of the Project tab pane.

- Right-click in the upper pane and select New Project.

Any of these options displays the New Project dialog (see Figure 20.2).

20

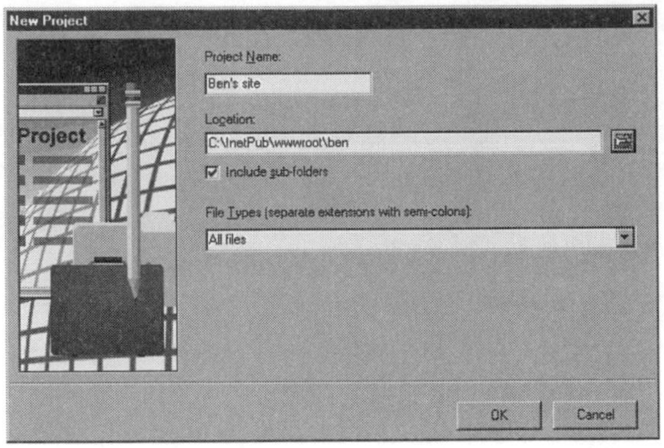

FIGURE 20.2

Use the New Project dialog to create new HomeSite projects.

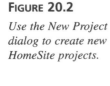

To create a new project by using the New Project dialog, do the following:

1. In the Project Name text box, specify a unique name for the project. Be as descriptive as possible, using punctuation or whatever special characters you need.

2. In the Location text box, specify the directory containing the files (or directories) to be included in the project. The .APJ file will be created in this directory.

3. By default, all subdirectories of the specified directory will be included in the project. To prevent this, deselect the Include Sub-folders check box.

4. Specify the files to be included from the File Types combo box. You can select the default All Files selection, any selection from the drop-down list, or enter the extensions of specific files you want.

After the project is created, it automatically opens (see Figure 20.3). The upper pane shows the directories in your project, and the lower pane shows the files within a selected directory.

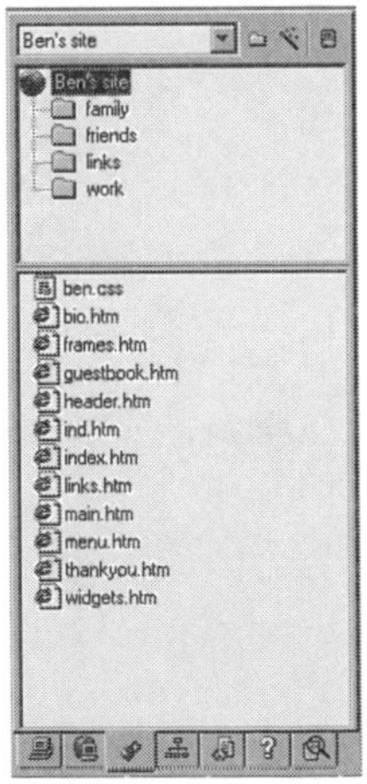

FIGURE 20.3

Open projects are displayed in the Project tab with directories in the upper pane and files in the lower pane.

For simple graphics manipulation, you might want to create a project called Graphics that contains all the GIF and JPEG images throughout your entire application (including files in all subdirectories).

Opening Existing Projects

To open an existing project, do any of the following:

- Choose Open Project from the Project menu.
- Click the Open Project button above the upper Project tab pane.
- Right-click in the upper pane and select Open Project.

Any of these options displays the Open dialog (see Figure 20.4).

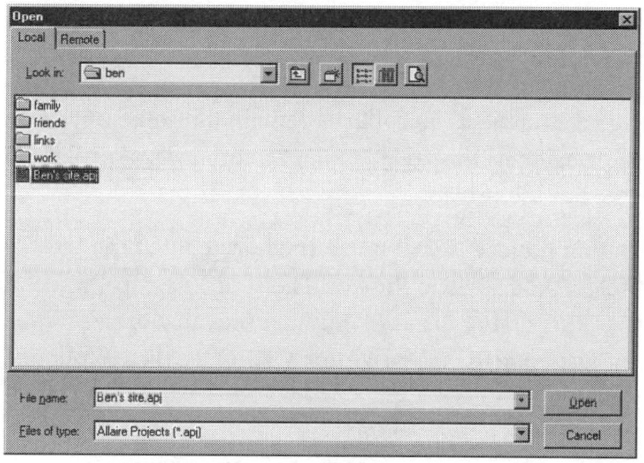

FIGURE 20.4

Use the Open dialog to open existing project files.

To open a local project (meaning, a project to which you have direct access via your PC), select the Local tab and locate the required .APJ file. After you find the .APJ file, click the Open button to open the project.

20

To reopen a recently used project, select that project name from the Recent Projects drop-down list box above the upper pane. You can also select the project by choosing Reopen Project from the Project menu.

Manipulating Project Files

HomeSite makes it very easy to manipulate or edit files in an open project. You can open individual files, all files, or files just in a selected directory:

- To open a single file, simply double-click it in the Project tab's lower pane. This opens the file for editing, just like any other file in HomeSite.

- To open all files, right-click on a project in the upper pane, and select Open All Documents in Project. This opens every file in your project for editing.

- To open the files in a specific directory within a project, select that directory in the upper pane, right-click it, and select Open All Documents in This Folder (this option will be labeled Open All Documents in Root Folder if you select the Project root directory).

After you open the files, you can edit them directly in HomeSite as you would any other file.

Modifying Projects

When a project is created, its contents remain the same unless you explicitly change them. This means that files added to a directory *after* a project is created aren't automatically members of the project.

To add files to a project, click on the directory containing the files to be added, right-click, and select Add Files to Project. The Add Files To Project dialog appears (see Figure 20.5). This dialog displays only the files that aren't currently in the project. Select the files you want added and then click OK. Only files explicitly selected will be added to the project.

FIGURE 20.5

Files can be added to existing projects by using the Add Files To Project dialog.

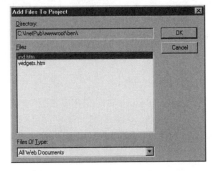

To remove a file from a project, select the file in the lower pane, right-click it, and select Remove From Project. Removing a file from a project does not delete the actual file.

To refresh the contents of specific project directories, right-click on the directory in the upper pane, and select Refresh. You also can update entire folders at once by choosing Synchronize Project from the Project menu.

Closing Projects

To close a project, choose Close Project from the Project menu. Any open project files in the HomeSite editor window are closed too. If you haven't saved any files, you will be prompted to save them before they are closed.

Using Remote Projects

As mentioned earlier in this chapter, HomeSite fully supports the use of remote projects. Remote projects are accessed via HomeSite's remote development features (as discussed in Hour 19, "Working Remotely").

To use remote projects, you must have already configured the remote server within HomeSite. If you haven't yet set up your remote servers, return to Hour 19 for step-by-step instructions.

Creating Remote Projects

The steps to create a remote project are as follows:

1. Make sure that the desired remote server is already set up within HomeSite.
2. Display the New Project dialog as explained earlier this hour.
3. In the Project Name text box, specify a unique name for the project. Be as descriptive as possible, using punctuation or whatever special characters you need.
4. To set the location, click the folder button to the right of the Location text box to display the Select Directory dialog. Select the Remote tab to show the remote server selector (see Figure 20.6). Expand the servers and directories to find the desired project root directory (where the .APJ file will be created).
5. By default, all subdirectories of the specified directory are included in the project. To prevent this, deselect the Include Sub-folders check box.

20

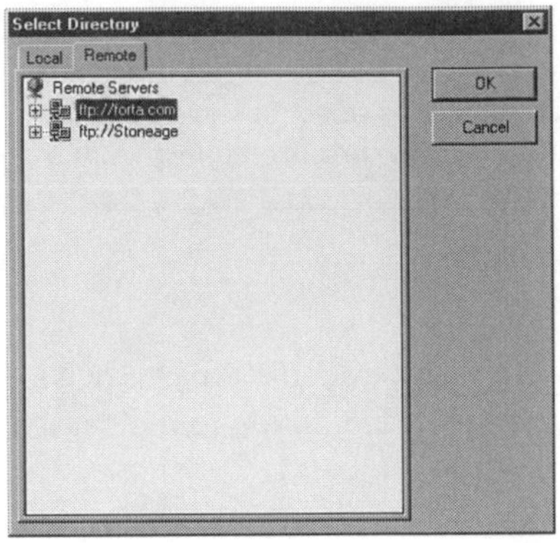

FIGURE 20.6

Use the Select Directory dialog's Remote page to create projects on a remote server.

6. Specify the files to be included in the File Types combo box. You can select the default All Files selection, any selection from the drop-down list, or enter the extensions of specific files you want.

Opening Remote Projects

To open an existing remote project, do any of the following:

- Choose Open Project from the Project menu.
- Click the Open Project button above the upper Project tab pane.
- Right-click in the upper pane and select Open Project.

Any of these options displays the Open dialog. Select the Remote tab as shown in Figure 20.7 to select the appropriate remote server. You need to expand the servers and directories to locate the required .APJ file.

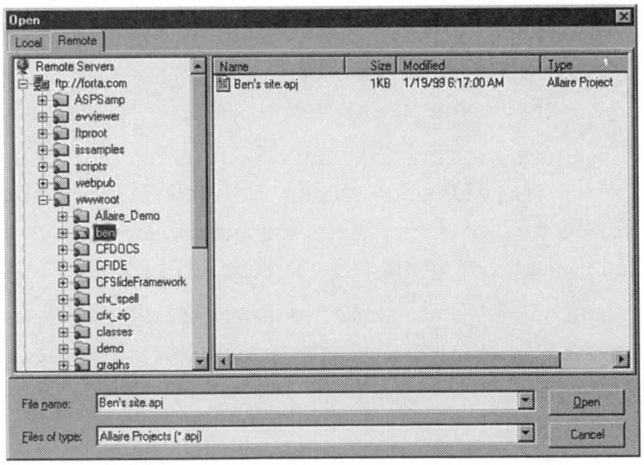

FIGURE 20.7

The Open dialog's Remote tab is used to open projects that reside on a remote server.

After you find the .APJ file, click the Open button to open the project.

> The reopen options described earlier can also be used to open remote projects.

Uploading Projects

Projects are especially useful when working remotely. The ability to open sets of files for editing can save you time and aggravation, particularly over slower connections.

Projects can also be used to simplify deploying sites developed locally. For example, imagine an ISP situation. If an ISP hosts your Web site, you likely are doing all development on a local host and deploying the finished site to the ISP's site only after it's complete.

The traditional way to do this is to develop the site locally, and then FTP the files one by one (each to its appropriate directory) over an FTP connection. Although this is workable, it's not an ideal solution. Manually sending files over an FTP connection involves creating individual directories, selecting the local files and the appropriate remote directories for each, checking which files have been changed and which haven't (you don't want to upload files that haven't changed because that takes extra time unnecessarily), and then transferring them one at a time. Obviously, this is both tedious and highly error prone (files can get easily missed or placed in incorrect directories).

HomeSite can fully automate the process of uploading sites to remote servers. HomeSite's project uploading feature lets you create a project locally (complete with any directory structure needed) and then deploy the entire project up to a server with the click of a single button.

To deploy a project to a remote server, do the following:

1. Make sure that a connection to the remote server is configured in HomeSite.
2. If the project to be uploaded isn't open, open it as described earlier.
3. Click the Upload Project button above the Project tab upper pane to display the Upload Project dialog (see Figure 20.8).
4. Select the remote server to upload the project to in the Upload Location server tree.
5. Expand the selected server to select the root directory into which the project should be saved.

20

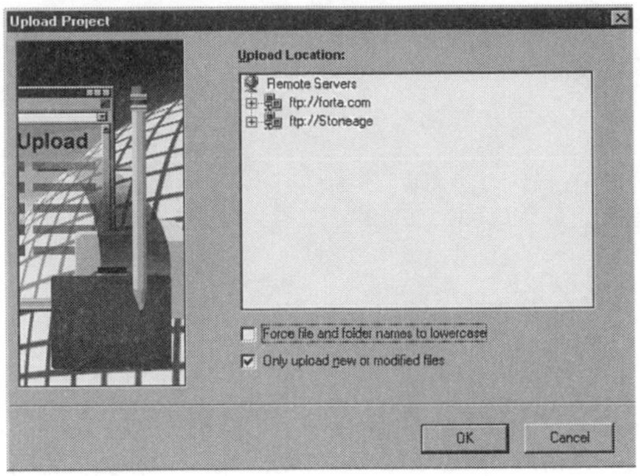

FIGURE 20.8

Use the Upload Project dialog to upload entire projects to a remote server in a single operation.

6. To save transfer time, HomeSite automatically checks the date and time stamp of files being uploaded so that only newer (changed) files are transmitted to the remote server. To force an upload of *all* files (to perform a complete refresh), deselect the Only Upload New or Modified Files check box.

7. Click OK to transfer the files.

> Some operating systems (such as Linux and Sun's Solaris) have case-sensitive file systems. If you are uploading the project to a server hosted on a computer with a case-sensitive file system, you might need to force all filenames and directory names to lowercase. To do this automatically, select the Force File and Folder Names to Lowercase check box.

Summary

Projects can greatly simplify the process of manipulating large sets of files. HomeSite supports the use of local and remote projects, the latter of which is particularly well suited for use in hosting environments.

Q&A

Q I use version control to manage my source files and changes made to them. Can HomeSite projects be checked in and out of version control?

A HomeSite supports two version control systems: Microsoft Visual Source Safe and Intersolv PVCS. If either system is installed on your computer, HomeSite automatically detects it and lets you manage your projects with them. Version control options are available by right-clicking in the Project tab.

Q Is there any way to make code changes to an entire project in one step?

A The extended search and replace functions (described in Hour 14, "Editing Your Pages") fully support projects.

Q Can projects be shared among developers?

A Yes, as long as all the developers have access to the .APJ files and all the member files. Remote projects are particularly well suited for this kind of development.

Workshop

The Workshop contains quiz questions and activities to help reinforce what you've learned in this hour. If you get stuck, the answers to the quiz questions can be found in Appendix A, "Answers to Quiz Questions."

Quiz

1. What's the primary purpose of projects?
2. True or false: Projects cannot contain other projects.

Exercises

1. Create a project containing all the files created thus far.
2. If you have access to a remote server, deploy the project you just created to that server by using the Upload Project button.

20

PART V
Using ColdFusion Studio

Hour

Hour **21**

Introducing ColdFusion Studio

ColdFusion Studio is an enhanced version of HomeSite designed especially for ColdFusion developers.

In this hour you'll learn the following:

- What ColdFusion and ColdFusion Studio are
- What advantages ColdFusion Studio offers over HomeSite
- What's contained in the ColdFusion-specific toolbars
- How to use ColdFusion Studio's Expression Builder

This hour (and the next three hours) discuss ColdFusion Studio, the advanced editor built on top of HomeSite and designed especially for ColdFusion programmers. If you are a ColdFusion developer and don't already run ColdFusion Studio, you owe it to yourself to download an evaluation version immediately from http://www.allaire.com.

ColdFusion is a Web application development system created by Allaire, the same folks who bring you HomeSite. ColdFusion lets you create and deploy complete Web-based applications with an easy-to-learn scripting language (it looks a lot like HTML; if you are comfortable working in HTML, you already have most of the skill sets you'll need to write ColdFusion applications). With ColdFusion you can process form submissions, create pages that interact (read from and write to) databases, send and receive email, create e-commerce Web sites, perform intelligent agent processing, interact with numerous other technologies and systems, and much more.

ColdFusion consists of two primary components: an application server that runs on the same computer as your Web server and a client development environment called ColdFusion Studio that runs on your own development computer. The application server executes the applications that you created by using ColdFusion Studio.

This book doesn't teach you ColdFusion (if you want to learn ColdFusion, look at my *ColdFusion 4 Web Application Construction Kit*, ISBN 0-7897-1809-X). This book will, however, teach you how to use the HomeSite-based ColdFusion development environment—ColdFusion Studio.

If you want to try ColdFusion for yourself (and you should), you can download an evaluation version from the Allaire Web site. An evaluation version is also provided on the CD-ROM that accompanies my ColdFusion book.

Understanding ColdFusion Studio

ColdFusion Studio (see Figure 21.1) is built on top of HomeSite (in fact, some developers affectionately refer to ColdFusion Studio as "HomeSite on steroids"). Whereas HomeSite is a tool oriented toward Web developers in general, ColdFusion Studio is oriented specifically toward ColdFusion developers. As such, almost everything you've learned in the past 20 hours applies to both HomeSite and ColdFusion Studio.

FIGURE 21.1

ColdFusion Studio is based on HomeSite, which it closely resembles.

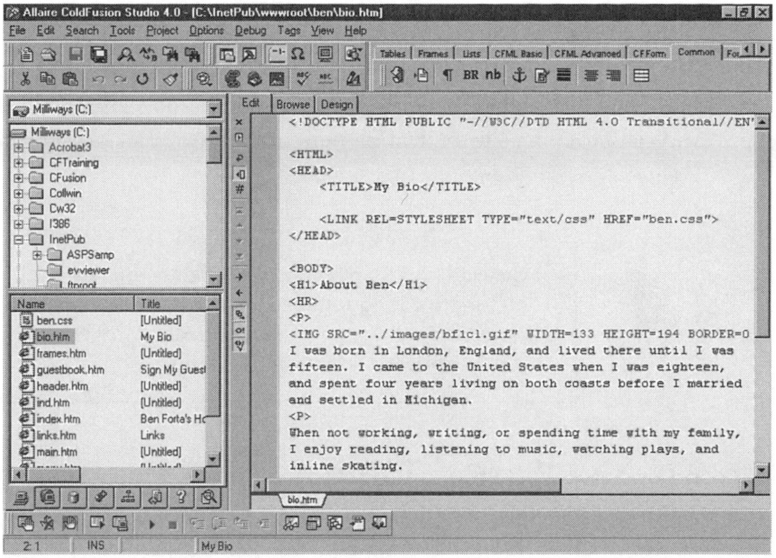

HomeSite Versus ColdFusion Studio

What distinguishes ColdFusion Studio from HomeSite? Here's a list of the primary differences:

- Additional toolbars to support ColdFusion tags
- Additional Tag Editors and Tag Inspectors to support the CFML tag set
- Extensive online ColdFusion and CFML (ColdFusion Markup Language) help
- An Evaluation Builder
- Support for remote development via Remote Development Services (covered in Hour 22, "Developing Against Remote ColdFusion Servers")
- Remote data source integration (covered in Hour 22)
- A SQL Query Builder (covered in Hour 23, "Using the SQL Query Builder")
- An integrated code debugger (covered in Hour 24, "Working with the Integrated Debugger")

Which tool is right for you? If you are a ColdFusion developer, you'll definitely want to use ColdFusion Studio instead of HomeSite. If you are developing Web sites only and don't need back-end processing support, HomeSite is the right choice for you.

21

Using ColdFusion Studio

For the most part, using ColdFusion Studio is much like using HomeSite. Files are opened and closed the same way, all the design tools and functions are used the same way, and even the customization options are the same. Remember, ColdFusion Studio is HomeSite with *additional* functionality.

> HomeSite and ColdFusion Studio can coexist on the same computer, but they don't share configurations. Changes made to one won't be recognized by the other. Similarly, snippets, code templates, wizards, and toolbars aren't shared between the two applications.

The ColdFusion Toolbars

ColdFusion is primarily a tag-based language. To simplify working with CFML tags, ColdFusion Studio features three toolbars containing CFML shortcuts (see Table 21.1). The CFML Basic toolbar contains commonly used CFML tags. The CFML Advanced toolbar contains advanced and less frequently used tags. The CFForm toolbar contains ColdFusion FORM extensions.

TABLE 21.1   CFML TOOLBAR BUTTONS

Button	Description
CFML Basic Buttons	
	Display ColdFusion server variable list
	`<CFQUERY>`
	`<CFOUTPUT>`
	`<CFINSERT>`
	`<CFUPDATE>`
	`<CFTABLE>`
	`<CFCOL>`

Button	Description
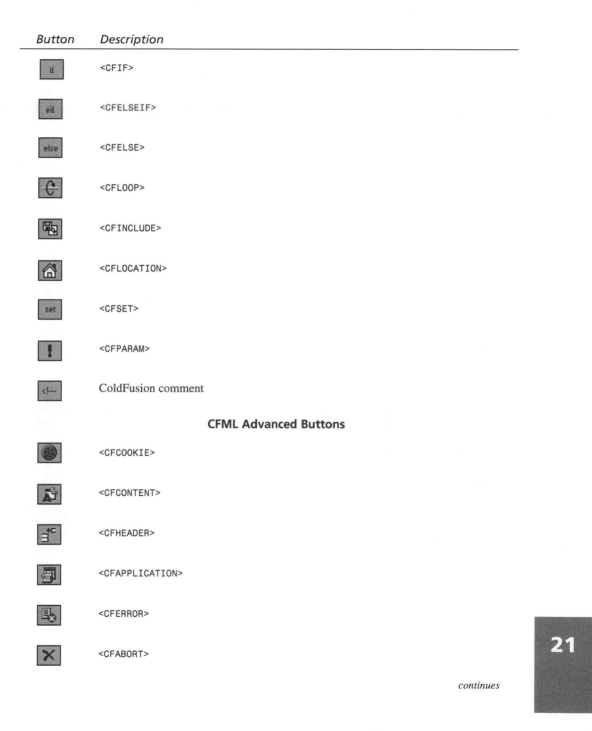	<CFIF>
	<CFELSEIF>
	<CFELSE>
	<CFLOOP>
	<CFINCLUDE>
	<CFLOCATION>
	<CFSET>
	<CFPARAM>
	ColdFusion comment

CFML Advanced Buttons

Button	Description
	<CFCOOKIE>
	<CFCONTENT>
	<CFHEADER>
	<CFAPPLICATION>
	<CFERROR>
	<CFABORT>

21

continues

TABLE 21.1 CONTINUED

Button	Description
	`<CFDIRECTORY>`
	`<CFFILE>`
	`<CFMAIL>`
	`<CFPOP>`
	`<CFHTTP>`
	`<CFHTTPPARAM>`
	`<CFLDAP>`
	`<CFFTP>`
	`<CFSEARCH>`
	`<CFINDEX>`
	`<CFMODULE>`
	`<CFOBJECT>`
	`<CFREPORT>`
	`<CFSCHEDULE>`

CFForm Buttons

Button	Description
	`<CFFORM>`
	`<CFAPPLET>`

Button	Description
	`<CFINPUT>` text field
	`<CFINPUT>` radio button
	`<CFINPUT>` check box
	`<CFSELECT>`
	`<CFTREE>`
	`<CFTREEITEM>`
	`<CFGRID>`
	`<CFGRIDCOLUMN>`
	`<CFGRIDROW>`
	`<CFGRIDUPDATE>`
	`<CFSLIDER>`

Except for the `<CFELSE>`, `<CFELSEIF>`, and ColdFusion comment buttons, all the buttons on the ColdFusion toolbars display a Tag Editor and don't insert code directly into your pages.

The Expression Builder

ColdFusion expressions are used to perform operations on data. Expressions are used to

- Manipulate text
- Perform calculations
- Manipulate or display dates, times, and numbers
- Manipulate lists, arrays, and structures

21

- Create conditional processing conditions
- Create evaluation conditions

Expressions consist of text, variables, function calls, and logical operators. For example, the following expression combines two CFML functions to return tomorrow's date:

```
#DateAdd('d', 1, Now())#
```

This next expression could be used in a `<CFIF>` statement to see whether two submitted passwords match:

```
password1 IS password2
```

Most ColdFusion expressions are easy enough to create. But writing complex expressions with multiple conditions and clauses can be tricky. To simplify the process of expression creation, ColdFusion Studio features an Expression Builder. To launch the Expression Builder (see Figure 21.2), do one of the following:

- Select Expression Builder from the Tools menu.
- Press Ctrl+Shift+E.
- Right-click in your editor and select Insert Expression.

FIGURE 21.2

The Expression Builder is used to simplify the creation of ColdFusion expressions (incorporating both functions and variables).

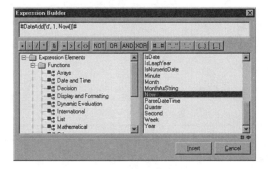

To demonstrate using the Expression Builder, follow these steps to create the date calculation expression I just showed you:

1. Open the Expression Builder by using any of the methods just listed.
2. Click the #...# button to embed starting and ending pound signs. (As you build the expression, it will be shown in the top part of the dialog.)
3. Expand the Functions branch, and then click Date and Time to display the date processing functions.

4. Locate the DateAdd function on the right and double-click it to insert it between the pound signs (the function will be displayed with placeholder values).

5. To specify the date part, delete the word datepart (leave the comma), click the '...' button to insert single quotes, open the Constants branch to select date formatting masks, and then double-click the d mask (yes, you could have just typed **d** too).

6. Replace the placeholder *number* with 1.

7. To set the base date, open the Functions branch, click Date and Time Functions, highlight the word date in the expression, and then double-click the Now function to replace the placeholder with the function.

8. To insert the new expression into your page, click the Insert button.

> The Expression Builder contains extensive integrated help that you can access by using the help buttons at the bottom of the Expression Builder dialog.

As you can see, the Expression Builder doesn't actually write expressions for you, but it can greatly simplify the process of building expressions (and thus the name *Expression Builder*).

Summary

ColdFusion Studio is an enhanced version of HomeSite designed especially for ColdFusion developers. In this hour we looked at some differences between HomeSite and ColdFusion Studio, and at the ColdFusion toolbars and the Expression Builder. We'll look at more ColdFusion Studio features in detail in the next three hours.

Q&A

Q Can HomeSite do anything that ColdFusion Studio cannot? Do I need both programs?

A No. ColdFusion Studio is a *superset* of HomeSite—everything you can do in HomeSite you can do in ColdFusion Studio (although there are some subtle interface differences as pointed out in earlier hours). As such, you don't need HomeSite if you have ColdFusion Studio installed.

21

Q Can I use the Expression Builder to edit existing expressions?

A Yes. To edit an expression, highlight it in your editor, right-click, and select Insert Expression.

Workshop

The Workshop contains quiz questions and activities to help reinforce what you've learned in this hour. If you get stuck, the answers to the quiz questions can be found in Appendix A, "Answers to Quiz Questions."

Quiz

1. How many toolbars appear in ColdFusion Studio and not in HomeSite?

2. What ColdFusion Studio tool would you use to build a `<CFLOOP>` WHILE condition?

Exercises

1. If you aren't currently a ColdFusion user and if you host your own Web server, download an evaluation version of ColdFusion from `http://www.allaire.com`, and install it on your computer.

2. By using the Expression Builder, create an expression that displays the current date formatted as a legible date string.

3. Using the Expression Builder, create an expression that shows the user's IP address (hint, the CGI Variables list in the Variables branch contains a list of CGI variables that return all sorts of information about both the client and the server).

HOUR 22

Developing Against Remote ColdFusion Servers

Just like HomeSite, ColdFusion Studio supports remote development via FTP. But unlike HomeSite, ColdFusion Studio also provides remote access via the ColdFusion Application Server's Remote Development Services (RDS).

In this hour you'll learn the following:

- What RDS is
- How to configure an RDS connection
- How to connect to an RDS server

Understanding RDS

In Hour 19, "Working Remotely," I explained how FTP is used to transfer files to and from a remote host. FTP isn't specific to HomeSite or ColdFusion Studio—it's a standard supported by many servers and many client applications.

Although FTP is invaluable for pure file and directory manipulation, it doesn't provide access to all server resources. Actually, it provides access to only a single resource—the file system.

ColdFusion developers who work over a remote connection usually need access to more than just files. They also need access to whatever databases are configured on the server, the actual application (for debugging purposes), and possibly files outside the FTP directory tree.

NEW TERM To empower ColdFusion developers with a greater degree of server interaction, ColdFusion features its own form of remote access—*Remote Development Services* (RDS). Unlike FTP, RDS doesn't require that a separate software application be running on your server. ColdFusion Application Server itself is the RDS server, so RDS is managed with the same administrative tools as ColdFusion .

To understand the difference between FTP and RDS access, look at Table 22.1.

TABLE 22.1 FTP AND RDS FEATURES

Feature	FTP	RDS
Transfer files	×	×
Create new files and directories	×	×
Delete files and directories	×	×
Browse server databases		×
Debug remote applications		×
Security managed by ColdFusion		×
Requires no additional software		×
Support for server-side source control		×
Can use clients other than ColdFusion Studio	×	

As you can see, from a feature perspective there's nothing you can do with FTP that you can't do with RDS. The only advantage of FTP over RDS is that FTP can be used by clients not using ColdFusion Studio.

Using RDS

Just like FTP access (covered in Hour 19), before you can access an RDS server, you need to configure that server in ColdFusion Studio. RDS servers are configured (and accessed) via the Remote Files tab in the Resource Tab.

Configuring RDS Server

To configure a remote server, follow these steps:

1. Contact your hosting company and have them give you the RDS server hostname and logon information.

2. Open the Resource Tab's Remote Files tab.

3. Right-click in the tab and select Add RDS Server to display the Configure RDS Server dialog (see Figure 22.1).

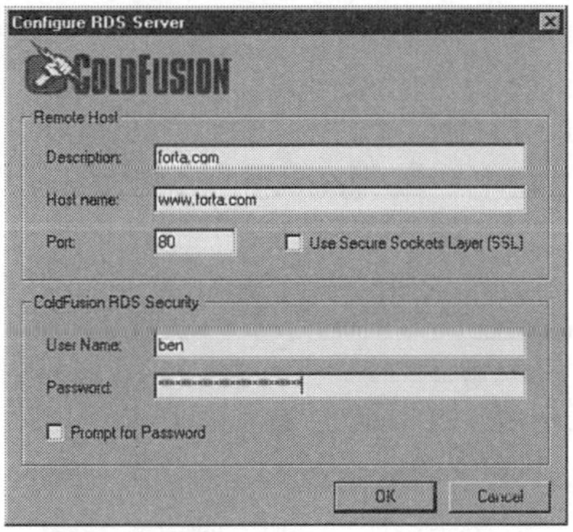

FIGURE 22.1

Use the Configure RDS Server dialog to add RDS servers to ColdFusion Studio.

4. Specify a unique name for your configuration in the Description text box (you might want to use the name of the site for which it will be used).

5. In the Host Name text box, specify the address of the RDS server (this will be the same as your Web site address). You can specify this address as a hostname or an IP address.

6. Enter your assigned logon name in the User Name text box.

7. Enter your assigned logon password in the Password text box.

8. If your hosting company gave you a port number, enter it in the Port text box; otherwise leave this text box alone.

9. For additional security, you can opt to be prompted for the RDS password each time you connect to the server. (This option should definitely be used if you share your computer with other users.)

10. The default values can be used for all the other options, so click OK to save the configuration.

The new server will be listed at the top of the Remote Files tab ready for use.

There's no limit to the number of RDS servers that can be configured in ColdFusion Studio. If you work on multiple sites hosted on multiple servers, you can create an RDS configuration for each one of them.

To edit or delete RDS server configurations, right-click the server name and select the appropriate option from the pop-up menu.

Using RDS for Remote Development

Now that your remote server is configured, you can use it like you would any other drive list:

1. Click the server name to connect to it. ColdFusion Studio will use the configuration information you provided to log on to the remote server. (If you opted to be prompted for a password, ColdFusion Studio will do so at this point.)

2. Click the + icon to expand the server and display a list of directories (the – closes a branch).

3. Click any directory to display the files stored in that directory (see Figure 22.2).

4. Double-click any file to open it. ColdFusion Studio retrieves the file over the RDS connection automatically (see Figure 22.3).

The ColdFusion Studio Remote Files tab lists both RDS and FTP servers. You can determine how a remote server is configured by looking at the beginning of its name—it'll say either FTP or RDS.

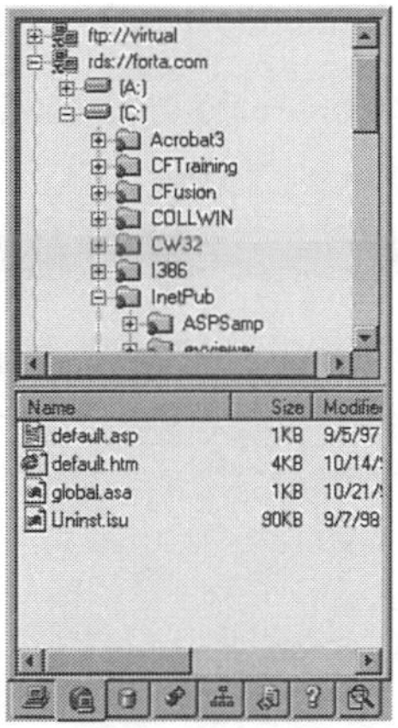

FIGURE 22.2

As you click a remote directory, ColdFusion Studio retrieves and displays a listing of that directory's contents.

FIGURE 22.3

ColdFusion Studio transparently opens files over an RDS connection.

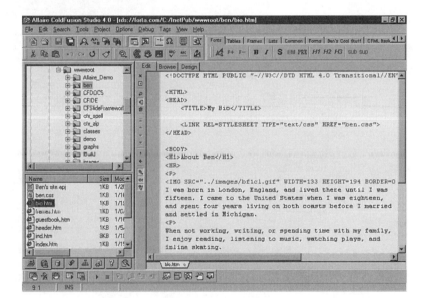

 To tell whether an opened file was retrieved over a remote connection, look at its editor tab. ColdFusion Studio displays a green dot after the filename if the file was retrieved from a remote server.

To save a new file on an RDS server, do the following:

1. Create the file as you would any other ColdFusion Studio file.

2. Click the Save button to display the Save As dialog, and click the Remote tab to display a list of available remote servers (see Figure 22.4).

FIGURE 22.4

New files are saved to remote servers by using the Save As dialog's Remote tab.

3. Browse the available servers and directories to locate the directory to save the file in.

4. Name the file in the File Name text box.

5. Click the Save button. ColdFusion Studio automatically opens an RDS connection and saves the file over it.

File lists displayed in the Remote Files tab aren't automatically updated if files are added or deleted. (Automatic updates would be terribly slow over slower connections.) To update the file list, right-click in the tab and select Refresh.

Summary

ColdFusion Studio extends HomeSite's remote development support by adding an interface to ColdFusion's Remote Development Services. An RDS configuration is configured in much the same way as an FTP connection. In the next two hours, we'll see some of the features available only via RDS.

Q&A

Q Can my Web server support both FTP and RDS connections at the same time?

A Yes, FTP and RDS can coexist. In fact, many sites run both FTP and RDS services on the same computer to ensure maximum compatibility while providing ColdFusion users with the advanced features they need.

Q My company has a firewall protecting our network. FTP is a standard protocol, so the firewall has been configured to allow FTP access. Can RDS work through the firewall?

A ColdFusion's RDS support is built on top of HTTP, the protocol used by your Web servers. As long as HTTP is allowed via the firewall (if you can get to the pages, it is), then RDS will work through it too.

Workshop

The Workshop contains quiz questions and activities to help reinforce what you've learned in this hour. If you get stuck, the answers to the quiz questions can be found in Appendix A, "Answers to Quiz Questions."

Quiz

1. What client applications support ColdFusion's RDS?
2. What's the recommended connection type to use if you're using ColdFusion Studio and ColdFusion Application Server, FTP or RDS?

Exercise

Configure an RDS connection to your ColdFusion server. If you're running ColdFusion locally, you can connect to it with RDS by specifying localhost as the hostname.

HOUR 23

Using the SQL Query Builder

All database access in ColdFusion occurs using SQL statements. To simplify the development process, ColdFusion Studio features a powerful and flexible SQL Query Builder.

In this hour you'll learn the following:

- What the SQL Query Builder is
- How to use the SQL Query Builder to retrieve, sort, and filter data
- How to use the SQL Query Builder to insert, update, and delete data

Understanding the SQL Query Builder

Almost every ColdFusion application uses some sort of database integration. Although database integration is probably the most commonly used ColdFusion feature, learning SQL—the language used to interact with these databases—remains the single biggest hurdle facing ColdFusion developers.

For this reason, Allaire added a graphical SQL generation tool to ColdFusion Studio. Some features built in to the Query Builder include

- Drag-and-drop interface for simpler field selection
- Simple drop-down lists for filter and sort selection
- Full support for relational queries and all JOIN types
- Ability to generate SELECT, INSERT, DELETE, and UPDATE statements
- Generated SQL shown in real time
- Ability to execute SQL statements and display any results
- Generates <CFQUERY> read code

Unlike other query builders built in to database client applications, the ColdFusion Studio SQL Query Builder has been designed from scratch with ColdFusion developers in mind. As such, learning to use the Query Builder effectively can dramatically improve the rate at which you roll out applications, and it can help you get the code right on the first try.

To use the SQL Query Builder, an RDS server must be configured. Even queries against local servers require a local RDS configuration. The SQL Query Builder can't be used over FTP connections.

As good as the SQL Query Builder is, it's no substitute for a good working knowledge of SQL. The Query Builder can help with your most common SQL statements, but at some point you will need to write SQL code directly. Whether it's to fine-tune the SQL code or to write statements not supported by the Query Builder, if you are serious about ColdFusion development, you must learn SQL.

Navigating the SQL Query Builder

First, let's look at the Query Builder screen. To start the SQL Query Builder, do one of the following:

- Select SQL Builder from the Tools menu, select a server from the drop-down list, select a table, and click New Query.

- Within the <CFQUERY> Tag Editor dialog, click the SQL Query Builder button (the button to the right of the SQL Statement text box), select a server from the drop-down list, select a table, and click New Query.

- Right-click any table in the Resource Tab's Database tab and select New Query.

This will open the Query Builder (see Figure 23.1).

FIGURE 23.1

Use the SQL Query Builder window to interactively construct SQL statements.

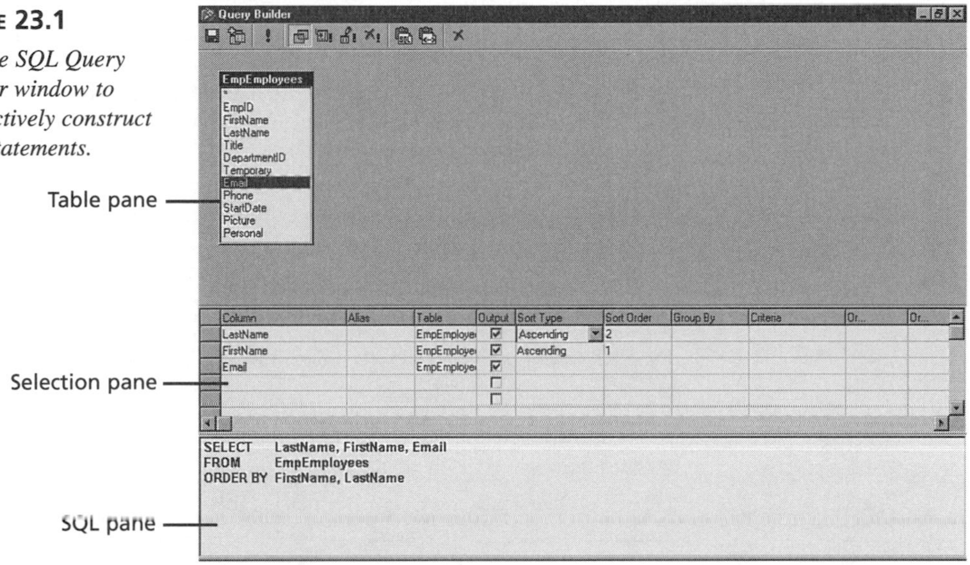

Table pane ——

Selection pane ——

SQL pane ——

The Query Builder window is divided into three sections, with standard Windows tool-bars at the top:

- The top portion of the window, the Table pane, is where you are presented with a graphical representation of the tables in your SQL query. You can add and remove tables, define relationships between tables, and select the columns you want included in the query.

- The middle portion of the window, the Selection pane, is where the list of currently selected columns appears. You can add and remove columns, attach criteria to perform data filtering, specify search orders and grouping, and pass subqueries.

- The bottom portion of the window, the SQL pane, is where the Query Builder shows you the SQL code being constructed. As you make changes in the two upper panes, the code in the SQL pane changes in real time. The final code, as it appears in this pane, is what gets pasted into your application.

Using the Toolbar

The SQL Query Builder window has no menus. All selections are made using the toolbar buttons and the items in the two upper panes. The toolbar buttons are described in Table 23.1.

TABLE 23.1   SQL QUERY BUILDER TOOLBAR BUTTONS

Button	Description
	Save Query lets you save the query for reuse. Queries are saved on the ColdFusion server, allowing queries to be shared by multiple users.
	Add Tables is used to add tables to a query.
	Run Query executes the SQL code appearing in the SQL pane. Results are displayed in a pop-up window.
	SELECT Query puts the Query Builder in SELECT mode, allowing you to create a SQL SELECT statement.
	INSERT Query puts the Query Builder in INSERT mode, allowing you to create a SQL INSERT statement.
	UPDATE Query puts the Query Builder in UPDATE mode, allowing you to create a SQL UPDATE statement.
	DELETE Query puts the Query Builder in DELETE mode, allowing you to create a SQL DELETE statement.
	Copy SQL to Clipboard copies the SQL code from the SQL pane to the Windows Clipboard so that you can paste it into other applications.
	Copy CFQUERY to Clipboard copies the SQL code formatted as a complete <CFQUERY> tag from the SQL pane to the Windows Clipboard.
	Close Query Builder quits the Query Builder.

Most SQL statements that you'll write are SQL SELECT statements, so the Query Builder window opens in the default SELECT mode. To generate SQL code for INSERT, UPDATE, or DELETE operations, you must switch the mode by using the toolbar buttons shown in Table 23.1.

Generating SQL SELECT Statements

Before you can start creating your SQL statement, you must select at least one database table. If you opened the Query Builder while a database table was selected, that table will be pre-selected in the Table pane (see Figure 23.2). If no database table was highlighted, the Query Builder prompts you for the initial table to use (see Figure 23.3).

FIGURE 23.2

By default, the highlighted table when you opened the Query Builder is opened for selection in the Table pane.

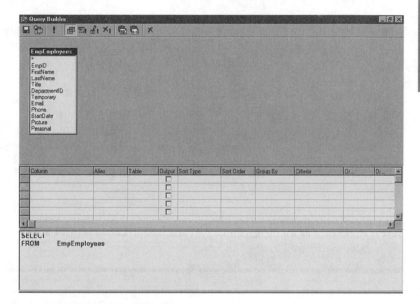

23

FIGURE 23.3

If no table was highlighted when the Query Builder was opened, you're prompted for the database table to use.

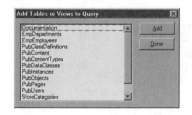

As soon as a table is selected, the Query Builder begins constructing your SQL statement (refer to the SQL pane in Figure 23.2).

Selecting Table Columns

The code in the SQL pane isn't a valid SQL statement yet; you need to select the columns to be retrieved. You can add columns to your statement in several ways:

- Double-click any column in any table in the Table pane to add that column to the Selection pane.

- Drag a column from the Table pane and drop it into the Column area in the Selection pane grid.
- Click any line in the Column area to display a drop-down list of all columns that can be added to the selection. Click any one to select it.

Notice how as you select each column, the SQL statement in the SQL pane reflects that change (see Figure 23.4).

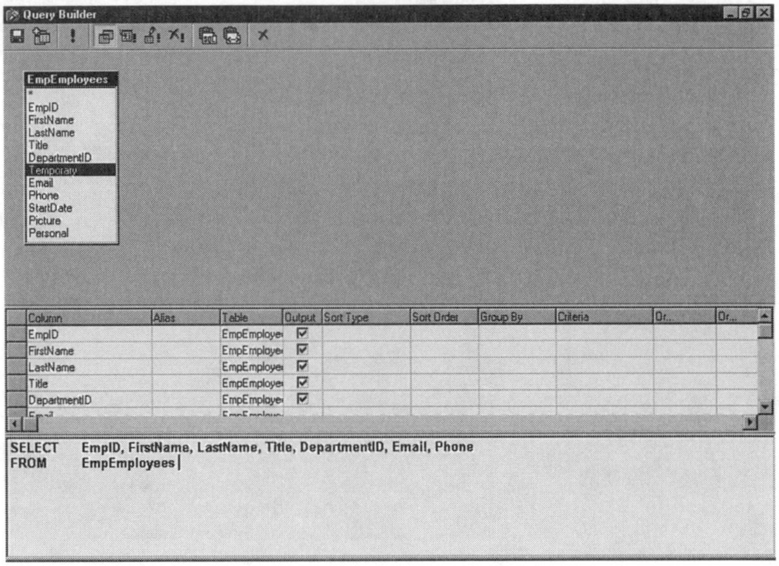

FIGURE 23.4

The SQL Query Builder allows you to add columns to your table in three different ways.

Testing SQL Statements

Now that you have a valid SQL statement, you next need to test that it works as intended. To test your SQL statement, simply click the Run Query button on the toolbar.

The Query Builder opens a results grid that displays the retrieved data for browsing. The title bar of the results window displays the SQL code executed, like the example shown in Figure 23.5.

To close the results window, click the Close Window button (the one on the right with an × in it).

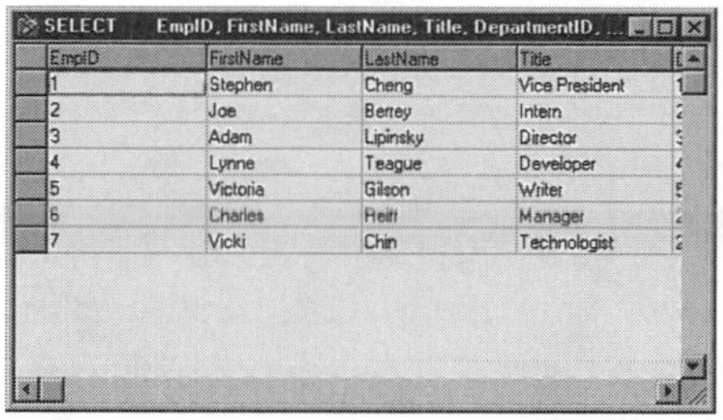

FIGURE 23.5

SQL statements can be tested directly in the Query Builder, and results are displayed in a results grid.

The Query Builder lets you execute any valid SQL statement. When you execute a SQL statement, the Query Builder submits the statement over the TCP/IP connection to the ColdFusion server for processing. The returned data is then displayed. Be careful not to execute a statement that could return very large result sets because this could take a very long time to return, giving you the impression that Studio has hung.

Sorting Results

Next, we'll sort the returned data. SQL results are sorted by columns in the retrieved columns list. Multiple columns can be selected, in which case the data will be sorted by the first column, and then by the second.

To sort results, do the following:

1. In the Selection pane grid, click the Sort Type column of the row containing the column you'd like to sort your data by. Select either Ascending or Descending.

2. Repeat step 1 for each additional sort column.

The SQL pane now shows an ORDER BY clause, which sorts the retrieved data. Data is now sorted by department name, and within each department, sorted by last name and then first name. To verify that this worked, try running the query by using the Run Query button.

To reorder the sequence within the ORDER BY clause, click the Sort Order column in the Selection pane and change the position as required.

Filtering Data

So far we've retrieved all the data in the tables. Next we'll add SQL WHERE clauses by using Query Builder's filtering tools.

To apply filtering within Query Builder, simply specify a search criteria in the Criteria column for the required row. As soon as you click anywhere out of that Criteria box, the SQL code in the SQL pane is updated to include your WHERE clause. You can test this query to verify that it returns the required data.

You can either enter your own search criteria or make a selection from the drop-down list (see Figure 23.6). You can select any of this to help you construct your SQL WHERE clauses.

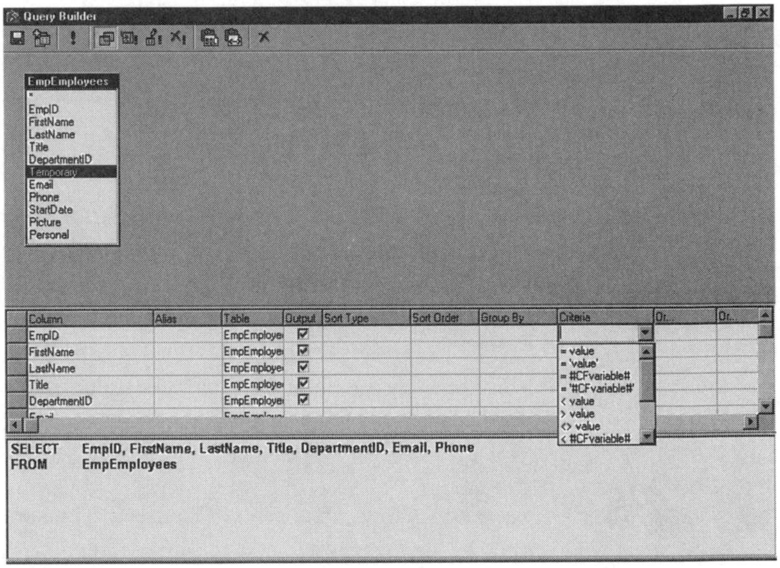

FIGURE 23.6

The Criteria drop-down list contains common WHERE clause conditions for selection.

Many selections in the drop-down list contain the text value or #CFvariable#. These are designed to be placeholders. You replace the word value with an actual value, and the word #CFvariable# with the name of a ColdFusion variable to be used within your WHERE clause.

There are two versions of each value and #CFvariable# in the Criteria drop-down list: one is enclosed within single quotation marks, the other isn't. Because SQL isn't typeless, it's your responsibility to enclose values and variables within single quotes when constructing WHERE clauses. Selecting the correct option from this list can help ensure that you don't inadvertently omit this.

Advanced Data Filtering

So far we have seen simple SQL WHERE clauses, with just a single criterion. You also can use the Query Builder to build more complex WHERE clauses, including AND and OR clauses, and any combination thereof.

AND clauses are created by making multiple selections of the fields to be filtered on, once for each condition. To create an AND clause, simply add the field to the grid again, and then specify the additional clause.

To create an OR clause, simply specify the alternate criteria in one of the additional Criteria columns (there are four of them per column).

23

> The SQL Query Builder supports an unlimited number of AND clauses and a maximum of four OR conditions per column in the WHERE clause.

Using Query Builder SQL Statements

After you create and test your SQL statements in the SQL Query Builder, you have several options: You can execute the SQL as is, copy and paste the SQL code, or save the code for reuse. To copy and paste the SQL code from the SQL pane, use the Copy SQL to Clipboard toolbar button.

Populating <CFQUERY> Tags

If you launched the Query Builder from within the <CFQUERY> Tag Editor dialog, you have the option of pasting the SQL code back into that dialog. To do this, follow these steps:

1. Click the Close Query Builder button.

2. You are prompted to save the query. If you plan to use this query again, choose Yes; otherwise, choose No.

3. You are prompted to insert the query back into your code; choose Yes.

The <CFQUERY> Tag Editor displays the final SQL code and automatically sets the data source correctly (see Figure 23.7).

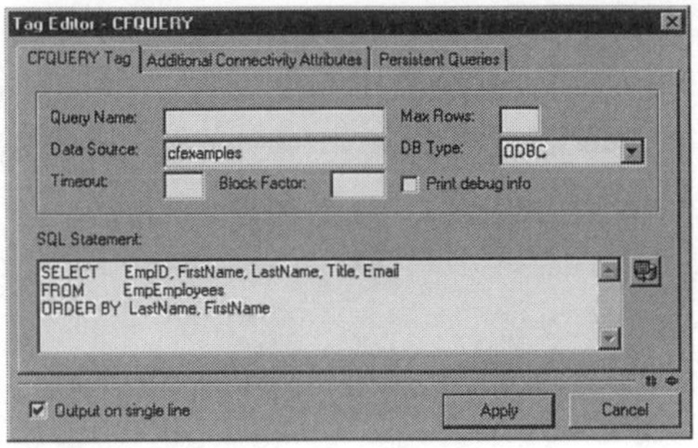

FIGURE 23.7

The Query Builder can insert generated SQL right into the <CFQUERY> Tag Editor.

Reusing Queries

As mentioned earlier, you can save SQL statements created with the Query Builder for future use. ColdFusion Studio saves generated queries on the ColdFusion server. This allows anyone connected to that ColdFusion server to reuse existing queries.

To reuse a saved query, do the following:

1. Open the Database tab in the ColdFusion Studio Resource Tab.

2. Connect to the desired ColdFusion server (providing the password, if required).

3. Expand the desired data source to display a selection titled Queries.

4. Expand the Queries option to display the list of saved queries.

5. Drag the desired query from the list to the editor window (see Figure 23.8). ColdFusion Studio creates a complete <CFQUERY> tag at the location that the query was dropped.

Generating Other SQL Statements

More often that not, you'll find yourself using the Query Builder to construct SQL SELECT statements. But that's not all the Query Builder can do. SQL INSERT, UPDATE, and DELETE statements are supported by the Query Builder too.

FIGURE 23.8

Drag and drop an existing database query to create a fully populated <CFQUERY> tag containing the query's SQL statement.

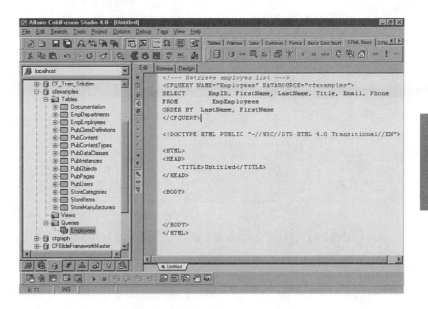

23

Generating SQL INSERT Statements

The SQL Query Builder can't be used generate simple SQL INSERT statements like this:

```
INSERT INTO Employees(FirstName, LastName)
VALUES('Ben', 'Forta')
```

The Query Builder can be used only to build SQL INSERT SELECT statements that insert the results of a SELECT statement into another table.

To generate a SQL INSERT statement, you must switch SQL Query Builder to Insert mode by clicking the INSERT Query toolbar button. The Query Builder then prompts for the name of the table into which you will be inserting data.

To create an INSERT statement, follow these steps:

1. Select the table into which data is to be inserted.
2. Right-click the table and select Remove Table. This removes it from the Table pane but retains the table as the destination for the inserted data in the SQL pane.
3. Click Add Tables (or right-click in the Table pane and select Add Table) to select the tables from which data is to be selected for insertion.
4. Select the columns to be inserted by using any of the selection methods described earlier.

5. Click the Append To column for the first row in the columns grid, and select the field into which the data is to be inserted from the drop-down list.

6. Repeat step 5 for every column listed in the Column area.

7. Select the columns to be used for the SELECT WHERE clause (if they aren't already selected).

8. Specify the criteria for the SELECT WHERE clause as explained earlier.

> Make sure that you *always* specify a WHERE clause criterion. Otherwise, you will insert every selected row into the destination table.

Generating SQL UPDATE Statements

To generate a SQL UPDATE statement, you must switch SQL Query Builder to Update mode by clicking the UPDATE Query toolbar button. The Query Builder then prompts you for the name of the table whose data you will be updating.

To create an UPDATE statement, follow these steps:

1. Select the table to be updated.

2. Select the columns to be updated by using any of the selection methods described earlier in the "Selecting Table Columns" section.

3. Specify the new value for each field in that field's New Value box. You can specify a literal value or a ColdFusion variable.

4. Select the columns to be used for the WHERE clause (if they aren't already selected).

5. Specify the criteria for the UPDATE WHERE clause as explained earlier in the sections "Filtering Data" and "Advanced Data Filtering."

> Make sure that you *always* specify a WHERE clause criterion. Otherwise, you will update every row in the table with the new values.

Generating SQL DELETE Statements

To generate a SQL DELETE statement, you must switch SQL Query Builder to Delete mode by clicking the DELETE Query toolbar button. The Query Builder then prompts you for the name of the table whose data you will be deleting.

To create a DELETE statement, follow these steps:

1. Select the table from which to delete data.

2. Select the columns to be used for the WHERE clause by using any of the selection methods described earlier.

3. Specify the criteria for the DELETE WHERE clause as explained earlier.

> Make sure that you *always* specify a WHERE clause criterion. Otherwise, you will delete every row in the table.

23

Summary

ColdFusion Studio's SQL Query Builder can greatly simplify the process of creating SQL queries for data retrieval and manipulation. Queries can pasted directly into a <CFQUERY> tag, and also can be saved and reused.

Q&A

Q Is there a way to browse database schemas by using ColdFusion Studio?

A The Resource Tab's Database tab supports schema browsing. You can expand any listed data source to browse its tables, and then expand any table to see the table definition.

Q I have a database on my hard drive that's not appearing as a database tab. How are databases added to the Database tab?

A The Database tab lists data sources that have been defined by using the ColdFusion Administrator. Refer to your ColdFusion documentation for information on how to create data sources for your own databases.

Q Does the SQL Query Builder support table joins?

A Yes. Standard joins are supported, as are INNER and OUTER joins. To create a join, click the SQL Query Builder's Add Tables button to add the various tables to your query, and then drag and drop the related fields together to define the joins. You also can right-click any join to specify the join type.

Q Can the SQL Query Builder be used to test queries containing clauses constructed using ColdFusion variables?

A Yes. If your SQL statement contains ColdFusion variables, the SQL Query Builder prompts you to provide variable values that can be used for testing.

Workshop

The Workshop contains quiz questions and activities to help reinforce what you've learned in this hour. If you get stuck, the answers to the quiz questions can be found in Appendix A, "Answers to Quiz Questions."

Quiz

1. True or false: The SQL Query Builder can be used to create SQL statements for local and remote databases.

2. Can the SQL Query Builder be used to generate INSERT VALUE statements?

3. What's the maximum number of OR clauses allowed in a WHERE clause?

4. What's the maximum number of AND clauses allowed in a WHERE clause?

Exercise

ColdFusion comes with a series of example data files (the ones used in the screenshots you saw this hour). Browse the available data sources to find the example data source, and use the SQL Query Builder to create test SELECT statements.

Hour **24**

Working with the Integrated Debugger

For most developers, application debugging is kind of like death and taxes—it's one those things that we never look forward to, even though we know it is inevitable. Debugging can be a harrowing experience even in tightly controlled environments. Debugging can be an absolute nightmare—and perhaps impossible—in distributed environments like the Web. As such, one of ColdFusion Studio's most impressive features is its integrated debugger. This tool combines the power and flexibility of high-end professional debuggers with the ability to debug any ColdFusion application anywhere (even over remote connections).

In this hour you'll learn the following:

- What the integrated debugger is
- How to set up the debugger mappings
- How to use the debugger
- How to work with the debugger panes

Understanding the Integrated Debugger

ColdFusion is a professional-strength development tool, and as such ColdFusion Studio features a complete integrated remote debugger. Key features of the debugger include the following:

- Debugging applications running on any server, local, or across any IP connection
- Creating breakpoints to examine code where needed
- Examining variables and expressions mid-execution
- Analyzing query results in real time
- Browsing the tag stack dynamically
- Monitoring output generation

The debugger can be used to debug only code on a server configured as a remote RDS server within ColdFusion Studio. To debug local files, you must have a local RDS server configured.

Setting Up the Integrated Debugger

More often than not, other than an RDS connection, no special setup is needed to use the debugger. Any files opened over an RDS connection can be debugged simply by starting the debugger.

The only exception to this is path mappings. Mappings are used to provide different applications with paths that they understand to a specific file. For example, if I opened the file ORDER.CFM over a network connection, there could be three different paths to that file:

- ColdFusion Studio would see the file as \\SERVER\share\forta\books\order.cfm.
- ColdFusion Application Server would see the file as C:\INETPUB\ WWWROOT\forta\books\order.cfm.
- Web Browsers would see the file as `http://www.forta.com/books/order.cfm`.

To debug an application over an IP connection, every component must be able to access the same file, and no ambiguity as to which file is being referred to may exist.

More often than not, ColdFusion and ColdFusion Studio can correctly work out which file is which by themselves. But if they can't, you have to set up explicit mappings by using the Remote Development Settings dialog (see Figure 24.1). (You'll know that you have to do this when you set debugger breakpoints, as explained later, and the debugger won't break as requested.)

FIGURE 24.1

The Remote Development Settings dialog is used to configure the debugger and to map directory paths.

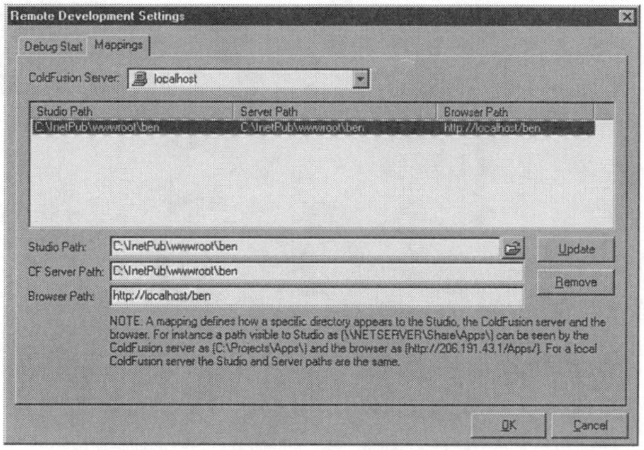

24

To set up a mapping, do the following:

1. Display the Remote Development Settings dialog's Mappings tab by selecting Development Mappings from the Debug menu.
2. Select the RDS server you are debugging against from the ColdFusion Server drop-down list. 
3. Enter the path that ColdFusion Studio will use in the Studio Path text box (click the browse button to interactively select the path).
4. Enter the path that ColdFusion will use in the CF Server Path text box.
5. Enter the URL to the file in the Browser Path text box.
6. Click Add to add the mapping (or Update to update an existing mapping).
7. Click OK to save your changes.

When the mapping is created, it's used automatically when you debug against the specified server.

Using the Integrated Debugger

The ColdFusion Debugger is controlled by using the Debug toolbar. This is usually at the bottom of the ColdFusion Studio window, as seen in Figure 24.2.

FIGURE 24.2

The ColdFusion Studio Debugger is controlled by using the Debug toolbar.

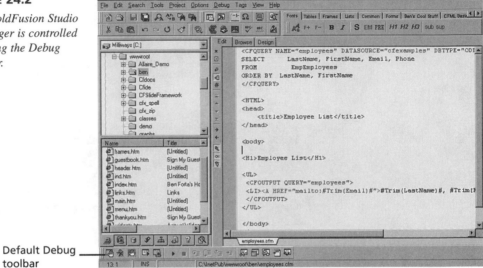

Default Debug toolbar

The Debug Toolbar

The Debug toolbar contains the 16 buttons shown in Table 24.1.

TABLE 24.1 DEBUG TOOLBAR BUTTONS

Button	Purpose
	Display list of breakpoints
	Clear all breakpoints
	Toggle the current breakpoint
	Debugger settings

Button	Purpose
	Debugger mappings
	Start debugger
	Stop debugger
	Step into code
	Step over code
	Step out of current code block
	Run to cursor
	Display watches
	Display record sets
	Display tag stack
	Display output
	Display variables

24

To use the debugger, open the page to be debugged in the editor window. You can set breakpoints (points in your code where the debugger should stop and wait for your input) by clicking the line number in the gray bar to the left of the editor window. You can put breakpoints only in CFML code.

Figure 24.3 shows a breakpoint on a <CFOUTPUT> tag. When a breakpoint is set, the line of code is displayed with a red background and a stop sign symbol is displayed in the page gutter on the left.

FIGURE 24.3

Breakpoints are set in the editor window.

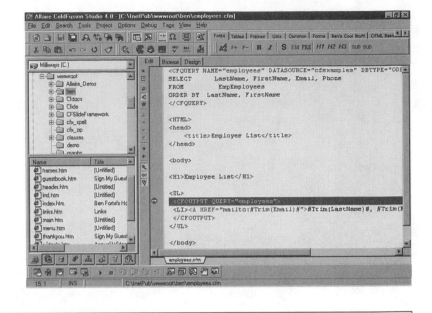

 To remove a single breakpoint, click the line number twice. To remove all breakpoints, click the Clear All Breakpoints button in the Debug toolbar.

 To start the debugger, simply click the Start Debugger button in the Debug toolbar, or choose Start from the Debug menu. You are prompted with a Remote Development Settings dialog, as shown in Figure 24.4.

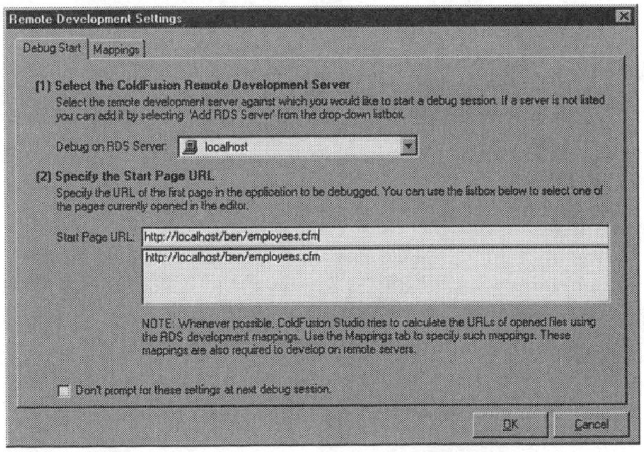

FIGURE 24.4

Debugger settings, including the initial file to load, are specified in the Remote Development Settings dialog.

In the Debug on RDS Server combo box, specify the server to debug against. The default value here is usually correct.

In the Start Page URL text box, specify the URL to start the debugger in. By default, ColdFusion Studio constructs a URL for the currently selected file. If you are debugging a page that must be called from another page (for example, a form action page), you must specify that initial page URL in this text box.

After you enter the information into these two fields, click OK to start the debugger. This will display the Debug window, as shown in Figure 24.5.

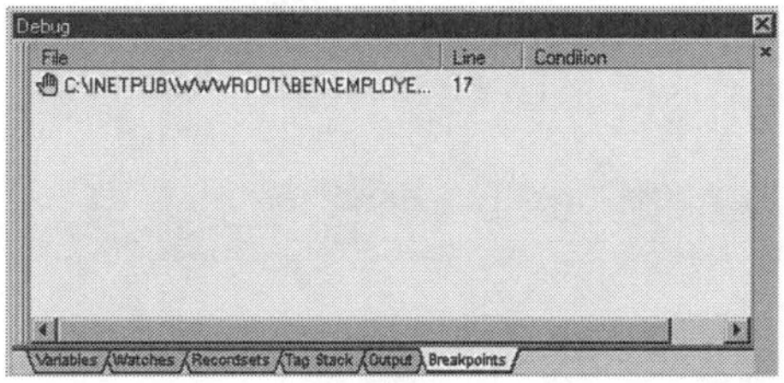

FIGURE 24.5

The Debug window hovers over the ColdFusion Studio window, allowing you to browse your files and access debug options at the same time.

After the debugger starts, you typically will want to execute the program until the first breakpoint is reached. To do this, just use the program in the ColdFusion Studio browse window. You might have to move the Debug window out of the way to get to the page.

The Debugger Panes

As soon as a breakpoint is reached, the debugger stops execution and highlights the breakpoint with a blue background. The Debug window displays the breakpoint that was reached, as shown in Figure 24.6.

FIGURE 24.6

The Breakpoints pane in the Debug window shows all breakpoints and allows adding, editing, and deleting of breakpoints.

After code execution stops, you can use any of the debugging options by selecting the tabs in the Debug window. To display a list of all variables and their values, click the Variables tab. The variables are categorized by type (see Figure 24.7), and each type can be expanded or closed as needed.

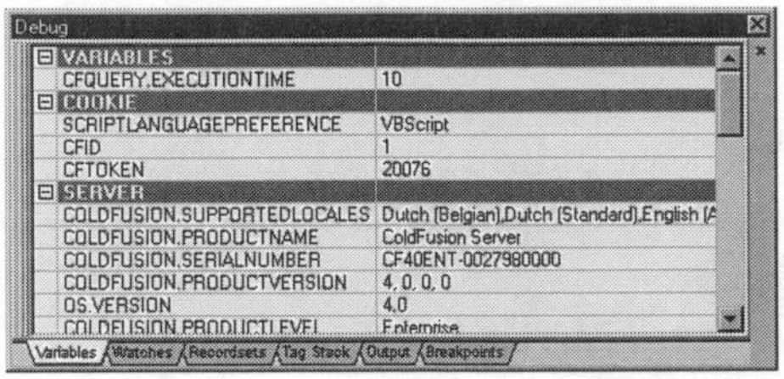

FIGURE 24.7

The Variables pane shows the current value of all variables, categorized by type.

The Watches pane lets you enter variables or expressions that you can monitor (see Figure 24.8). As they change, their values are updated in this window. To evaluate an expression once, type it in the expression field and click the Evaluate button. To watch (monitor) an expression, type it in the expression field and click the Watch button.

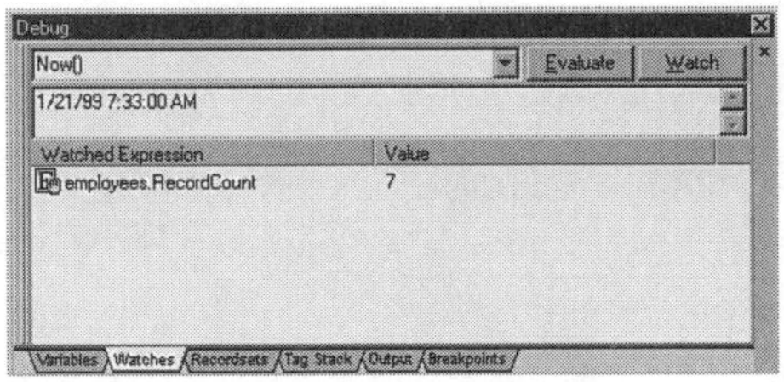

FIGURE 24.8

The Watches pane shows the all expressions being watched and allows for the real type evaluation of expressions.

The Recordsets pane lists all queries that have been executed up to the breakpoint. As Figure 24.9 shows, the query name, number of rows retrieved, and the SQL statement are listed in this tab.

FIGURE 24.9

The Recordset pane shows all executed queries and their details.

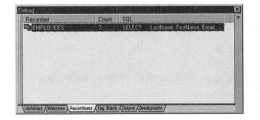

The Tag Stack pane (see Figure 24.10) shows the current page being executed and, if there is one, the calling tag stack. If you're debugging a page that has been called or included from any other page, those pages will be listed in descending order.

FIGURE 24.10

The Tag Stack pane shows the tag call stack.

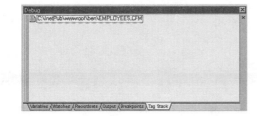

The Output pane (see Figure 24.11) displays the HTML output as it's being generated. The data shown here is post-processing data, the same data that will be sent back to the client browser.

FIGURE 24.11

The Output pane shows generated client output as it's being generated.

24

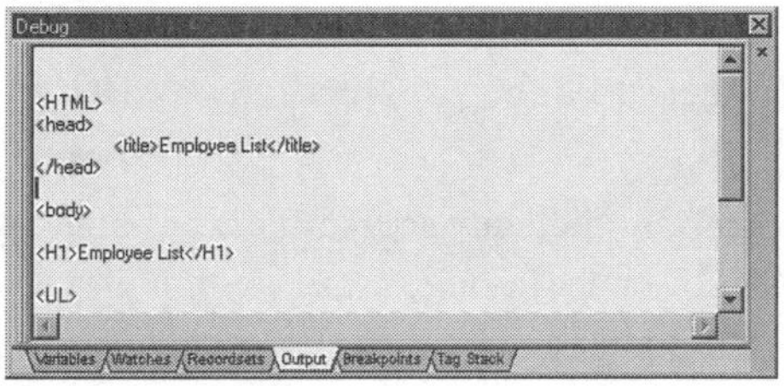

You can open, close, move, and break the Debug window into multiple panes . Each pane can be undocked and repositioned as needed (see Figure 24.12). To move a pane, select and then drag it by clicking the double vertical lines to the left of the pane. To redock a pane simply close it by clicking on the X on its upper right.

FIGURE 24.12

Debugger panes can be undocked and displayed as separate windows if needed.

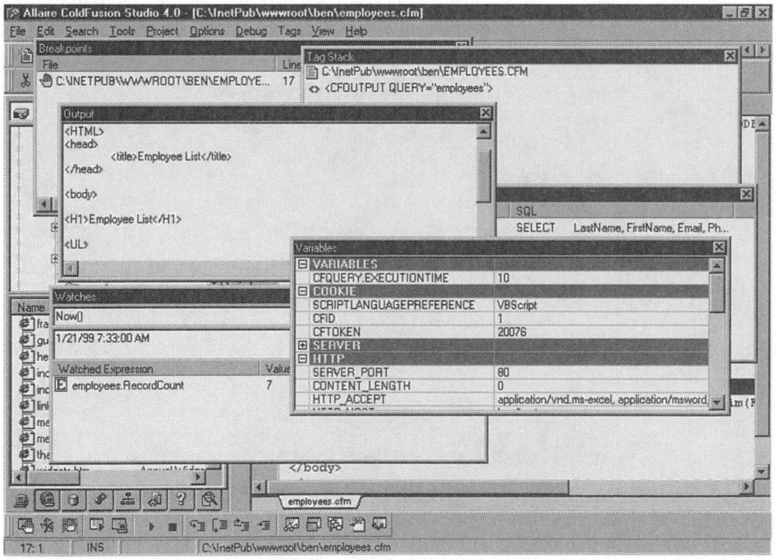

As you can see, the remote debugger provides you with industrial-strength tools to help you pinpoint and code trouble spots, the kind of tool previously not seen in the Internet application development space.

Summary

The ColdFusion Studio integrated debugger is a powerful and invaluable feature, one that provides the Web developer community with tools previously only available in traditional development environments. The debugger requires an RDS connection and a ColdFusion Studio client.

Q&A

Q Can I use the debugger to debug applications written in languages other than ColdFusion?

A The debugger can step through any source files, but breakpoints can be set only on lines containing CFML code. In other words, although you can run non-ColdFusion pages through the debugger, doing so won't accomplish very much.

Q What impact does debugger use have on the performance of my ColdFusion applications?

A When you debug an application by using ColdFusion Studio, you're actually debugging on the remote server. ColdFusion Studio is simply a view port into the ColdFusion server. The process of stepping through code line by line (not to mention sending debugging data back and forth) definitely degrades overall ColdFusion server performance. For this reason, Allaire recommends (and good development processes dictate) that you do testing on separate development and testing servers—never on production servers.

Workshop

The Workshop contains quiz questions and activities to help reinforce what you've learned in this hour. If you get stuck, the answers to the quiz questions can be found in Appendix A, "Answers to Quiz Questions."

Quiz

1. What's required to debug an application?
2. Which Debug pane lets you enter expressions and evaluate them?

Exercise

Create a small test application consisting of a <CFQUERY> and a <CFOUTPUT>. Place a breakpoint at the start of the <CFQUERY> and step through line by line watching the various panes.

24

APPENDIX A

Answers to Quiz Questions

Hour 1

1. The *Internet* is the public Internet, the world's biggest network. *Intranets* are private networks (often connected to the public Internet) built on top of Internet technologies and standards. *Extranets* are intranets that span more than one location or organization.

2. True. Every page on the Internet has an URL that uniquely identifies it.

3. False. Host IP addresses must be unique; DNS names don't need to be. In fact, it's very common to find a single DNS hostname map to multiple IP addresses.

Hour 2

1. Unfortunately, the same Web pages often look different in different Web browsers. Professional Web developers make a habit of checking what their pages look like in multiple browsers to ensure that all visitors see the desired result, regardless of the browser they're using.

2. False. HomeSite's Design mode is intended to simplify the creation and manipulation of specific graphical elements (such as HTML tables). It's not a full WYSIWYG page layout tool, as those tools greatly limit Web developers.

Hour 3

1. Tag Completion.

2. Tag Editors, Tag Insight, Tag Inspector.

Hour 4

1. Because HTML is not case sensitive, `<table>`, `<TABLE>`, and `<Table>` all do the same thing. There's no right or wrong case for tags within your pages, but you should be consistent—pick one standard and stick with it to make editing and maintaining your code much easier. HomeSite lets you control the case of inserted tags so that embedded text matches your chosen case convention.

2. It makes pinpointing specific lines of code easier, it breaks the monotony of long pages of code, and it helps locate typos and errors.

Hour 5

1. False. *Local files* means files that can be accessed directly from your computer without requiring you to use FTP on some other transfer mechanism. Local files include files on your own computer, as well as any files that can be accessed via the Network Neighborhood.

2. True. As long as you have access to the file (can connect to it with a browser), HomeSite can open it by using the Open from Web feature.

Hour 6

1. False. As a rule, whitespace is ignored. But there's one exception—preformatted text. All text between `<PRE>` and `</PRE>` tags is honored, even whitespace characters such as carriage returns.

2. Entity references enable you to use text within your Web page that otherwise wouldn't be allowed. For example, < > & and " are all characters that can't be used within Web pages because they have special meanings to your browser.

3. Whenever possible, widths should be specified as relative values using percentages. This will ensure maximum compatibility with as many browsers as possible, on as many screen sizes as possible.

4. False. This one is wishful thinking. Life would be that much easier if styles rendering was consistent, but unfortunately that's just not the case. This means that although styles should be used when needed, it's up to you to ensure that the results look good in as many different browsers as possible.

Hour 7

1. False. HTML color constants aren't supported by older browsers. As a rule, it's safer to use RGB values because they are supported by more browsers.

2. The Browser Safety Palette.

3. False. As long as you take precautions (using only commonly available fonts, and specifying alternate font face choices), there's no reason not to take advantage of font face specification.

4. Actual sizes (1 through 7) don't correspond to any real sizes. Relative sizes are safer to use because although the actual font size is still unknown, the desired effect (larger or smaller text) can still be achieved.

Hour 8

1. Image size and how it affects download time.

2. True. It's a good idea to compare image sizes in multiple file formats to find the one that's most bandwidth- friendly.

3. False. First, it's not safe to assume that all browsers can display graphics. There are actually text-based browsers that are designed to not display graphics. Also, users of many online services (for example, America Online) routinely turn on an option that improves browsing speed without downloading graphics unless they are explicitly requested. To be on the safe side, always provide ALT text.

Hour 9

1. True. Relative URLs are preferred because they are less likely to break if the site directory structure changes.

2. `HREF`.

3. False. Although text and graphics are the most commonly used links, any HTML code can be specified between the anchor tags (for example, list items as I showed you earlier this hour).

4. `VLINK`.

Hour 10

1. HTML tables provide flexible control over the placement of Web page elements, allowing layout that's impossible without them.

2. The Table Sizer (also called Quick Table).

3. False. Although it's true that code indentation increases code size (all those blank spaces can add up), the benefit gained by having pages that are easier to maintain makes it worthwhile. Some developers, however, like to have their cake and eat it too—leaving the indentation in their code during development (simplifying development), and then stripping it out once the page is complete (reducing page size).

4. The text `First name:` and `Last name:` isn't within `<TD>` or `<TH>` tags. This illegal table syntax will cause all sorts of display problems.

Hour 11

1. Frames are well suited for navigation controls because they allow controls to remain consistently in one place onscreen.

2. `<NOFRAMES>` allows developers to specify text and HTML to be displayed or processed by browsers that don't support frames. This includes search engines and spiders, many of which will ignore frame links (but will honor `<NOFRAMES>` content).

3. True. `<FRAMESET>` defines the frame layout, and `<FRAME>` defines the name and contents of each frame. All other frame tags are optional.

Hour 12

1. True. Depending on what browser you are using, form controls that aren't within form tags might or might not be displayed. Regardless of whether they are displayed, they will be useless unless enclosed within `<FORM>` and `</FORM>` tags.

2. Check boxes are used for on/off states. Radio buttons are used to select one of a set of mutually exclusive options.

3. Radio buttons would be your best bet here. Check boxes would be highly inappropriate (asking visitors if they were male or not or female or not would undoubtedly upset 50 percent of them). Similarly, a list box would be inappropriate.

Hour 13

1. False. I have heard many HomeSite developers claim this, but I must disagree with them. Although Design mode isn't the answer to all page layout problems, it does solve specific needs and simplify specific operations. And I believe that any tool that makes a developer's life easier is a good thing.

2. Bulleted list is a formatting style, so you would select the text to be formatted, and then select Bulleted List from the format drop-down list.

Hour 14

1. Extended Replace.

2. Removing the extra characters reduces the page size, which in turn reduces file download time. In practice, however, the download time saved is usually minimal at best.

3. True. Indenting your code will help prevent code errors and help pinpoint those errors more quickly.

Hour 15

1. The <STYLE> tag defines style blocks for use by an entire Web page. The STYLE attribute defines style information for a specific tag.

2. False. Tag-level styles should be avoided. You can't do anything in tag-level styles that can't be done in page-wide styles. Plus, if you use page-wide styles your pages will look more consistent.

3. Using the <LINK> tag.

Hour 16

1. False. We all wish that were true, but alas, it isn't. Not all browsers are created equal—in fact, barely any browsers are created equal. That your page works in one browser doesn't guarantee that it'll work in other browsers.

2. Unknown tag names (usually means a typo was made), and version compatibility issues.

3. As many as you possibly can—the more, the better.

A

Hour 17

1. Code templates.
2. The ¦ character indicates the post-insertion cursor position.

Hour 18

1. Chart View and Tree View.
2. False. Any link can be verified, internal or external, and absolute or relative. The only restriction is that the file being verified must be local.
3. The primary factors that affect estimated download times are bad connections and cached files.

Hour 19

1. Server name, login name, and login password.
2. Directory and file manipulation.
3. True. As with almost all Internet services, IP addresses and hostnames can be used interchangeably. Your hosting company will give you the address or hostname to use.

Hour 20

1. Grouping files for simplified manipulation.
2. True. A single file can be a member of multiple Projects, but Projects cannot be nested.

Hour 21

1. 3.
2. The Expression Builder.

Hour 22

1. Only ColdFusion Studio.
2. RDS.

Hour 23

1. True. As long as the database is available via RDS, SQL Query Builder can use it.

2. No, the only supported INSERT statement is the INSERT SELECT statement.

3. There is a limit of four per column, but because each column can be selected multiple times there is no real limit.

4. There is no limit.

Hour 24

1. A ColdFusion Server, a ColdFusion Studio client, and an RDS connection between them.

2. The Watches pane.

A

INDEX

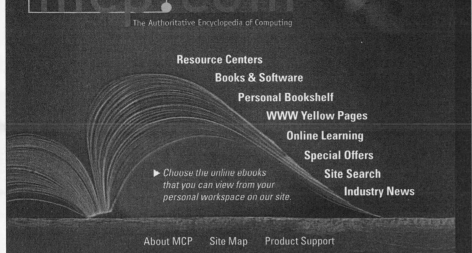

Other Related Titles

The ColdFusion 4.0 Web Application Construction Kit

Ben Forta
ISBN: 0-7897-1809-X
$49.99 U.S/$71.95 CAN

Sams Teach Yourself Dynamic HTML in a Week

*Bruce Campbell,
Rick Darnell, and
John Jung*
ISBN: 1-57521-335-4
$29.99 US/$42.95 CAN

Sams Teach Yourself JavaScript 1.3 in 24 Hours

Michael G. Moncur
ISBN: 0-672-31407-X
$19.99 US/$28.95 CAN

Advanced ColdFusion 4.0 Application Development

Ben Forta
ISBN: 0-7897-1810-3
$49.99 US/$71.95 CAN

Sams Teach Yourself HTML 4 in 24 Hours

*Dick Oliver and
Molly E. Holzschlag*
ISBN: 0-672-31369-3
$19.99 US/$28.95 CAN

www.samspublishing.com

All prices are subject to change.